TRADE-OFFS

TRADE-OFFS

Negotiating the Omnibus Trade and Competitiveness Act

SUSAN C. SCHWAB

HARVARD BUSINESS SCHOOL PRESS

Boston, Massachusetts

Library of Congress Cataloging-in-Publication Data

Schwab, Susan Carol, 1955–
    Trade-offs : negotiating the Omnibus Trade and Competitiveness
Act / Susan C. Schwab.
      p.   cm.
    Includes bibliographical references (p.) and index.
    ISBN 0-87584-510-X (alk. paper)
    1. Tariff —Law and legislation—United States—History.
2. Foreign trade regulation—United States—History.   3. United
States—Commercial policy—History.   4. United States. Omnibus
Trade and Competitiveness Act of 1988—History. I. Title.
KF6659.S39   1994
343.73'087—dc20
[347.30387]   94-10392
                                              CIP

98 97 96 95 94   5 4 3 2 1

The paper used in this publication meets the requirements
of the American National Standard for Permanence of Paper for
Printed Library Materials Z39.49-1984.

For Joan and Gerald Schwab
and for Teresa and David Herring
For everything

CONTENTS

PREFACE

This study began as a few ideas about U.S. trade policymaking that, as a Senate staffer, I would use in speeches on "how Washington works." I used some of the concepts in journal articles and then, in early 1987, started to write a monograph for the Council on Foreign Relations on the emerging Omnibus Trade Act. But action on the bill never seemed to end, and by the time it did, I was moving on to a new job with the U.S. and Foreign Commercial Service. Fast-forward to 1993, when, after several years of intermittent research and writing, the monograph had become a dissertation for my Ph.D. at George Washington University.

This book is adapted from the dissertation and is, therefore, much shorter, somewhat less scholarly, and, I hope, a lot more fun. It is meant to be read by anyone seriously interested in public policy and how it is made, particularly those in business or government who think U.S. trade policy is of some importance to the nation's economic well-being. International trade is, in many ways, a microcosm of contemporary U.S. political-economy, involving the convergence of domestic politics, foreign policy, and economics; Congress, the president, and their respective staffers; big business, small business, big labor, the media, and a panoply of other interests.

Above all, I wanted to tell a story, a story that was substantive and important, but not without its moments of drama and humor. And I wanted it to be readable. So this is a case study, a rather intimate history of the Omnibus Trade and Competitiveness Act of 1988, written by one who was there.

The 1988 act is the law that set the stage for negotiation of the NAFTA and the Uruguay Round GATT accords, and dictated the terms of their approval by Congress. And while the research and most of the writing predate these events, the book's themes and conclusions have largely been reinforced by them. Moreover, until Congress and the president negotiate the terms of an entirely new law granting presidential authority to implement the next generation of major trade agreements, the 1988 act will remain the basis for much of U.S. trade policy.

The book moves between chronology and context, enabling a variety of readers to be served. Those seeking a conceptual framework for understanding U.S. trade policy and policymaking, for example, should be sure to read Chapters 1–3 on history and context. Those interested primarily in the "inside story" of how this law came into being can skip to the narrative contained in Chapters 3–7.*

What sets this book apart is the level of detail about the internal deliberations and decisions of the principal congressional and executive branch actors involved in writing the bill. While the study draws extensively on the historical record of U.S. trade law, and on works by others with special insights into U.S. trade policy, the heart of this work was based on sources uniquely available to an insider—an insider with thoughtful and caring colleagues. These sources include notes and observations that, as Senator John C. Danforth's legislative director, I was able to compile during the process; interviews with or recorded observations of congressional members and staff, administration officials, and people in the private sector who had a fundamental say in the bill's outcome; and internal working documents, memoranda, and scrap notes used by participants at the time.

This particular vantage point, however, also risks bias. I was very much involved in the writing of the 1988 act and, as a former trade negotiator, have rather strong opinions about U.S. trade policy. I did take sides, but for purposes of this book, I have presented what I believe to be a balanced view.

Efforts to ensure balance were aided by the dissertation process, which required articulating and justifying methodologies and decision rules. It meant learning about participant-observers, elite-interviewing, and the use of what are known as "informants" or surrogate observers. And it meant the extensive use of footnotes and other means of attribution throughout the text. For example, although I agreed with them, quotes attributed to Senator Danforth are entirely his own, taken from transcripts of extemporaneous remarks. When my own involvement made a particular difference in an event, I have flagged it with a reference to "Danforth staff." Finally, it should be evident that the interests and episodes described in the text were chosen because they were either pivotal to the outcome or because they are illustrative of individuals, events, and decisions that are daily features of the policy-making process.

Some critics may find this story somewhat "unfashionable" because it does not dump all over the Congress. Yes, there are episodes noted in the book about which I doubt the members will be particularly proud

---

* Those interested in extensive background material, detailed analysis, and/or formal citations of primary source quotes, should probably read the dissertation. All 688 pages and 732 footnotes are available through U.M.I. of Ann Arbor, Michigan.

or that may puzzle some outside the Washington beltway. That I have chosen not to dwell on these events may reflect my own bias and the many years I spent in government service. Yet even in retrospect, and now from the private sector and the heartland of America, I still recall working on the trade bill with a lot of well-intentioned, hard-working people who felt they were contributing something of value to their country.

Another conclusion to be drawn from this study is that while policy-making is a very human business, a remarkable number of the events, decisions, and motivations that characterized the writing of the 1988 act clearly transcend it. For example, several provisions and trade policy concepts considered extreme in 1988—such as results-based assessments of trade agreement compliance—are practically mainstream today. In fact, very few of the trade policy issues evident in the law have proven time-bound, and many of the forces underlying them are just as applicable to developments in other policy areas. In this regard, the book both benefits and suffers from the life-goes-on nature of focusing on recent history. Since pen was first put to a 5″ × 8″ card for this work, much has transpired in the worlds of trade policy and politics. In addition to various new trade agreements, a great many of the faces in the executive and legislative branches of government have also changed. Of the individuals most closely associated with the bill's evolution, several have retired or have been retired by voters, shareholders, or scandals; a few have died; some have moved up or out, and many have moved on to new phases in their lives, involving, in several cases, responsibility for implementing the law they helped create.

For those involved in negotiating the Omnibus Trade and Competitiveness Act, this book will remind you of events you were certain you would never forget. For many, it may bring to mind the time I asked all those questions, borrowed those books, or had you read a draft—for some paper I was planning to write. Guess what? I did it. And given the years it took for both the law and this work to be completed, there are many individuals to whom I owe thanks:

Very special thanks to I. M. Destler, Jeffrey M. Lang, William A. Reinsch, and Rufus Yerxa, who let me draw on their expertise, memories, and wisdom for most of those years, and who read my dissertation drafts and cared enough to correct me. Special thanks, as well, to Susan J. Tolchin, who read and commented on numerous drafts, and who suggested the Ph.D. in the first place.

I will always be grateful to Jack Danforth for inspiration and friendship, and for convincing me an activist trade policy need not be protectionist. Without him and Alex Netchvolodoff, and without the help of my friend and associate, Marjorie Chorlins, this book would probably not have been written. Thanks, as well, to the members of Congress and the administration officials who made this a book worth writing, and to my colleagues at Motorola, for being willing to wait for me to finish it.

Others who shared insights, information, and background materials with me; read and commented on drafts; or otherwise made this study and, in many cases the 1988 act, a better product: C. Michael Aho, John W. Anderson, William T. Archey, Thelma J. Askey, Stuart Auerbach, Judith H. Bello, Joshua B. Bolten, Phyllis O. Bonanno, Carol Brookins, Sheila Burke, Robert C. Cassidy, Jr., Calman J. Cohen, Dan Crippen, Bill Cunningham, C. Richard D'Amato, Alan F. Holmer, Gary N. Horlick, Charles S. Levy, Alisa Learner Maher, John K. Meagher, Marcia Miller, Kevin C. W. Mulvey, Janet A. Nuzum, Nicholas Philipson, Joanna R. Shelton, Bruce Stokes, Dick Warden, George J. Weise, Michael Wessel, Mary Jane Wignot, and Robert B. Zoellick.

Finally, for typing, editing, printing, computer stuff, and lots and lots of moral support, I am ever so grateful to my parents, Joan and Gerald Schwab, and to my sister and brother-in-law, Teresa and David Herring.

Susan C. Schwab
Chicago, Illinois
1994

1

THE EVOLUTION OF LAW AS A FRAME
OF REFERENCE

*In a very dark Chamber at a round Hole, about one third Part of an Inch
broad, made in the Shut of a Window, I placed a Glass Prism, whereby the
Beam of the Sun's Light, which came in at that Hole, might be refracted
upwards toward the opposite Wall of the Chamber, and there form a colour'd
Image of the Sun.*
—Isaac Newton[1]

INTRODUCTION

On August 23, 1988, the president of the United States signed into law
the Omnibus Trade and Competitiveness Act of 1988. It comprised over
a thousand pages of text, running the gamut from trade, tariff, and
customs law to worker retraining to repeal of the oil windfall profits
tax. It was the first major trade law since the Smoot-Hawley Tariff Act
of 1930, drafted almost entirely by the Congress. Its enactment was a
prerequisite to active U.S. participation in a round of global trade talks
and, unknown to its authors at the time, in the negotiation of a North
American Free Trade Agreement (NAFTA). It was the law likely to
dominate U.S. trade policy for the balance of the century.

Yet for all of this bulk, complexity, and significance, the "legislative
history" printed in minuscule type at the end of Public Law 100–418
simply reads:

---

[1] Isaac Newton, *Opticks, Or a Treatise on the Reflections, Refractions, Inflections
and Colours of Light*, Book I, Part I, Prop. II; quoted in Philip P. Wiener, ed. *Dictionary
of the History of Ideas* (New York: Charles Scribner's, 1973), vol. III, 391.

LEGISLATIVE HISTORY—H.R. 4848:
CONGRESSIONAL RECORD, Vol. 134 (1988):
  July 13, considered and passed House.
  Aug. 2,3, considered and passed Senate.
WEEKLY COMPILATION OF PRESIDENTIAL DOCUMENTS,
Vol. 24 (1988):
  Aug. 23, Presidential remarks.

In fact, the law had its origins in several different House and Senate bills and its enactment entailed an odyssey closer to three years than to three months. The legislative process involved over two hundred members of Congress, twenty-three different committees, a dozen federal agencies, hundreds of amendments, and innumerable policy papers, statements, letters, and drafts. The bill faced a presidential veto, a failed attempt to override, and, in an unusual twist, was eventually split into two bills—both of which became law.

This study is a history of the Omnibus Trade and Competitiveness Act of 1988. It is designed to open a unique window on the legislative process and on contemporary U.S. trade policy, and to help make sense of an important trade law. By exploring the process of enactment, we observe the messy interplay of history, humans, and events that somehow fails to emerge in Civics 101. By examining the law in the context of its structural, economic, and political underpinnings, we better comprehend the dominant themes and countervailing trends of U.S. policy.

This is not the first—nor will it be the last—book written about the writing of a law or about U.S. trade policy. A review of the literature reveals three basic categories of books and articles similar in some way to this study. The first category is composed of works on U.S. trade policy, law, and economics. It includes fundamental texts such as those by John Jackson (1969) and Kenneth W. Dam (1970) on trade law and the General Agreement on Tariffs and Trade (GATT), as well as historical works on U.S. trade policy by William S. Culbertson (1925, 1937) and F. W. Taussig (1931).

A second category comprises books and articles on policymaking, including the "process politics" of governmental organizations or of a particular field. Here one finds insightful commentaries about the Congress by Norman J. Ornstein (1975), Ornstein and Thomas E. Mann (1981), Walter J. Oleszek (1984), and others. Also included in this subcategory are important pieces on actors and organizations in policymaking, such as those by V. O. Key, Jr. on political parties (1942), Douglass Cater on the media (1959), and Robert A. Dahl on pluralism (1967); along with an almost unlimited supply of books about lobbying and lobbyists. A second subcategory examines the policy process in the context of a specific field—in this case, U.S. trade policy. Books and articles in this group tend to focus on the political context of the policy process such as the Raymond A. Bauer, Ithiel de Sola Pool, and Anthony Lewis Dexter study on U.S. business (1963) or Robert A. Pastor's work on economic policymaking in Congress (1980). Others address a wider array of influences on U.S. trade policy, as with various works written or co-authored by I. M. Destler on U.S. trade politics (1986, 1992).

A final—and particularly significant—category of literature pertains to specific events and decisions in governmental policymaking. Non-trade examples here include works on individual pieces of legislation, such as Richard E. Cohen on clean air (1992), Jeffrey H. Birnbaum and Alan S. Murray on tax reform (1987), T. R. Reid on waterways (1980), and Eric Redman on health care (1973). Within the trade arena, books and articles have been written on entire GATT negotiations, such as Gilbert R. Winham on the Tokyo Round (1986) or Ernest H. Preeg on the Kennedy Round (1970), and on individual factors key to the implementation of such rounds, including works by Destler (1980), Winham (1980), and Robert C. Cassidy (1981).

Yet despite this plethora of resources, the real conceptual basis for this study is to be found in a 1935 work by one E. E. Schattschneider. *Politics, Pressures and the Tariff* provided an in-depth look at enactment of the Smoot-Hawley Tariff Act and is considered a seminal work on pluralist theory. It focused on the relationship between economic interests and political behavior—namely, the role of pressure groups during consideration of the Tariff Act of 1930. At the crux of his model was the concept of "reciprocal noninterference"[2] or political logrolling, whereby congressional distribution of tariff increases snowballed into thousands of protectionist changes in the U.S. tariff schedule. However, even though Schattschneider offered a fairly accurate model for understanding the 1930 act and several that preceded it, Smoot-Hawley itself helped bring an end to that era in U.S. trade policy. Therefore, while the notion of policy as the product of certain fundamental influences is a good start, a new conceptual framework is necessary for understanding the evolution of the 1988 act and its place in U.S. trade policy.

A TRADE LAW PERSPECTIVE

By 1988, almost six years of planning had gone into the Uruguay Round of multilateral trade negotiations. The round had been the topic of

---

[2] E. E. Schattschneider, *Politics, Pressures and the Tariff* (New York: Prentice-Hall, 1935), 145.

heated debate during at least two ministerial meetings of the GATT and an agenda item at no less than four presidential economic summits. To be credible in the negotiations, however, the executive branch needed statutory authority, authority to cut U.S. tariffs and to implement non-tariff measure agreements through a special "fast-track" legislative process. Congress also wanted to legislate on trade at the time, and while the round was not its principal objective, it was ultimately the reason a bill was enacted into law. In this and other ways, the Omnibus Trade and Competitiveness Act of 1988 was remarkably consistent with patterns in U.S. trade law and policy since 1934.

A nation's trade policy can be thought of as the product of the varied and often competing forces that affect it. Folded into the policy-making process are domestic and international economic factors and the inescapable tug of the political imperative. In the United States, the equation is further complicated by the unique interaction of Congress and the executive in the management of trade. Therefore, one conceptual framework for understanding U.S. trade policy would place it in the context of three forces that dominate the policy mix: the fundamental structure of the policy process, including the attitudes of and control exercised by dominant policymakers; the prevailing economic circumstances and philosophies; and the positions and political influence of other participants. As the nature of these forces has changed over time, so, too, have the governing themes of U.S. trade policy.

While the history of U.S. trade policy and the economic, political, and institutional forces that shape it have been researched in some detail, systematic analyses of how those forces have come together in U.S. trade law are few. This history of the origins and passage of the Omnibus Trade Act focuses on the policy-making process and its substantive outcome, treating the legislation as a tangible manifestation of the more complex set of themes in U.S. trade policy. The use of a single piece of legislation as a frame of reference for U.S. trade policy offers an analytical approach comparable to treatment of the law as a prism: The "colors" that make up a beam of light are always there, but are generally invisible to us until refraction and diffusion make the spectrum apparent. In this case, close examination of a piece of trade legislation and the events and processes that saw its enactment into law allows us to observe and better understand its context in time, the convergence of forces it represents, and its implications for U.S. trade policy in general.

Forces in U.S. Trade Policy

Institutional forces. Trade policymaking in the United States is ultimately governed by the awkward marriage of the Constitution's commerce clause and the power vested in the president to make treaties. As with most decision-making processes, he who dictates the terms of the process generally commands a disproportionate say in its outcome. In this regard, in 1987 Chairman[3] Dan Rostenkowski (D-Ill.) of the House Ways and Means Committee, commented at the National Press Club that the first eighteen powers detailed by the Constitution belong to the Congress; and of these, the first three resided in his committee.[4] It was a not-so-subtle reminder that to the extent the executive branch of government makes trade policy, it does so on "borrowed" authority. It also served to remind listeners of the key role played by the House Ways and Means and Senate Finance Committees, whose jurisdictions span tax and trade matters, as well as a substantial chunk of federal spending on Social Security, health care programs, and the like.

While the institutional factor is obviously the most stable of the forces in U.S. trade policy, history demonstrates that it, too, can be the subject of accommodations and shifts in the balance of power. This is because those in the executive and legislative branches of government in a position to exert the most influence over U.S. trade policy have periodically redefined their own roles and relationships through statute. These elite actors in the policy process include members of Congress serving on those committees with jurisdiction over trade, appointed officials in key executive branch agencies, and many of the staffers who support them.

Economic context. The second major set of forces influencing U.S. trade policy includes both the economic circumstances faced and perceived by policymakers and the economic philosophies that shape their responses to these circumstances. A number of important elements have a bearing on this economic environment, ranging from domestic economic performance and the relative position of the United States in the world economy to more fundamental issues of market economics and the appropriateness of government intervention.

The history of U.S. trade policy spans the emergence of the United States from a relatively minor player on the international economic scene to that of its dominant superpower to more of a first among equals. During the same period, the United States moved from an agrarian-based economy to one dominated by manufacturing and services,

---

[3] Throughout the study, the terms "chairman" and "chairmen" are used in their generic sense, i.e., irrespective of gender. In fact, during the period covered by the study, all standing committees of the Congress were chaired by men. Similarly, "he" is used in this study as a generic pronoun, including in references to the U.S. Trade Representative, whose first woman incumbent, Carla Hills, was appointed in 1989.

[4] Taken from "Text of remarks by Ways and Means Committee Chairman Dan Rostenkowski for delivery at a National Press Club lunch, March 3, 1987."

affecting the composition of both its work force and its international accounts. Cyclical economic developments of growth, stagnation, recession, and depression also had an impact.

Over time, American political leaders have embraced the market-oriented philosophies of Adam Smith and David Ricardo as well as approaches more akin to the economic nationalism of the early mercantilists. They have treated trade variously as a domestic jobs issue, as a foreign policy issue, or as simply a source of federal revenue. Similarly, trade policy has been accorded both priority status as a concern in its own right and the lowly status of an afterthought or byproduct of other policy determinations.

Trade politics. The last major category of forces governing U.S. trade policy are those derived of politics. In this context, trade politics constitutes the totality of positions and perceptions of those who influence trade decision making.

In the pluralistic U.S. environment, views on trade matters are as diverse as the interests of those who hold them. Some groups gain from exports, while some are threatened by imports; still others have legitimate claims in both camps. As the composition of the U.S. economy and its foreign commerce have changed over time, so too have the make-up and positions of the coalitions seeking to influence U.S. trade policy. Traditional participants in the policy process include agriculture, light and heavy industry, certain service providers, and organized labor. The nature of their involvement has comprised both contacts through grass roots constituencies and active lobbying by organized interest groups, as well participation in more formal government processes such as hearings and advisory committees. Consumers and the voting public also have played a role in U.S. trade policy, albeit a less active one. Finally, there are the observers, including journalists and editorial writers, who periodically come to influence the very policies that are the subject of their conjecture and commentary.

Themes in U.S. Trade Policy

Taken together, these structural, economic, and political forces have made the making of U.S. trade policy the epitome of the adage about the production of laws and sausage—namely, not recommended for the faint of heart. Efforts to accommodate and, to the extent possible, manage these contending forces fall into two distinct periods in U.S. history. Each of these eras reflects a unique phase in the U.S. approach to international trade. Each has been subject to its own policy-making framework, economic context, and trade politics. Each has been characterized by distinct trade policy themes. And each can be observed and traced through the enactment of major U.S. trade laws.[5]

The first era encompassed the period between 1789 and 1930. It was characterized by a strict interpretation of the constitutional authority of Congress to regulate foreign commerce, a U.S. economy of limited global significance, a prevailing philosophy of economic nationalism, and the politics of partisanship and special interests. The era culminated with the passage of the Smoot-Hawley Tariff Act, when its dominant themes reached their most extreme manifestation and came to a timely end.

The trade policy themes these forces produced were relatively constant throughout this 140-year period. They included congressional dominance and micromanagement of the policy process, with U.S. trade policy dictated almost exclusively through enactment of highly specific trade laws. Bouts of intense trade politics were not uncommon, bringing with them a unilateral policy activism as politicians sought to respond to import-sensitive constituencies seeking remedial assistance. Statutory oscillations between relatively open and closed markets moved progressively in a protectionist direction with the passage of time.

The second era in U.S. trade policy dates from approximately 1934 and continued into the 1990s. It was officially ushered in with enactment of the Reciprocal Trade Agreements Act of 1934 and has been referred to as the Trade Agreements Program. This regime was the product of an entirely different set of forces and has been characterized by radically different themes. The U.S. economy was a growing and increasingly important influence on the world scene. U.S. policy formulation came to be dominated by elite participants sharing a definite market-oriented bias. And, in the realm of trade politics, bipartisanship and the depoliticization of trade as an issue became the order of the day.[6]

Of most significance to this era were the structural changes made in

---

[5] For purposes of this study, the phrases "trade law" and "trade policy" encompass the treatment of imports and matters involving foreign market access, including trade agreements. "Major" trade bills include substantive new law or fundamental changes to existing U.S. trade law. Therefore, generally excluded from the scope of this study are foreign policy or national security export controls, export promotion, regulation of U.S. business practices, authorization and appropriations measures, and lesser or routine bills and amendments.

[6] The term "politicization" as used during the course of this study relates to the role of trade as an issue in electoral and partisan politics. It also implies policymaker motivations influenced more by political pressures from fairly narrow constituencies than by considerations of the broader national economic interest. Used in this way, the term has primarily negative connotations.

trade policy formulation. Here, Congress opted for an executive-legislative partnership where policymaking became the product of a new balance of interests. This was institutionalized through a distinct legislative formula comprising periodic delegation to the executive of authority for the negotiation and implementation of trade agreements, but only in exchange for limits on its use and a statutory framework to ensure executive attention to other elements of the congressional trade agenda. Creation of the "Special Trade Representative" in the Executive Office of the President in 1962 contributed to the focus and coordination of U.S. trade policy. Enactment of fast track legislative procedures for implementing trade agreements in 1974 expanded the scope of agreements beyond tariffs into the realm of nontariff barriers.

The convergence of these new forces, including as they did the delegation of authority and discretion to the president, provided the executive with a heretofore unimaginable role in trade policymaking. They enabled the United States to lead internationally in the pursuit of bilateral and multilateral trade-liberalizing agreements, bringing with them a dramatic increase in global commerce. Day-to-day policy formulation and implementation were left largely to the control of elites in the executive branch and on a few congressional committees who had the accumulated knowledge of years of experience with hearings, negotiations, and legislation. Trade remedies to assist unhappy constituencies were established through a system of generic statutes, administered by the executive, that also served as a quasi-judicial buffer between Congress and interest groups pressuring it to intervene directly.

The 1980s: Evidence of Countervailing Trends

America's trade policy in the 1980s and trade legislation in the 100th Congress (1987–1988) were the product of this second era in U.S. trade policy. Yet, while the dominant forces and themes of this policy regime remained, there was growing evidence of countervailing trends, often with roots in earlier decades whose emergence only became apparent as legislative initiatives moved toward enactment.

Shifts in the forces influencing trade policy that evolved through the 1980s began with a decline in the U.S. economy relative to that of its trading partners. This was accompanied, particularly in the second half of the decade, by an increasing number of policymakers questioning the virtues of the marketplace and the Reagan administration's perceived blind adherence to laissez-faire economics. Congressional frustration with and disdain for the executive in the post-Vietnam/post-Watergate era also was felt to an extent in the trade realm, bringing with it some limited congressional reassertion of prerogative. Finally, a growing number of traditionally free-trade-oriented constituencies in industry and agriculture began to exhibit more concern with import competition than with the development of export markets, and urged their politicians to respond accordingly.

Virtually all of the trends in U.S. trade policy generated by these forces were apparent in the Omnibus Trade and Competitiveness Act of 1988 and in the process leading to its enactment. Among the most noteworthy were (1) shifts in the balance of control over trade policy away from the executive branch towards the Congress, and away from a trade policy elite towards a broader group of interests; (2) a proliferation of issues considered under the trade policy umbrella, with growing pressure to use trade tools to address problems not previously associated with trade; and (3) increased support for sustained U.S. activism in trade—even if it meant unilateral action.

CHAPTER OUTLINE

The chapters of this study move back and forth between chronology and context. The first set of chapters establishes the historical and policy framework for congressional action on the 1988 act. The premise that U.S. trade policy can be divided into two distinct periods is the focus of Chapter 2, which details the forces and themes relevant to each era and their manifestation in U.S. trade law. The chapter also introduces the legislative formula for the executive-legislative partnership underlying the post–Smoot-Hawley era. Chapter 3 sets the stage for the 1988 act by examining trade policy developments in the 1980s, including specific events indicative of the rift that emerged between the Congress and the administration, and growing concerns in the private sector about the future of the U.S. economy.

The second set of chapters represents the work's primary focus— namely, the evolution of the Omnibus Trade and Competitiveness Act. It encompasses the period from early 1987 through enactment in August 1988, with each chapter detailing a distinct phase of the legislative process. Chapters 4 and 5 explore House and Senate treatment of the bill, from introduction to committee consideration to passage on the floor. In the process, the narrative considers the motivations of key participants in each chamber, distinctive characteristics of the two legislative bodies, and the substantive trade provisions of primary interest to each.

Chapter 6 introduces the complex House-Senate conference committee formed to reconcile the two bills. It considers conference atmospherics, including its composition and principal actors, the state of executive-legislative relations, and the impact on proceedings of external developments and interest groups. Chapter 7 represents the crux of conference developments as they related to U.S. trade law, addressing the outstanding differences between trade portions of the House and Senate bills and the decisions that enabled them to be reconciled. The chapter also touches briefly on provisions that emerged from other parts of the conference and explores the legislation's political denouement, including the pivotal decisions that resulted in the bill's veto, reemergence, and ultimate enactment into law.

The study closes with observations and conclusions about the 1988 act, along with a discussion of trends that might signal the end of this era in U.S. trade policy.

2

TWO ERAS IN U.S. TRADE POLICY

*Our Constitution is in actual operation; everything appears to promise that it
will last; but in this world nothing is certain but death and taxes.*
—Benjamin Franklin (1789)[1]

*It is incumbent upon some great nations . . . to come forward with a broad,
constructive program calculated to displace gradually the policies which have
proven so futile and so destructive during these past several years.*
—Cordell Hull (1935)[2]

"DEATH AND TAXES"

The first era in U.S. trade policy began with the nation's first tariff act
in 1789 and closed with enactment of the notorious Smoot-Hawley
Tariff Act of 1930. It was an era dominated by Congress, the need to
finance war, and the politics of trade, and it was punctuated by the
enactment of highly specific tariff laws. Fluctuating U.S. tariff rates
moved steadily upward over time, driven by government revenue needs
and political constituencies seeking protection from imports. It was an
era in which Congress dictated trade law and trade law largely dictated
trade policy.

The origins of U.S. trade law can be traced back to the Boston Tea
Party when the colonials reacted to import tariffs imposed by Britain's
Townshend Acts. This fundamental objection to taxation without repre-
sentation is found in the Declaration of Independence and is the source
of the constitutional vesting of power under Article I, Section 8, "to lay
and collect taxes, duties, imposts and excises" and "to regulate commerce with foreign nations" in the Congress of the United States.

[1] Benjamin Franklin, from a letter to M. Leroy, 1789.
[2] Cordell Hull, Address to the U.S. Chamber of Commerce, May 2, 1935, in *Memoirs
of Cordell Hull* (New York: Macmillan, 1948), 377.

Congressional dominance over U.S. trade interests set out in the Constitution was the single most significant force influencing U.S. trade policy between 1789 and 1930. This factor, combined with the limited importance of trade to the U.S. economy and the limited importance of the United States to the world economy prior to World War I, enabled political motivations in trade to dominate and a basic philosophical bias in favor of economic isolationism to flourish.

In actual fact, the philosophical genesis of U.S. economic policy of the era can be found in the writings of philosophers and thinkers as far back as Plato. Earliest economic thought focused on the regulation of economic relationships as a means to contribute to broader social or moral ends. Economic doctrine involved issues that could not be separated from other aspects of man's behavior.

At that time, theories about economic relationships were rarely, if ever, described in terms of a system of objective or predictive laws. As concepts of scientific method, social and political equity, and the desire for improvement in this life (as opposed to salvation in another) were introduced into society, these and other concepts helped to shape economic doctrines. As they evolved, most economic doctrines remained instruments for the furtherance of broader moral or social policy objectives. Not surprisingly, the economic concept of welfare maximization, when applied to international commerce, differed greatly depending on whose welfare was considered at a premium.

The philosophical foundation of the classical school of economics, with its emphasis on global welfare maximization and the doctrine of laissez faire, was grounded in the works of Adam Smith (1723–1790) and David Ricardo (1772–1823). Smith, the patriarch of the classical school, developed the philosophy of the marketplace, on the basis of which he and the physiocrats who preceded him launched their attack on mercantilism. The physiocrats believed in the rule of nature, of a "natural law" wherein the state should leave individuals to practice their own self-interest. In contrast to the mercantilist emphasis on the welfare of the producer, Smith maintained that "consumption is the sole end and purpose of all production." Smith's interest in the division of labor and Ricardo's doctrine of comparative advantage revolved around the conviction that allowing individuals to pursue their self-interest results in competition, and that competition results in the most efficient allocation of resources and production of goods valued by the consumer. Basically, it assumed that what worked for Plato's village should also work for the nation-state and—by extension—what works for one nation should also be applicable among nations. Therefore, any barriers to trade between nations would, by definition, protect the less efficient through the creation of monopolistic enclaves, dampen economic growth, and damage the interests of the consuming public.

Other economic philosophers and philosophies, however, placed far greater value on national welfare maximization. The view that a trade surplus increases national wealth and power, and that exports increase aggregate demand, thereby increasing economic growth, originated with the mercantilists. Mercantilism (a label later applied to this school of thought by its critics) was the view advocated by men like Thomas Mun (1571–1641), who believed that an export surplus should be a chief goal of national policy. The mercantilists considered the nation to be akin to a merchant, where each is better off selling more than he buys. Long after Adam Smith had decimated mercantilist doctrine, however, others found reasons for governments to intervene in the marketplace to offset its perceived negative effects on society.

During the United States' early years, the practical considerations of raising money to finance the government far outweighed any single economic philosophy of trade. Until shortly before World War I, U.S. trade policy was, in essence, tariff-as-revenue policy. Executive branch motivations and objectives were only important to the extent they mirrored those of Congress. In fact, until the Reciprocal Trade Agreements Act of 1934 instituted the broad statutory role that the executive branch enjoys today, U.S. trade policy was almost exclusively a product of the legislature.

The first U.S. trade law, the Tariff Act of 1789, was the second law enacted by the Congress under the new Constitution—the first having established the oaths of office for senators and congressmen. While its principal purpose was to raise tariffs to generate funds for financing the new government, it did contain a hint of what later became known as "infant-industry" protection. In the century that followed the Tariff Act of 1789, Congress periodically embraced and discarded high-tariff policies. In fact, until the emergence of a federal income tax after 1913, the revenue raising and import protection objectives of U.S. tariff measures were virtually indistinguishable in law. As a general rule, periods of war or domestic economic strife were marked by tariff increases, while periods of growth were characterized by moderate reductions.

Although tariff levels fluctuated throughout the period from 1789 to 1930, trends in U.S. tariff rates fit readily into three distinct intervals: From the first tariff act through the notorious "Tariff of Abominations" of 1828, U.S. import duties grew progressively higher. During this period, the initial manifestations of trade politics also became evident. From 1832 through the Civil War, the nation enjoyed a brief interval during which there occurred some moderate reductions in tariffs.

Finally, the period between the Civil War and the Tariff Act of 1930 was marked primarily by tariff increases. With adoption of the Sixteenth Amendment to the Constitution in 1913 and the growth in America's world role, the stage was set for the transition to U.S. trade policy as we know it today.

As noted earlier, the most important economic factor influencing U.S. trade policy prior to 1913 was war and the need to finance it. Until the federal income tax became an integral part of the operation of government, customs duties were the principal source of revenue for the Congress in the event of war. Only when revenues from customs duties proved insufficient were other taxes levied—and then subsequently reduced and replaced by increased tariffs once the conflict subsided.

Emergency tariff increases were imposed to finance the War of 1812, for example, but when trade and, therefore, customs revenues fell off because of the conflict, new internal taxes were imposed on houses, land, and slaves. These were later repealed and the tariff regained its prominence as the government's principal source of income.

The Civil War brought with it an unprecedented need for government revenue as the federal budget reached and surpassed the $1 billion mark for the first time in 1865. Between 1861 and 1867, Congress sought to foot the bill by enacting various excise taxes (including "sin" taxes on alcohol and tobacco), the nation's first income tax, and, of course, by raising tariffs. Following the war, federal expenditures dropped and Congress accommodated a growing public call for tax reductions by lowering excise taxes and, in 1872, by repealing the Civil War income tax.

The 1890s were marked by growing disillusionment with high tariffs among farmers and laborers, on whom the burden fell most sharply. By 1894, their call for reinstatement of a federal income tax and a growing populist influence in the Democratic party resulted in Congress enacting—as part of a tariff bill—an individual and corporate income tax of 2 percent. Unfortunately for the income tax proponents, the Supreme Court declared it unconstitutional in 1895 on the grounds that as a direct tax, it could not be levied unless apportioned among the states on the basis of population.

The turning point in the tariff-as-revenue approach came in 1913 when the Sixteenth Amendment to the Constitution was ratified, allowing for "taxes on incomes from whatever source devised without apportionment among the several States. . . ." Shortly thereafter, with the passage of the Underwood Tariff Act of 1913, came a modest income tax and a reduction in tariff rates to their lowest level since the Civil War.

World War I marked the first time in American history that tariff rates were not raised to finance a war. Although federal expenditures following the war remained high, the income tax became the predominant source of government financing. By 1929, customs duties, while still on the increase, accounted for less than 16 percent of total federal revenue. The enactment of the federal income tax in 1913 meant the need for federal revenue, that had for over a century obscured any of the philosophical and political influences on U.S. trade policy, had disappeared as a dominant motivating factor. Following the imposition of the income tax, the role of tariffs became almost exclusively that of protecting domestic industry. Moreover, with the end of the war the United States found itself a relatively mature economy, moving in four years from a net debtor of \$3–4 billion to a net creditor of more than \$5 billion. This eliminated yet another justification for protective tariffs. From then on, considerations of economic philosophy and trade politics became the dominating forces in U.S. trade policy.

POLITICS AS ECONOMICS

Notwithstanding the overriding influence of the revenue motive in the early history of U.S. trade policy, broader philosophical and political considerations were also evident in congressional trade activities of the era. But to the extent any economic philosophy dominated the thinking of American policymakers prior to the 1930s, it bore little resemblance to that advocated by Adam Smith. As early as 1782, for example, Alexander Hamilton suggested that "to preserve the ballance [*sic*] of trade in favour of a nation ought to be a leading aim of its policy."[3] He went on to temper this sentiment, however, by noting:

> Experience has shown that moderate duties are more productive than high ones. When they are low, a nation can trade abroad on better terms—its imports and exports will be larger—the duties will be regularly paid, and arising on a greater quantity of commodities, will yield more in the aggregate, than when they are so high as to operate either as a prohibition, or as an inducement to evade them by illicit practices.[4]

Another form of economic nationalism that enjoyed widespread acceptance in the decades that followed was that of infant industry

---

[3] "The Continentalist No. V" of April 18, 1782, in Alexander Hamilton, *Selected Writings and Speeches of Alexander Hamilton*, ed. Morton J. Frisch (Washington, D.C.: American Enterprise Institute, 1985), 55.

[4] Ibid., 58.

protection, justified by Hamilton in his 1791 *Report on Manufactures* as follows:

> To maintain between the recent establishments of one country and the long matured establishments of another country, a competition upon equal terms, both as to quality and price, is in most cases impracticable. The disparity . . . must necessarily be so considerable as to forbid a successful rivalship, without the extraordinary aid and protection of government.[5]

This call for the use of protection as a means to stimulate industry served as the basis for the Republican party's advocacy of protective duties well into the last half of the nineteenth century. Hamilton's further concerns about foreign government "bounties, premiums and other aids"[6] that enabled imports to undersell U.S. producers also contributed a basis for several of the "unfair trade practice" concepts that eventually became—and remain—a fundamental precept of U.S. trade policy.

In this regard, the first 140 years of U.S. trade policy were marked by several events, punctuated by the passage of trade laws, that offer some additional insight into the themes of the era and the forces that generated them. The first U.S. tariff law exhibiting clear evidence of protective intent was enacted in 1816. It canceled the emergency duties enacted to finance the War of 1812 and replaced them with levies averaging 42 percent higher than their prewar levels. New England's newly established cotton textile industry was a principal beneficiary of the act, which included minimum valuation requirements that became more prevalent in subsequent legislation. By 1824, the average tariff on the entry of goods into the United States had reached 33.5 percent. This movement toward increasingly protective tariffs culminated with the so-called Tariff of Abominations of 1828, which began as an effort by lawmakers to discredit protectionist philosophy, then backfired when it passed both houses of Congress and was signed into law.

There followed growing dissatisfaction with high tariff policies, as regional economic considerations began to dominate the trade politics of the time. As the "free trade" versus "protectionism" debate began to grow, the protagonists were split largely along geographic, rather than partisan, lines. Southern politicians and their agrarian constituencies opposed high tariffs, while Northerners continued to demand protection for their infant manufacturing interests.

The 1828 Tariff Act represented the high-water mark of tariff protec-

---

[5] "Report on Manufactures" of December 5, 1791, in Hamilton, *Selected Writings*, 298.
[6] Ibid., 298–299.

tion prior to the Civil War and prompted the constitutional crisis of "nullification." Although tariff reduction legislation was enacted in 1832 to placate the South, the South Carolina legislature still declared the 1828 act unconstitutional and, therefore, null and void in that state. And while the legislature's move was as much an endorsement of Senator John Calhoun's interpretation of the Constitution as it was a reaction to high tariffs, the subsequent "Compromise Tariff of 1833" set in motion a reduction in tariffs in the ten years that followed.

By the late nineteenth century, the regional debates over U.S. tariff policy between the agrarian and industrial sectors of the economy gave way to partisan political differences. Something of an open trade philosophy developed in the Democratic party, although it continued to encompass moderate tariff rates for revenue purposes and some degree of protection—so long as it did not favor the industrialists who provided Republican financial backing. The Democrats also hoped that U.S. tariff reductions would encourage a similar foreign response, thereby enabling American farmers to sell their surplus production abroad. This approach was never embraced by all Democrats, but appealed to the southern farmers and urban consumers who were the backbone of the party's support. The Republicans, on the other hand, uniformly supported their high-tariff policy as a means of protecting the wages of workers in the industrial East and the "home market" of their farm supporters in the agrarian Midwest. As a general matter, however, the partisan debate over the tariff during most of this period was limited to its relative importance as a political issue, the appropriate level at which duties should be imposed, and the types of goods that should benefit from them.

In 1887, President Grover Cleveland devoted his entire State of the Union message to the tariff, and the issue subsequently played a central role in the presidential election of 1888. Although Cleveland received a plurality of the popular vote, Republican Benjamin Harrison gained an electoral college majority, and with it, the presidency. The highly protectionist McKinley Tariff of 1890 was the fulfillment of Harrison's campaign pledge as he, with the aid of Republican majorities in both houses of Congress, increased average tariff rates to 49 percent.[7] When Cleveland and congressional Democrats regained control of their respective seats, modest downward revisions in tariff rates were enacted in

---

[7] John M. Dobson, *Two Centuries of Tariffs* (Washington, D.C.: U.S. Government Printing Office, 1976), 19, 63. Dobson notes that the 1890 act also contained a limited reciprocity clause used to negotiate bilateral tariff agreements with several Latin American countries. Congress allowed the authority to lapse shortly thereafter.

1894—only to be increased again in 1897 with the return of the Republicans to control.

In the decades that followed, the generally upward trend in tariff rates was also accompanied by several innovations in U.S. trade law of a more generic[8] and policy-oriented nature than the strict micromanagement of specific tariffs evident until that time. Many of the trade policy concepts contained in these measures remain fundamental to U.S. trade law to this day, including those involving U.S. responses to foreign unfair trade practices and discrimination against U.S. exports. The Dingley Tariff Act of 1897, for example, contained the first generic countervailing duty law to respond to foreign export subsidies, following earlier tariff acts in 1890 and 1894 that imposed countervailing duty actions solely to protect the sugar industry. While the 1897 act "generified" the provision for the first time, it, too, was immediately put to use on behalf of the sugar industry.

The Payne-Aldrich Act of 1909 contained a form of reciprocity in its so-called "maximum-and-minimum clause." This provision gave the president the authority to impose a 25 percent tariff on top of existing U.S. duties to respond to "discriminatory" tariffs abroad. Although it was the first time the president was given any real latitude in dealing with international trade, the authority was only available for trade-restrictive purposes. President William Howard Taft, however, declined to use the authority until he received advice from a special panel set up to conduct a "scientific" study on the impact of tariffs on international trade and, in 1912, the Democratically controlled Congress canceled the board's appropriations. The maximum-and-minimum principle was repealed a year later, as part of the Underwood Tariff Act of 1913.

Finally, in 1916, a law was passed making it a misdemeanor to import foreign goods at a price lower than that in other markets, referred to as "dumping." However, the law's requirement of proof of intent to injure domestic producers proved too stringent to be useful. Congress, having failed in an attempt to add a civil antidumping law to the Underwood Tariff, tried again in 1919 and eventually saw enactment into law of the Antidumping Act of 1921, which remained fundamentally unchanged until 1954.

As the United States assumed a growing role in the world economy, its leaders became increasingly cognizant of the global implications of national trade policies. This factor, along with the widely held view that

---

[8] The term "generic" is used throughout this work to describe trade law written in a form that makes it generally applicable to any product or sector, as distinct from explicitly product- or sector-specific.

there existed some rational statistical basis for calculating appropriate tariff levels, gave rise to enactment in 1916 of a law creating the United States Tariff Commission. While Congress was willing to delegate to this independent body its technical and fact-finding work on tariff legislation, many years were to pass before the Commission would contribute to depoliticizing U.S. trade policy.[9]

With the end of World War I, the United States found itself in a more dominant position than ever in world trade. In spite of the fact that enactment of a federal income tax effectively eliminated the revenue justification for tariffs, it had no impact on the political impetus for import protection. It was at this point that the Congress, reflecting a period of profound political and economic isolationism, rejected the internationalist foreign and foreign economic policies incorporated in the Treaty of Versailles. The philosophy embodied in the third of President Woodrow Wilson's Fourteen Points, calling for "the removal, so far as possible, of all economic barriers and the establishment of an equality of trade conditions among all nations consenting to peace,"[10] would have to wait for the next era in U.S. trade policy.

The isolationist mood reflected in the failure of Congress to approve the treaty also brought with it the election of Republican Warren G. Harding in 1920 and a new tariff act in 1922. The Fordney-McCumber Tariff Act of 1922 raised the average tariff rate on all products entering the United States to a level 50 percent higher than that of the Underwood Tariff of 1913, and permanently increased tariffs on many agricultural products that had been imposed on an "emergency" basis in 1921. In most ways that counted, the protective intent and effect of the act far outpaced even that of the later Smoot-Hawley Tariff Act.[11]

---

[9] In this regard, it is worth noting that the commission was specifically designed to be a bipartisan agency insofar as the statute creating it allows no more than three of its six members to be of a single political party. Several of its initial commissioners, in particular its first chairman, F. W. Taussig, and William S. Culbertson, were also among the earliest members of America's trade policy elite.

[10] Woodrow Wilson, "The Fourteen Points: Address to the Congress of the United States, January 8, 1918," in *The Record of American Diplomacy*, ed. Ruhl J. Bartlett (New York: Alfred A. Knopf, 1948), 460.

[11] With the exception of U.S. tariff schedules involving agriculture and related products (such as sugar, spirits and other beverages, wool and woolens, and so forth), the average U.S. tariff rate by schedule was raised less than ten percentage points between the 1922 and 1930 acts. In F. W. Taussig's words: "The outcome was a tariff with rates higher than any in the long series of protective measures of the whole period. It went beyond the acts of 1890, 1897, 1909 . . . to an extreme of protection which few had thought possible." F. W. Taussig, *The Tariff History of the United States*, 8th ed. (New York: G.P. Putnam's, 1931), 453.

The 1922 act also introduced a number of concepts into U.S. trade policy that were to play an important role in our commercial relations for years to come. For the American chemical industry, for example, it provided higher tariff protection through the American Selling Price (ASP) method of calculating duties by assessing the value of imports on the basis of similar products manufactured in the United States, rather than on the actual price of the import. The act also revived and built on the maximum-and-minimum clause concept of the Payne-Aldrich tariff by introducing the so-called flexible tariff into U.S. trade law. Contained in Sections 315, 316, and 317 of the act, the flexible tariff was based on the principle of equalization of domestic and foreign costs of production—the same principle used to explain the high tariffs embodied in the remainder of the act.[12] Section 315, for example, authorized the president, pursuant to a recommendation of the Tariff Commission, to adjust rates on particular products up or down by as much as 50 percent in order to offset and equalize relative costs of production between American producers and their principal foreign competitors. Although the provision bore little resemblance to market economics, some of its drafters were in fact trade moderates who hoped that the combination of delegated flexibility and a more "scientific" basis for determinations would ultimately result in lower tariff rates.

Sections 316 and 317 of the Fordney-McCumber Act introduced two additional policy elements into U.S. trade law and into the Tariff Commission's investigatory repertoire. These pertained, respectively, to determinations of "fairness" involving unfair trade practices by importers and to foreign discrimination against U.S. exports. Both provisions were incorporated into the Tariff Act of 1930 and remain a part of U.S. law to this day. Section 316, for example, was designed to supplement the Antidumping Act of 1921, enabling the president to raise tariffs on, or to exclude from entry, products subject to unfair methods of competition—as defined by criteria then applied to U.S. interstate commerce. Renumbered Section 337 in the 1930 act, the provision is now used primarily to address patent and copyright infringement by imports.

Section 317 authorized the president to impose a 50 percent ad valorem tariff on the "product of any foreign country . . . [that] discrimi-

---

[12] Taussig and others writing about the 1922 act cite the fundamental importance of this concept in the bill's evolution. "The notion of equalizing costs of production had become a sort of fetish among the protectionists," wrote Taussig. "The principle . . . was embodied for the first time in statutory language,—declared by Congress to be the principle on which the tariff system is founded. . . . [And] it was pushed to further extremes than ever before, both in the rates themselves and in their advocacy or justification." Taussig, *Tariff History of the United States*, 480, 487.

nates . . . against the commerce of the United States," in order to offset the discriminatory "burden." Were the foreign country to maintain or increase the discrimination in response, the president was then authorized to exclude that country's products from entry into the United States. Although never applied, Section 317 became an important footnote to contemporary U.S. trade policy as the basis cited for the adoption of an unconditional most-favored-nation (MFN) policy in 1923. At the prompting of Tariff Commission vice chairman William S. Culbertson—who suggested that the provision "expresses the desire of Congress to extend the principle of equality of treatment in commercial relations"[13]—Secretary of State Charles E. Hughes used this provision to justify the inclusion of MFN clauses in all future commercial treaties.

As it turned out, Section 317 did little to counteract the discriminatory treatment faced by U.S. exports abroad. It proved extremely hard to administer, and as long as the United States maintained a high-tariff policy with a non-negotiable tariff, the promise of MFN was correctly interpreted by trading partners to mean nondiscriminatory bad treatment. It was not until the tariff became negotiable with enactment of the Reciprocal Trade Agreements Act of 1934, that unconditional MFN treatment had a profound impact on U.S. trade policy and performance.

THE PROCESS IMPLODES

The Smoot-Hawley Tariff Act of 1930 established the highest tariffs in U.S. history. It brought about massive retaliation by America's trading partners, resulted in a drastic shrinkage in international trade flows, and deepened and prolonged the Great Depression. It had a profound impact on the history and direction of U.S. trade policy. And it was the last time Congress ever initiated a general revision in U.S. tariffs.

The act, which began in response to President Hoover's call for a special session of Congress to enact a "limited" revision in agricultural tariffs, was quickly expanded in the House Ways and Means Committee to include a large number of industrial products. Many more were added

---

[13] William S. Culbertson, "Letter of W. S. Culbertson to Secretary of State Hughes, 29 September 1922," in *Reciprocity* (New York: Whittlesey House, 1937), 245. It is worth noting that others dispute this interpretation. William B. Kelly, Jr., in a review of events leading to the bill's enactment notes: "The United States had adhered to a conditional MFN policy for 144 years. If it were the intent of Congress . . . to inaugurate a new and different MFN policy, it is reasonable to expect that there would have been some discussion of this intent." Kelly, "Antecedents of Present Commercial Policy, 1922–1934," in *Law of International Trade*, ed. Stanley D. Metzger (Washington, D.C.: Lerner Law Book Co., Inc., 1965), 300. Regardless, the policy was not repudiated by Congress at the time and eventually received its formal endorsement in 1934.

on the House floor. The Senate Finance Committee moved the bill in the same direction, and by the time it reached the Senate floor, the process was largely beyond the control of the leadership. This process of political logrolling, termed "reciprocal noninterference" by E. E. Schattschneider, saw congressional distribution of tariff increases rapidly snowballing into a bill that contained thousands of adjustments in the U.S. tariff schedule. According to Schattschneider, reciprocal noninterference was a form of political pluralism that enabled potentially conflicting interests to join together into mutually supportive ones— where each special interest walked away with something, and where little thought was given by policymakers to the broader implications of the bill.[14] "Congress," he wrote, "seeks political support for the system, not by giving ample protection to a few industries whose stimulation is required by the public welfare, but by giving limited protection to all interests strong enough to furnish formidable resistance to it . . ."[15]

The act was the final product of the forces that had governed U.S. trade policy since 1789: congressional dominance of the process, economic isolationism, and trade politics run rampant. It represented the most extreme manifestation of the trade policy themes of the era through the massive and unilateral U.S. imposition of tariff increases in response to constituent pressure. And while congressional support for the bill was by no means universal—Senate passage was by a narrow 44 to 42—it was indeed approved by both houses.

Although action on the bill was already well underway by the time of the stock market crash in October 1929, the latter stages of Senate consideration of the measure did coincide with the intense politics of economics that came with the Great Depression. By the time the bill left the Senate, it had been amended 1,253 times, 1,112 on the Senate floor.[16] The bill adjusted tariffs on over twenty thousand items, resulting in an average ad valorem rate on dutiable U.S. imports of almost 53 percent.

On June 17, 1930, the bill received President Herbert Hoover's approval, in spite of a written appeal by over a thousand leading economists who predicted that ". . . such action would inevitably provoke other countries to pay us back in kind by levying retaliatory duties

[14] Schattschneider, *Politics, Pressures and the Tariff* (New York: Prentice-Hall, 1935), 145.

[15] Ibid., 85.

[16] Congress, Senate, Committee on Finance, *History of the Committee on Finance*, 95th Cong., 1st sess., 1977, Senate Document 95–27, 35. The amendment process in 1930 still fell far short of the Senate record—some 2,436 amendments to the Tariff Act of 1922.

against our goods." Between 1929 and 1933, world trade declined approximately 70 percent in volume terms, and 35 percent in dollar terms. During the same period, U.S. exports declined from $5.2 billion to $1.7 billion; U.S. imports fell from $4.4 billion to $1.4 billion.

It was time for the United States to reconsider its approach to trade policy.

THE SECOND ERA

Congressional passage of the Reciprocal Trade Agreements Act of 1934 signaled a turning point in U.S. trade policy. The law, barely three pages in length, heralded a fundamental restructuring of U.S. decision making in trade that enabled policies derived of an open trade philosophy to flourish. It was the start of a new era, characterized by executive-legislative partnership, progressive market opening, and the dominance of policy over politics.

The most important feature of the law's new approach was congressional delegation of authority to the president to implement trade-liberalizing agreements with foreign countries. With this delegation came the development of generic trade remedy statutes, administered by the executive, that were to substitute for Congress as the focal point for constituent trade complaints. Congress had acknowledged its shortcomings in the trade policy arena and opted to hand over the day-to-day responsibility to the executive, subject to these remedy laws and periodic renewal of market-opening authorities. It was a profound structural shift in the balance of trade decision making that had an equally profound impact on the substantive outcome of the policy process. For the Congress, it offered a buffer against extreme constituent demands while still providing a means for responsiveness to constituent needs. For the executive, it afforded sufficient flexibility and control in the management of U.S. trade policy to enable a president to incorporate trade in his policy portfolio.

By the 1950s, this marriage of the power of Congress to regulate foreign commerce with the president's treaty-making authority was further enhanced by a growing bipartisan appreciation for more market-oriented trade policies and for the use of trade as a tool in U.S. international endeavors. Together, they formed the basis of what became known as the Trade Agreements Program, and while the forces that influenced the era (and the trade policy themes they produced) have evolved over time, the fundamentals remain with us today.

Since the beginning of this second era, the economic philosophy that has dominated the U.S. approach has been reflected in a commitment to the promotion of an open world trading system. In its most basic form, it is derived from the theories of Smith and Ricardo and has manifested itself in the conventional wisdom that "free trade is good; protectionism is bad." Ricardo described it this way:

> Under a system of perfectly free commerce, each country naturally devotes its capital and labour to such employments as are most beneficial to each. This pursuit of individual advantage is admirably connected with the universal good of the whole. By stimulating industry, by rewarding ingenuity, and by using most efficaciously the peculiar powers bestowed by nature, it distributes labour most effectively and most economically: while, by increasing the general mass of productions, it diffuses general benefit, and binds together, by one common tie of interest and intercourse, the universal society of nations throughout the civilised world.[17]

However, just as important to international trade developments in the second era in U.S. trade policy has been the influence of John Maynard Keynes (1883–1946), both in terms of the implied role for government and with respect to multilateral agreements as a vehicle to effect a policy based on liberal trade. Keynes believed that government had a responsibility to compensate for the vagaries of private capitalism and emphasized, in particular, the use of domestic economic policies to promote employment, economic growth, and general well-being. Keynes' philosophical approach, particularly regarding government intervention in trade matters, reflected above all his pragmatic inclinations:

> There are strong presumptions of a general character against trade restrictions unless they can be justified on special grounds. The advantages of the international division of labour are real and substantial, even though the classical school greatly overstressed them. The fact that the advantage which our own country gains from a favourable balance is liable to involve an equal disadvantage to some other country . . . means not only that great moderation is necessary, . . . but also that an immoderate policy may lead to a senseless international competition for a favourable balance which injures all alike. And finally, a policy of trade restrictions is a treacherous instrument even for the attainment of its ostensible object, since private interest, administrative incompetence and the intrinsic difficulty of the task may divert it into producing results directly opposite from those intended.[18]

---

[17] David Ricardo, *The Principles of Political Economy and Taxation*, 3d ed. (1821; reprint, London: J.M. Dent & Sons Ltd., Everyman's Library, 1911), 81 (page reference is to reprint edition).

[18] John Maynard Keynes, *General Theory of Employment Interest and Money* (New York: Harcourt Brace, 1936), 338.

While the philosophical basis for favoring liberal trade was embraced by some in the United States prior to 1934, its impact on U.S. trade policy was, at best, minimal. But the Smoot-Hawley Tariff Act did more than simply discredit overt protectionism, it also made way for a U.S. trade policy more reflective of the enhanced status of the United States in the world economy. By 1934, the United States enjoyed ever-increasing economic and political clout among nations, and the global response to the Smoot-Hawley Tariff Act had provided a clear lesson in how damaging an isolationist U.S. economic policy could be. The United States had started to run a relatively small but steady trade surplus beginning in the 1880s, which had grown dramatically prior to and during World War I before sliding downward and then collapsing in the early 1930s. The interwar period was also the point where the proportion of U.S. raw material and agricultural commodity exports began to decline relative to that of manufactured products, accompanied by a comparable shift in composition of U.S. imports. Although there was a halt in the U.S. emergence as a net creditor during this period, by the early 1940s the United States was once again moving forward as a strong net creditor and exporter. Without this growing measure of economic superiority, a market-oriented trade philosophy might not have prospered. And the politics of prosperity, combined with executive branch flexibility under the new law, also offered a unique opportunity for a U.S. trade policy that ran parallel to its foreign policy objectives.

Between enactment of the Reciprocal Trade Agreements Act in 1934 and early 1947, the United States negotiated bilateral trade agreements with twenty-nine countries. It then invited a number to participate in the negotiation of a multilateral trade agreement in Geneva, Switzerland. By the time the negotiation of the General Agreement on Tariffs and Trade (GATT) was complete in October 1947, it encompassed a governing protocol and the results of bilateral tariff agreements (applied on an MFN basis) between each of twenty-three participating nations.[19] Provisions of the governing protocol, which generally resembled those in bilateral agreements to which the United States was already a party,

---

[19] The original signatories to the GATT included Australia, Belgium, Brazil, Burma, Canada, Ceylon, Chile, China, Cuba, Czechoslovakia, France, India, Lebanon, Luxembourg, the Netherlands, New Zealand, Norway, Pakistan, Southern Rhodesia, Syria, the Union of South Africa, the United Kingdom, and the United States. The Soviet Union had been invited, but declined to participate in the negotiations. United States Tariff Commission, *Operation of the Trade Agreements Program June 1934 to April 1948* (Washington, D.C., 1948), Report No. 160, Second Series, Part I, Summary; reprinted in Andrew J. Kress, ed., *The Economics of Diplomacy* (Washington, D.C.: Georgetown University, School of Foreign Service, 1949), 6 (page references are to original).

were also to be applied multilaterally: Article I of the protocol incorporated the concept of unconditional MFN. Article II contained the new schedules of tariff concessions and prohibited the use of currency conversion techniques to impair the value of agreements. Article III provided for the extension of national treatment to imported products.

Other significant GATT articles included parameters for the imposition of antidumping and countervailing duties (Article VI), principles for customs valuation (Article VII), and a prohibition on the use of quantitative restrictions (Article XI). Articles XXII and XXIII established a dispute settlement mechanism providing for the withdrawal of concessions in response to another signatory's "nullification or impairment" of its concessions under the agreement. Finally, Article XIX contained a general escape clause or "safeguard" provision whereby countries could temporarily withdraw concessions if the product involved was "being imported . . . in such increased quantities and under such conditions as to cause or threaten serious injury to domestic producers."[20] In return for such action, other countries could expect compensatory tariff cuts or withdraw concessions of their own.

The countries participating in the GATT agreement considered it a provisional document, pending creation of an International Trade Organization (ITO) that had been proposed as the trade counterpart to the International Monetary Fund (IMF) and International Bank for Reconstruction and Development (World Bank) at the Bretton Woods conference of 1944. The GATT agreement was to remain in place only until the charter was ratified by the contracting parties. When the U.S. Senate refused to ratify the ITO charter, the GATT was left the principal organization and body of rules governing international trade. To comply with its GATT commitments, the United States implemented its new tariff schedule by executive order, using tariff reduction authority contained in the Trade Agreements Extension Act of 1945. Compliance with the new GATT protocols was facilitated by their consistency with other existing executive authorities. Under the 1947 GATT agreements, the average U.S. tariff was reduced to 15.3 percent on dutiable imports and to 6 percent on duty-free and dutiable imports combined. While this represented a relatively small drop from the rates at the beginning of 1947, the levels attained were dramatic by comparison with, for example, the average U.S. duty rates of 52.8 percent for dutiable and

---

[20] *General Agreement on Tariffs and Trade: Basic Instruments and Selected Documents* IV (Geneva, Switzerland: GATT, 1969). Other exceptions (such as for balance of payment purposes, developing countries, or the establishment of customs unions) were also enumerated in the agreement, with the specific circumstances, conditions, and procedures related to each.

17.7 percent for all imports under Smoot-Hawley and the 37.3 and 14.4 percent rates still in effect five years after enactment of the 1934 law.

By 1949, manufacturing had far outpaced agriculture as a source of employment and income in the United States. The relative strengthening of the position of U.S. manufacturing was reflected in the trade politics of the day. Although Republicans had initially remained committed to high-tariff policies, by 1948 Republican party opposition to reciprocal trade had been reversed. In Bauer, Pool, and Dexter's *American Business and Public Policy*, the authors note that "until 1943, no more than five Republican votes had ever been cast for a reciprocal-trade bill in either house. From 1943 through 1951, a majority of Republicans supported it in six of nine roll calls on renewal."[21] Until 1953, however, each renewal effort was still characterized by battles along partisan lines, where "internationalism vs. isolationism, creeping socialism vs. vested interests, executive bureaucracy vs. congressional logrolling were among the specters raised."[22]

When Dwight D. Eisenhower assumed the presidency in 1953, his initial inaugural address contained a request for extension of the Reciprocal Trade Agreements Act. It was the first major Republican legislative initiative in trade since Smoot-Hawley. It was also a move consistent with Eisenhower's call for a policy of "trade, not aid," and it signaled the new Republican willingness to embrace an internationalist approach to foreign economic policy.

Although since the early 1950s free trade has been widely accepted as both the norm (against which deviations are measured) and the goal of U.S. trade policy, it has by no means been the only theme evident during this era. From the outset, the overriding objective of the Trade Agreements Program was to increase U.S. exports, with trade agreements accepted as the best means to that end. While this era in U.S. trade policy brought with it a global movement towards freer trade, the processes that made it possible also saw many of the more political themes in U.S. trade policy codified in the very public laws that allowed successive administrations to engage in negotiations. And with virtually every new delegation of trade-liberalizing authority, the trade-restrictive "price" for attaining such agreements has grown, both in statute and

---

[21] Raymond A. Bauer, Ithiel de Sola Pool, and Anthony Lewis Dexter, *American Business and Public Policy*, 2d ed., (New York: Aldine Publishing Company, 1972), 27–28. The extremely lopsided Republican showing in favor of the 1948 act (47 in favor and 1 against in the Senate, 218 for and 5 against in the House) was, however, considered anomalous in that it was largely attributable to the "peril point" clause added to the bill.

[22] Ibid., 26.

in the context of preemptive administration action designed to influence the outcome.

The themes and trends in U.S. trade policy of the era are all evident in the trade laws that they produced. All major pieces of trade legislation since 1934 can be explained in the context of executive-legislative compromise derived of the post-1934 policy-making structure. All reflect relative U.S. economic strength in the world and the dominance of elite decision makers who placed value on free trade. Yet, all also incorporate the trade-offs between this prevailing open market philosophy and the political imperative that inevitably influences the democratic process. As a result, presidential desire for reasonably unfettered authority to implement trade-liberalizing agreements has been granted by Congress, but only in exchange for limits on its use and a variety of trade-related riders.

THE FORMULA: EVIDENCE OF THEMES IN U.S. TRADE LAW

To appreciate the impact of the structural, economic, and political forces in U.S. trade policy since 1934, it is useful to observe the parallel evolution of U.S. trade law. The laws represent concrete manifestations of these competing influences and of the trade policy themes they produced.

A convenient formula for appreciating the pattern evident in U.S. trade law since 1934 is the illustrative equation $(X - Y) + Z$, showing that virtually every major trade law enacted since 1934 has contained new presidential authority (X), limits on its use (Y), and congressional quids pro quo (Z). The authority component is that delegated by Congress to the president to implement trade-liberalizing agreements. Limits placed on its use encompass the procedural and substantive restrictions imposed on the president's exercise of the authority. The quids pro quo come in a variety of forms, including any measures and actions upon which the granting of the authority appear conditioned by Congress in the first place. The statutory products of this formula have guided U.S. trade policy since 1934, making trade-liberalizing agreements possible simply by providing a realistic means for their implementation.

With the 1934 act, tariffs became a negotiable commodity in international relations, as U.S. trade negotiators acquired a measure of credibility unknown during the period when trade agreements were submitted as treaties requiring a two-thirds vote of Congress. Up until 1974, congressional delegation of power took the form of presidential proclamation authority in advance of trade negotiations, enabling tariff cuts to be implemented by executive order. When U.S. trade negotiators returned from the Kennedy Round Multilateral Trade Negotiation (MTN) in 1967 with nontariff measure agreements beyond the scope of existing authority, Congress refused to implement them. So, with the Trade Act of 1974, the nature of the delegated authority was expanded dramatically to accommodate nontariff measure agreements, including those likely to involve policies previously considered solely in the domestic domain. Other examples of delegated authorities to negotiate and/or implement trade-liberalizing initiatives include those related to bilateral or plurilateral Free Trade Area (FTA) agreements, unilateral grants of duty-free treatment to certain developing countries, and the occasional sectoral or commodity agreement.

Agreement implementing authority has remained the linchpin of the legislative formula throughout the second era in U.S. trade policy. Without such delegation, a market-oriented president has had little incentive to sign a trade bill. All major pieces of trade legislation lacking this authority, or offering it at a time when the president could do without, have failed to be enacted into law. They have fallen by virtue of a presidential veto (sustained by like-minded members of Congress) or have failed to survive the legislative process in anticipation of that outcome.

Inevitably, however, the delegation of authority has arrived on the president's desk with constraints on its use. These limits have been Congress' means of retaining its constitutional say over U.S. trade policy, taking the form of substantive and procedural parameters on the timing, scope, and degree of barrier reduction that the president is allowed to undertake. All major trade laws enacted since 1934, for example, have included a sunset clause for the implementation of agreements. These time limits provide Congress with the option of periodic renewal of the authority, along with some insurance against its abuse with respect to import-sensitive constituencies. They also afford Congress the opportunity to renegotiate the terms of the executive-legislative partnership with succeeding delegations. Another constraint placed on the use of tariff adjusting authority has taken the form of statutory limits on the percentage cuts allowed and/or the exemption of certain classes of product from cuts altogether. In addition, virtually all major trade bills subject to the legislative formula have contained procedural or quasi-procedural assurances that congressional negotiating objectives are taken seriously by executive branch negotiators. The establishment of private sector advisory committees, mandated public hearings, consultative requirements and procedures, side letters, commitments, and the consideration of International Trade Commission (ITC) advice are all examples of this phenomenon.

With each successive delegation of congressional authority, the limits placed on its use have also generally tightened. Reasons for this vary, but the principal one has probably been that the cumulative effect of each delegation (and presumed reduction in U.S. import restrictions) has meant an enhanced risk of impact on politically sensitive domestic production. As noted earlier, when the executive sought authority in the 1970s to implement trade agreements moving beyond tariff cuts into nontariff barriers, Congress provided expansive new authority. It was, however, made subject to post-agreement congressional scrutiny and implementation through a new legislative fast-track process.

Under the fast track, any modifications to U.S. law mandated by the agreements had to be submitted for congressional approval under special procedures involving accelerated treatment and no amendments. This balance between enhanced executive authority and a post-negotiation guarantee of an up or down vote became the mechanism by which the United States implemented the Tokyo Round MTN in 1979. When the president sought authority to negotiate and implement FTA agreements in 1984, involving the bilateral elimination of virtually all import restrictions, Congress again granted access to the legislative fast track. However, this time Congress expanded its application to encompass the tariff as well as the nontariff portions of any agreements and added a new pre-clearance process for the initiation of negotiations.

The final element of the legislative formula, the "Z" factor or quids pro quo, represent the remainder of the congressional trade agenda at the time the laws have been enacted. Falling into this category are both measures contained in the legislation and administration action or commitments in connection with the legislative activity. Statutory additions have varied and multiplied over the years since 1934. They range from establishment of significant new provisions of trade law, such as generic trade remedy statutes or the denial of MFN treatment to Communist countries, to the tightening of existing remedy laws to the granting of Trade Adjustment Assistance (TAA) for displaced workers. They also include mandated studies, reports, and a plethora of hortatory resolutions and report language stating congressional desires or intent. In addition, this category includes action taken by the executive to preempt protectionist legislation or to influence the nature of the add-ons. Executive reorganization of trade functions, negotiated voluntary restraint agreements, and stepped up attacks on foreign barriers are all examples of this kind of administrative response.

The add-on component of the formula has facilitated enactment of authority for trade-liberalizing agreements, but often at a trade-restrictive price. Usually incremental in nature, these changes in U.S. law have progressively institutionalized many of the more political themes in U.S. trade policy. They have become law regardless of the outcome of the authorized trade negotiations, and generally have remained in law long after the temporary negotiating authority has expired.

Between 1934 and 1979, eleven major trade bills were enacted consistent with the $(X - Y) + Z$ legislative formula. During this period, hundreds of other trade measures not conforming to the formula failed to become law. The era saw the successful negotiation of a great many trade-liberalizing agreements, including seven rounds of multilateral trade negotiations under the auspices of the GATT. As noted in Table 2.1, seventeen major trade laws were enacted between 1934 and 1988. The eleven major trade bills cited above include those enacted in 1934, 1945, 1948, 1949, 1951, 1953, 1954, 1955, 1958, 1962, and 1974. Trade laws enacted in 1984 and 1988 also conform to the pattern. Three laws implementing trade agreements approved pursuant to the fast-track legislative mechanism in 1979, 1985, and 1988 could be said to fit the formula as well, along with a regional trade preference bill enacted in 1983. Congressional resolutions extending the 1934 Act in 1937, 1940, and 1943 are more difficult to characterize as "major."

The Trade Agreements Act and Extensions

The Reciprocal Trade Agreements Act of 1934, formally titled the "Act to Amend the Tariff Act of 1930," was Secretary of State Cordell Hull's vision of a new U.S. trade policy and policy process. It also reflected lessons learned about trade politics during his earlier tenure on the Senate Finance Committee. It was a pragmatic and seemingly simple amendment to the 1930 act, avoided a frontal assault on Smoot-Hawley and emphasized the benefits of increased U.S. exports.[23] The three-page bill had as its stated purpose:

> Expanding foreign markets for the products of the United States (as a means of assisting in the present emergency in restoring the American standard of living, in overcoming domestic unemployment and the present economic

---

[23] "It was immaterial," Hull wrote later, " . . . whether the Trade Agreements Act was a separate Act or an amendment to an Act. The point was that it was to be fully effective and independently operated just as if it were a separate enactment. Actually it would have been folly to go to Congress and ask that the Smoot-Hawley Act be repealed or its rates reduced by Congress. This had been the old system; and, with the exception of the Underwood Act in 1913, it always resulted in higher tariffs. . . . " Hull, *Memoirs*, 352–356. Even then, Hull recalled, he still faced opposition from the high-tariff Republicans, Democratic flirtation with a high tariff policy in 1931–1932, and President Roosevelt and cabinet colleagues who wanted to protect the New Deal NRA and AAA programs.

TABLE 2.1
Major Trade Laws (1934–1988)

Provision/Issue	1934	1937 1940 1943	1945	1948	1949	1951	1953	1954	1955
Tariff-cutting authority	X	X	X	X	X	X	X	X	X
Nontariff measure authority									
Time limits	Y	Y	Y	Y	Y	Y	Y	Y	Y
Quantitative limits	Y	–	Y	–	–	–	Y	Y	Y
Negotiating objectives/ mandates	Y	–	–	–	–	Y	–	–	Y
Sensitive product exceptions				Y	Y	Y	–	–	–
Post-agreement approval required									
Pre-clearance required									
Consultative requirements	Y	–	Y	Y	Y	Y	Y	–	Y
Trade reorganization									
Escape clause–related			Z	Z	Z	Z	Z	–	Z
Adjustment assistance									
Treatment of export-related unfair trade practices/barriers	Z	Z	–	–	–	–	–	–	Z
Treatment of import-related unfair trade practices	–	–	–	–	–	–	–	–	–
National security/ NMEs/Communism						Z	–	Z	Z
Sectoral or country provisions	Z	–	–	–	Z	Z	Z	–	Z
Reports/investigations				Z	Z	Z	Z	–	Z

Note: "Major Trade Laws" included in table:
Act to Amend the Tariff Act of 1934 (Reciprocal Trade Agreements Act)
Joint Resolutions of 1937, 1940, and 1943 to extend the Reciprocal Trade Agreements Act
Trade Agreements Extension Acts of 1945, 1948, 1949, 1951, 1953, 1954, 1955, and 1958
Trade Expansion Act of 1962
Trade Act of 1974
Trade Agreements Act of 1979
Caribbean Basin Economic Recovery Act of 1983
Trade and Tariff Act of 1984
United States–Israel Free Trade Area Implementation Act of 1985
United States–Canada Free-Trade Agreement Implementation Act of 1988
Omnibus Trade and Competitiveness Act of 1988

TABLE 2.1
(continued)

Provision/Issue	1958	1962	1974	1979	1983 CBI	1984	1985 IFTA	1988 CFTA	1988
Tariff-cutting authority	X	X	X	X	X	X	X	X	X
Nontariff measure authority		X	X	–	X	X	X	X	X
Time limits	Y	Y	Y	Y	Y	Y	Y	Y	Y
Quantitative limits	Y	Y	Y		Y	Y	Y	Y	Y
Negotiating objectives/ mandates	Y	Y	Y	–	Y	Y	Y	Y	Y
Sensitive product exceptions	–	Y	Y	Y	Y	Y	Y	Y	–
Post-agreement approval required			Y	Y	Y	Y	Y	Y	Y
Pre-clearance required						Y	–	–	–
Consultative require- ments	Y	Y	Y	Z	Z	Y	–	Y	YZ
Trade reorganization		Y	Y	Z	–	Z	–	Y	Z
Escape clause–related	Z	Z	Z	–	Y	Z	Y	Y	Z
Adjustment assistance		Z	Z	–	–	–	–	⊥	Z
Treatment of export-related unfair trade practices/barriers	Z	Z	Z	Z	Z	Z	–	Y	Z
Treatment of import-related unfair trade practices	–	–	Z	Z	Z	Z	–	Y	Z
National security/ NMEs/Communism	Z	Z	Z	–	Z	Y	Y	–	Z
Sectoral or country provisions	Z	Z	Z	Z	Z	Z	Z	Z	Z
Reports/investigations	Z	Z	Z	Z	Z	Z	–	Z	Z

Guide to symbols: The presence of a symbol reflects the presence of a provision, not the provision's trade-liberalizing or trade-restrictive nature or magnitude.
"X"   indicates delegation of or change in trade-liberalizing authorities
"Y"   indicates limits or change in limits placed on the use of such authorities
"Z"   indicates provisions or change in provisions not directly related to such authorities or agreements
"–"   indicates continuation of provisions in previous law(s)

depression, . . .) by regulating the admission of foreign goods into the United
States in accordance with the characteristics and needs of various branches
of American production so that foreign markets will be made available to
those branches . . . by affording corresponding market opportunities for
foreign products in the United States . . . [24]

This focus on U.S. barrier reduction for purposes of increasing exports was central to Hull's approach, later described by him as "a sound
middle course between extreme economic internationalism and extreme
economic nationalism."[25] The law suggested that whenever the president found that "duties or other import restrictions of the United States
or any foreign country are unduly burdening and restricting the foreign
trade of the United States," he could enter into reciprocal trade agreements. For this purpose, he was provided proclamation authority for a
three-year period for U.S. tariff cuts of up to 50 percent from Smoot-
Hawley levels. Tariff elimination was not permitted, but existing duty-
free rates could be "bound." Duty reductions could be extended to third
countries on an MFN basis, excepting those found to "discriminate
against U.S. exports."[26] Although not appearing in the law itself, the
administration also apparently committed to use the tariff authority
solely on a selective basis, rather than for linear or across-the-board
formula cuts.[27]

The principal source of legislative history for the act appeared in the
report issued by the Committee on Ways and Means. It focused on the
decline in world trade since 1929, attributing it to "the almost universal
existence of high trade barriers built up in a frenzied effort to gain a
so-called 'favorable balance of trade' by shutting out foreign goods."

[24] *An Act to Amend the Tariff Act of 1930*, Public Law 73-316, 73d Congress, 48
Stat. 943, 19 USC 1001, 1201, 1351–1354.
[25] Speech before the U.S. Chamber of Commerce on April 30, 1936. Quoted in Bartlett, *The Record of American Diplomacy*, 514.
[26] This resulted in a two-column U.S. tariff schedule, with the first column containing
the lower MFN agreement rates and the second column retaining the Smoot-Hawley
rates. Column 2 rates are still applied to countries to which the U.S. denies MFN treatment. The 1934 law was the first explicit statutory authority for "unconditional" MFN
concessions. Noted Hull in this regard, "the phrase is not of the happiest. It gives an
impression of getting or giving favored or special treatment. It merely means: 'I won't
treat you any worse than the person I treat the best of all, provided you don't treat me
any worse than the person you treat best of all.' " Hull, *Memoirs*, 359.
[27] A reference to this "Y" commitment appears in Hull, *Memoirs*, 359. When Hull
originally conceived of the idea of tariff agreements to lower trade barriers in 1916, he
had wanted the agreements to be multilateral, regional, or bilateral in nature. He had,
however, concluded in the 1920s that few countries were as yet willing to consider a
multilateral approach and so opted for "the next best method of reducing trade barriers,"
bilateral agreements subject to unconditional MFN principles. Ibid., 356.

The report went on to suggest that "if the United States is to compete successfully with other countries to regain a fair share of foreign trade, it is necessary that the United States should create machinery whereby it can bargain successfully for such trade." That mechanism required a means to negotiate with other nations, and that "the very nature of international negotiations requires that it should be in the hands of the Executive." Nevertheless, the committee concluded, while "the exigencies of present-day conditions require that more and more of the details be left to presidential determination, the Congress must and always will declare the policy to which the Executive gives effect."[28]

In this regard, the Congress included several conditions on the use of the new presidential authority. The Senate Finance Committee, for example, added language to ensure that interested constituencies would have an opportunity to comment during negotiations, including requirements that the president seek advice from the Tariff Commission and various federal agencies and that public notice be provided "in order to protect American producers and manufacturers, who may fear hasty or ill-considered action without their knowledge and without their being given a chance to present their views. . . ."[29] Congress also added a prohibition on the reduction or cancellation of foreign debts to the United States, made an exception to the MFN rule for Cuba, and added a provision involving flour produced by imported wheat. Finally, the committees noted in their reports that they were leaving intact the 1921 Dumping [sic] Act, as well as various 1930 act provisions pertaining to unfair trade practices and countervailing duties.

The 1934 act, approved by a vote of 274–111 in the House and 57–33 in the Senate, was extended verbatim by three separate joint resolutions of Congress, making the original authority available for use in trade agreements through 1944. Between 1945 and 1958, the Congress approved eight Trade Agreements Extension Acts, extending the original for periods ranging from one to four years. In one instance when the previous authority had lapsed, the new authority was applied retroactively. In another case, the law offered a one-year extension to provide continuity—in exchange for an administration commitment not to use it! Several of the extension measures contained adjustments to both the base year from which tariff cuts could be proclaimed and the

[28] U.S. Congress, House, Committee on Ways and Means, *Amend Tariff Act of 1930: Reciprocal Trade Agreements; Report of the Committee on Ways and Means to accompany H.R. 8687*, 73d Cong., 2d sess., 1934, Report No. 1000.

[29] Congress, Senate, Committee on Finance, *Reciprocal Trade Agreements: Report of the Committee on Finance to accompany H.R. 8687*, 73d Cong., 2d sess., 1934, Report No. 871, 3.

allowable rate of reduction from the base. The initial extender, for example, allowed for 50 percent reductions from 1945 tariff levels, while the 1958 version only permitted 20 percent cuts below that year's levels.

Among the more significant limitations placed on the use of tariff authorities were those involving import-sensitive products. The 1948 act, for example, included a "peril point" provision where in advance of any negotiations, the Tariff Commission was required to investigate whether a threat of injury existed to any producer whose tariff was being considered for a cut. This was in contrast to an executive branch commitment in connection with the 1945 act and an executive order issued in anticipation of the 1948 act providing for escape clause investigations only after a concession had been granted. The peril point limitation on tariff concessions was repealed in the 1949 act and then reinstated in 1951, this time requiring the president to provide an explanation to Congress any time he chose to ignore Tariff Commission findings.

Most of the extender measures enacted during this period also contained a variety of add-ons. To expand the protection available to constituencies concerned with duty reductions, for example, the "escape clause" concept was progressively expanded beyond its role limiting the use of tariff-cutting authority to that of a stand-alone trade remedy law.[30] Examples of other add-ons during this period included a denial of MFN treatment for Communist countries and a ban on the importation of furskins from the Soviet Union and China (1951), multiple admonitions that "enactment [of this Act] . . . not be construed to determine or indicate the approval or disapproval by the Congress of the Executive Agreement known as the General Agreement on Tariffs and Trade" (1951–1958), establishment of a bipartisan commission to review the future of reciprocal trade (1953), and enactment of a national security import relief statute (1955). The 1955 act provided particularly good examples, as well, of the unwritten "Z" factors that often accompanied enactment: While the law's escape clause changes and national

---

[30] In the context of adoption of the 1945 act, the executive had committed to include an "escape clause" provision in all negotiated agreements. The executive order issued in connection with the 1948 act also established an escape clause process available to any industry able to prove injury from imports. With the 1951 act, Congress enacted this generic escape clause remedy into law, delineating the ITC's investigative process and criteria, and authorizing the president to grant import relief in response to an injury finding. The statutory remedy was modified in 1955 and again in 1958, with, for example, the addition of a legislative veto enabling Congress to override presidential escape clause decisions with a two-thirds vote.

security import relief provision were generic in nature, both were used by the administration shortly after the law's enactment to assist specific industries understood to be of interest to the provisions' authors. Fifty percent tariffs were imposed on bicycle imports under the escape clause, and the national security provision was used to assist the oil industry. Also related to the law's enactment was a Department of Defense decision to exclude the (low) British bidder in a procurement of heavy equipment.[31]

The Trade Expansion Act of 1962

Upon expiration of the 1958 law, the Kennedy administration requested a new law in lieu of another renewal measure. In particular, the executive sought authority to negotiate multilateral tariff agreements through reductions across broad categories of goods, rather than solely on an item-by-item basis. By the time the Trade Expansion Act of 1962 was enacted, it contained the most wide-ranging authorities delegated by Congress to the executive until that time, including five-year tariff proclamation authority for cuts up to 50 percent from 1962 levels and permission for linear (across-the-board) tariff reductions. Authority was also granted for the first time for the elimination of tariffs, but was confined to tropical products, certain agricultural commodities, items with tariffs under 5 percent ad valorem, and products where the U.S. and the European Economic Community (EEC) together accounted for at least 80 percent of the aggregate world export value. Staging requirements for implementing cuts were also imposed.

Explanations for the generous nature of the authorities contained in the 1962 law are many, including the perceived growth in export opportunities for U.S. manufactured goods in Europe, concerns about the EEC's new agricultural policies, and active private sector backing for the legislation related to both. This was also the last major trade-liberalizing bill enjoying the support of organized labor. But the 1962 act came at a cost to executive branch autonomy in administering U.S. trade policy. In addition to the limits on the use of the authorities noted above, the act required the president to obtain Tariff Commission advice on the probable impact of any change in U.S. import restrictions in advance of negotiations, and it precluded any tariff cuts on products subject to an affirmative injury determination. Congress also superimposed on the process its own executive branch structure—by creating the Special Representative for Trade Negotiations (STR) and an inter-

---

[31] These and other events are detailed in Bauer, Pool, and Dexter, *American Business and Public Policy*, 59–73.

agency trade organization chaired by the STR, and by appointing official congressional advisors to the U.S. negotiating delegation.[32]

The remainder of the bill was similarly expansive. Congressional add-ons of particular note included major new TAA programs for import-impacted industries and another revision of the statutory escape clause. One of the adjustment assistance programs provided for funding, tax relief, and technical assistance to injured firms. The other program provided for readjustment allowances, training, and relocation expenses for workers. Under the revised escape clause, the Tariff Commission could receive petitions from industries or workers seriously injured by imports that had benefitted from prior U.S. tariff concessions. The negotiation of orderly marketing agreements (OMAs) and the granting of trade adjustment assistance were added to tariff relief as presidential import relief options. And the number of votes needed to override a presidential escape clause decision was changed from a two-thirds majority to a simple majority in both houses of Congress. Other import-related provisions in the 1962 act included a Section 232 reformulation of previous national security import relief language and a stricter version of a 1951 act provision denying MFN treatment to Communist countries.

The last major provisions added to the bill involved U.S. responses to foreign trade barriers, including "unjustifiable . . . restrictions [that] impair the value of tariff commitments made to the United States, oppress the commerce of the United States, or prevent the expansion of trade on a mutually advantageous basis." Parallel provisions were added with respect to nontariff barriers (NTBs) inconsistent with trade agreements (including variable levies), "discriminatory" policies (including the toleration of international cartels), and "unreasonable" import restrictions. In all such cases, the president was to take appropriate and feasible steps to eliminate the restrictions or, to the extent he deemed necessary and appropriate, to retaliate against the products of the foreign country.[33]

Although none of these provisions had been requested by the administration, it was prepared to accept them in exchange for agreement au-

---

[32] The Special Trade Representative was to hold the rank of ambassador, be appointed by the president and confirmed by the Senate, and was to be the chief U.S. representative for any negotiations under the trade agreement title of the bill. The new interagency organization was tasked with making recommendations to the president on policy issues under the trade agreements program and on action under various trade statutes. The four official congressional advisors to the trade negotiations (two from each political party) were to be chosen from the Senate Finance and House Ways and Means Committees by the leaders of their respective chambers.

[33] *Trade Expansion Act of 1962*, Public Law 87–794, 87th Congress, 76 Stat. 879, 19 USC 1351.

thority. The same was true with respect to several restrictive trade initiatives undertaken in conjunction with the bill's passage and subsequent MTN negotiations. These included the multilateral Long-Term Arrangement Regarding International Trade in Cotton Textiles (LTA),[34] pledges to negotiate a voluntary restraint arrangement (VRA) on lumber with Canada and to offer Defense Department purchasing preferences to U.S. producers, and tariff increases on carpets and glass in connection with escape clause cases.

The Kennedy Round MTN was completed in 1967, involving fifty-three participant nations that together accounted for 80 percent of global commerce. More than $40 billion in trade was subject to some form of liberalization, including tariff cuts on industrial products averaging 35 percent. Negotiations in agriculture were far less successful, as the European Community proved unwilling to concede anything considered fundamental to its emerging Common Agricultural Policy (CAP). As for the two NTB commitments made by U.S. negotiators involving a new GATT antidumping code and elimination of the American Selling Price (ASP) system of customs appraisals, Congress simply refused to approve the changes in U.S. law necessary to implement them. And while Congress eventually adopted legislation related to the GATT antidumping code in 1968, it still required that domestic U.S. law always take precedence over the code.

The year 1967 marked the first time that presidential tariff-cutting authority was allowed to lapse for a sustained period since its initial enactment in 1934. This was due to a number of factors, not the least of which was evidence of growing protectionist pressures on the Congress as labor unions and several import-impacted industries made their concerns known. Both the Johnson and Nixon administrations faced battles with Congress over trade-restrictive legislation. Two of the most prominent were a major textile and footwear quota bill, known as the

---

[34] Throughout the second era in U.S. trade policy are examples of major sectoral exceptions to the era's general orientation towards freer trade. Textile and apparel import restrictions, and periodic arrangements to limit U.S. imports of steel and certain agricultural commodities are examples of this phenomenon. Such sectoral initiatives have been undertaken by the executive branch using various statutory authorities and voluntary restraint arrangements. I. M. Destler writes with great insight about these "special cases" in U.S. trade policy in *American Trade Politics*, 2d ed. (Washington, D.C.: Institute for International Economics and New York: The Twentieth Century Fund, 1992), 24–27. In the context of the $(X - Y) + Z$ legislative formula, these "special cases" constitute "Z" initiatives by the executive attributable to the unusual political clout of the sectors, executive desire to enact reasonably unfettered "$X - Y$" trade legislation, and/or a fear that in the absence of such preemptive action, a trade bill containing only "Z" might be enacted into law.

"Mills bill," that passed the House in 1970 and the labor-backed "Burke-Hartke" bill of 1971. Both were examples of bills not meeting the post-1934 trade law "formula," and ultimately neither became law.[35]

Partly as a means to offset growing congressional pressure on trade, the Nixon administration convened a Commission on International Trade and Investment Policy, known as the "Williams Commission" for its chairman, Albert L. Williams of IBM. In July 1971, the Williams Commission issued a lengthy report detailing major structural changes in the world economy related to trade, investment, and capital flows, and calling for negotiations with a view to eliminating "all barriers to international trade and capital movements within 25 years."[36] It proposed that the U.S. and its trading partners launch a comprehensive new round of multilateral trade negotiations to focus on the removal of nontariff trade barriers, reform of the international monetary system, and the elimination of trade-distorting practices involving agriculture, discriminatory procurement policies, trade preferences, export subsidies, foreign investment, and international aspects of environmental policies. Within a year, an Organization for Economic Co-operation and Development (OECD) group reported similar conclusions and, as one prominent U.S. trade official noted, "The idea caught on of using multilateral negotiations to solve some . . . domestic complaints and to offer a positive alternative to protectionism."[37]

Richard Nixon's August 1971 suspension of the dollar's convertibility and temporary import surcharge helped to precipitate the Smithsonian Agreement and, eventually, U.S. involvement in what would become the GATT Tokyo Round. It was obvious from the start, however, that

[35] The textile quota provision of the Mills bill, named for Rep. Wilbur D. Mills (D-Ark.), chairman of the House Ways and Means Committee, was originally supported by the administration in the context of failed textile negotiations with Japan. It opposed other quota measures in the bill, however, which was eventually blocked by a Senate filibuster led by Walter Mondale (D-Minn.) and Jacob Javits (R-N.Y.). The Burke-Hartke bill, named for Rep. James A. Burke (D-Mass.) and Sen. Vance Hartke (D-Ind.), employed statistical formulas based on import growth and market share to trigger U.S. import quotas and to impose restrictions on overseas investment by U.S. multinational corporations. It never reached the floor for a vote, but two of its quota provisions were later offered (and rejected) as amendments during House markup of the Trade Act of 1974.

[36] Commission on International Trade and Economic Policy, *United States International Economic Policy in an Interdependent World*, Report to the President submitted by the Commission on International Trade and Investment Policy, July 1971 (Washington, D.C.: GPO, 1971), 10.

[37] Harald B. Malmgren, "The United States," in Wilfred L. Kohl, ed., *Economic Foreign Policies of Industrial States* (Lexington, Mass.: Lexington Books, 1977), 9.

were such comprehensive negotiations to be undertaken, U.S. negotiators would need sufficiently expansive authority to implement agreements that might be forthcoming. It was evident that nontariff barriers were rapidly overtaking tariffs as the more pervasive form of impediment to global trade. Therefore, after failed efforts to obtain such authority in 1969 and 1970, the administration proposed legislation in 1973 containing tariff proclamation authority, advance authority for implementing certain NTB agreements (including one on ASP valuation), and authority to implement other NTB agreements in the absence of a negative vote of either chamber. The administration also included in its bill generally discretionary provisions to facilitate the granting of relief to import-impacted industries, authorities for presidential action against foreign barriers to U.S. exports, some tightening of laws relating to dumped and subsidized imports, tariff preferences for developing countries, and the provision of MFN status to the Soviet Union. Several of these provisions were designed to contribute to the bill's chances in Congress, along with administration negotiation of voluntary restraints (VRAs) on steel in 1972 and the Multi-Fiber Arrangement on textiles and apparel in 1974.

The Trade Act of 1974

Where the 1962 law had taken eight months to enact, the Trade Act of 1974 took closer to twenty. And while it contained significant new trade agreement authorities, it also embraced an expanded role for Congress in the negotiation and agreement implementing processes. The Trade Act of 1974 was signed into law by Gerald Ford on January 3, 1975. It had passed the House by a vote of 272–140 and the Senate by an overwhelming 77–4. Like the 1962 measure, the new law was written as a stand-alone bill rather than as a series of amendments to a previous trade law.

The statute's most significant and innovative contribution to U.S. trade law and policy came with its five-year "fast-track" authority to implement nontariff measure (NTM) trade agreements. Unlike tariff proclamation authority provided in advance of a negotiation and unlike the legislative veto proposed in the Nixon bill, the new procedure established an affirmative process for approval or disapproval of such agreements after their completion. The fast track was based on legislated changes in internal House and Senate rules of procedure and allowed trade agreement implementing bills to be considered on a specified time line and without amendment. It required the president to notify Congress at least ninety days in advance of entering such an agreement and later to submit a copy of the agreement, an implementing bill, statements of other administration intent, and various justifications for the agreement and its implementation. Upon submission, the implementing measure would be introduced in both chambers, after which the committees of jurisdiction would have forty-five legislative days in which to act before the bills automatically went to the floor for action during a final fifteen day period. Although the implementing bill would not be subject to filibuster or change during any point in the process, and only required a simple majority of each house to clear it, executive branch negotiators would still need to satisfy enough constituencies (with improved access abroad or trade remedy measures at home) and/or avoid the wrath of enough import-sensitive interests (by limiting reductions in U.S. barriers) to prevent a critical mass of interests from coalescing to defeat the entire bill.

With respect to tariff agreements, the 1974 act contained five-year proclamation authority, providing for maximum cuts up to 60 percent from 1974 levels and elimination of tariffs of 5 percent ad valorem or below. Commitments were also made by the STR in connection with this delegation to avoid cuts with a negative impact on import-sensitive products, to consult on any potential footwear and dairy product concessions, and to avoid negotiating agreements that would undermine the Multi-Fiber Arrangement (MFA). Finally with respect to tariffs, the act also included authority for the administration to adopt a new Generalized System of Preferences (GSP) program extending duty-free status to imports from developing countries. The GSP authority was made available for ten years and came with its own set of limitations on use. These included country and product eligibility criteria such as the exclusion of Organization of Petroleum Exporting Countries (OPEC) members; and of watches and most import-sensitive textile, apparel, footwear, electronic, steel, and glass products from the program entirely.

Both the House Ways and Means and the Senate Finance Committees made it clear in report language accompanying the trade bill that they expected use of the new authorities to involve "a degree of consultations and oversight activity not previously considered under past extension of trade agreements authority."[38] To this end, the 1974 act placed heavy

---

[38] U.S. Congress, House, Committee on Ways and Means, *Trade Reform Act of 1973: Report of the Committee on Ways and Means to accompany H.R. 10710*, 93rd Cong., 1st sess., 1973, House Report 93–571, 42. Throughout consideration of the 1974 act, the measure was titled "The Trade Reform Act." At the end of the legislative process, however, Senator Russell Long (D-La.), chairman of the Finance Committee, insisted that the bill did not deserve the "reform" label and the word was dropped.

emphasis on provisions designed to ensure ongoing consultations between executive branch negotiators, the Congress, and the range of interested private sector constituencies. In particular, the new law established an innovative official private sector advisory committee structure whose members were to play an integral part in the negotiating and implementing processes. The Section 135 advisory committees, topped by a CEO-level Advisory Committee for Trade Negotiations (ACTN), were to be comprised of labor, industry, agriculture, and consumer representatives. They were tasked with providing policy and technical advice to executive branch negotiators and with reporting to Congress on the outcome of negotiations. For purposes of the Tokyo Round, the system essentially institutionalized key aspects of previously informal links between the branches of government and between government and business. It enabled interest groups to work directly with administration trade negotiators, forced the negotiators to face interest group demands directly rather than filtered through the political process, made explicit to the interest groups (and to Congress) the trade-offs among them necessary to conclude a comprehensive multilateral trade agreement, and eventually helped the executive to harness the external groups on behalf of efforts to obtain congressional approval of negotiated agreements.[39]

Consistent with the formula for U.S. trade law since 1934, a raft of other provisions also appeared in the 1974 act. Principal among these was the Jackson-Vanik amendment, named for Senator Henry M. (Scoop) Jackson (D-Wash.) and Congressman Charles A. Vanik (D-Ohio), which conditioned any waiver of the law denying MFN trading status to Communist countries on freedom of emigration. Other major 1974 act provisions addressed expansion of existing law pertaining to the escape clause, responses to foreign unfair trade practices, and TAA, along with various amendments to antidumping and countervailing duty statutes. While several of these resembled proposals in the administration's original bill, all went beyond that submission with respect to accessibility of the processes to constituencies and limits on executive flexibility in response.

---

[39] Official advisors received security clearances and had access to many U.S. negotiating documents as the talks developed and progressed. To keep the negotiator-adviser dialogue as open as possible while still protecting the confidentiality of U.S. positions, the Trade Act had exempted the advisory system from certain provisions of the Federal Advisory Committee Act with respect to the openness of meetings, public notice and participation, and the availability of documents. To protect the advisors and to encourage them to provide as much unbiased information to U.S. government officials as possible, the act further provided for a limited statutory exemption to the Freedom of Information Act.

The new escape clause, contained in Sections 201–203 of the act, set out the various authorities, procedures, and criteria whereby the Tariff Commission (renamed International Trade Commission [ITC]) could investigate claims of injury from imports, issue a determination and, in affirmative cases, make a remedy recommendation for import relief. The injury criteria were relaxed from previous versions by no longer requiring a causal linkage between the injury and a U.S. trade concession, and by requiring industries only to show that increased imports had been "a substantial cause" of serious injury, rather than "the major factor in causing" that injury. Following an ITC injury finding, the president was then required to grant some form of relief to the industry, a shift from the discretionary "may" language in the earlier escape clause to "shall." The new statute did, however, allow the president to waive the requirement if he considered it contrary to the national economic interest. Congress retained its right to have the ITC-recommended remedy imposed by concurrent resolution of disapproval of the president's decision.

The 1974 act's unfair trade practice provision, contained in Sections 301 and 302, was also expanded significantly. It was transformed from a statute with presidential authority to respond to such foreign practices into more of a remedy vehicle through the addition of complaint procedures for concerned industries. Its definition of unfair trade practices was expanded to encompass foreign government subsidies as well as import restrictions, and its coverage was extended to trade in services as well as goods. The new law also placed responsibility for receipt of complaints in the hands of the STR.

In many ways, the Trade Act of 1974 rounded out and framed the network of U.S. trade laws and the executive-legislative-private sector interaction that characterize contemporary U.S. trade policy. In exchange for delegating to the executive a generous measure of flexibility, the Congress gave itself and its constituents some assurance of ongoing input in the negotiating process and remedies should the process still have an undue negative impact on any one constituency. In spite of the fact that it emerged in the midst of the post-Watergate congressional reforms, the 1974 act also had the effect of strengthening the control exerted by the House and Senate committees with principal jurisdiction over trade issues. Similarly, the law served to enhance the roles of the ITC and the STR, two congressionally mandated trade entities, in terms of the ITC's independence from the executive and the STR's status and position within that branch.[40] In fact, the act effectively brought to-

---

[40] With respect to the ITC, the 1974 act included a number of other provisions beyond

gether, formalized, and reinforced many of the elements in U.S. trade policy making that had been evolving since 1934: a network of authorities and processes for the conduct of U.S. trade policy and negotiations, control of the apparatus in the hands of an experienced executive-legislative policy elite, and a means to harness and channel external influences in trade in a generally productive (or at least nondisruptive) direction.

The Tokyo Round and the Trade Agreements Act of 1979

The Tokyo Round was the most comprehensive multilateral trade negotiation ever undertaken until that time. Emerging from over five years of negotiations were tariff cuts that reduced the average U.S. tariff on dutiable industrial goods to around 5.7 percent. Some limited gains were also made in agriculture. Potentially far more significant in terms of global trade, however, were the new GATT codes of conduct pertaining to rules and principles governing nontariff barriers to trade. These were designed to minimize the trade-distorting impact of domestic practices through standards of accountability, transparency, and procedures for the settlement of disputes. Specific codes addressed government procurement practices, licensing, customs valuation, subsidies, trade in civil aircraft, and the use of standards as technical barriers to trade.

In 1979, when the process for implementing the Tokyo Round MTN agreements went into high gear, STR Robert S. Strauss sold the agreement to the Congress on the basis of its potential for increasing U.S. exports. The overwhelming vote margins in favor of the Trade Agreements Act of 1979 of 395–7 in the House and 90–4 in the Senate reflected more, however, than just approval of its contents. They also signaled the success of the consultative mechanisms and procedures that had been put in place.

Beyond those formally established by the 1974 act, additional consultative arrangements had been negotiated between Ford and Carter administration trade representatives and the Ways and Means and Finance Committees. These included a 1975 memorandum of understanding in which the STR committed to keep the committees "currently informed" of developments during the negotiations (involving the sharing of position papers and classified cable traffic) and an exchange of letters in

---

those in Section 201 designed to strengthen its role and independence. These included removal of the ITC's budget from the control of the Office of Management and Budget (OMB), and transfer of the president's decision-making authority in Section 337 (intellectual property rights) cases to the ITC, subject to a presidential override.

1978 pertaining to procedures for committee action on implementing legislation. It was agreed, for example, that in advance of formal presidential submission of the nonamendable implementing bill, executive branch draft legislative proposals would be subject to a "mock" markup by each committee, followed by a "mock" conference between the committees. While everyone understood that the president would not be bound by committee recommendations emerging from this process, the fact that only one significant element of the MTN agreement had to be renegotiated,[41] and all but a handful of minor provisions in the jointly drafted implementing bill later appeared in the president's formal submission, evidenced its success.

In addition to the tariff and nontariff measures cited earlier, the Tokyo Round also resulted in several U.S. concessions of particular concern to key constituencies. Among others, these involved the dairy sector (with an increase in the volume of cheese entering under U.S. quotas), customs valuation (including elimination of the ASP standard), the addition of a material injury test in subsidy/countervailing duty cases, a change in the method of assessing tariffs and taxes on imported distilled spirits, and various tariff concessions that went beyond the levels authorized in the original proclamation authority. As a result, the executive took a number of other actions to offset potential opposition from affected constituencies. Examples included additional import protection provided to the textile and steel industries outside the negotiations (through a tightening of U.S. enforcement of the MFA and a new Trigger Price Mechanism [TPM] to address steel dumping), and an expansion in the product coverage of U.S. cheese quotas. In addition, the Congress was able to use the implementing bill to rewrite U.S. antidumping and countervailing duty (AD/CVD) laws, imposing strict criteria for determinations of dumping or subsidization, establishing time limits for action, and adding a mechanism for judicial review; and to enact provisions tightening various other U.S. trade statutes, including the 1974 act's Section 301 unfair trade practice provision. Finally, in connection with the bill's passage, the Carter administration was also forced to reorganize executive branch trade functions, including the transfer to the Commerce Department of the Treasury Department's responsibility for implementing AD/CVD laws and of the State Department's export promotion functions (through creation of the Foreign Commercial Service).

---

[41] The committees insisted that U.S. procurement from minority-owned businesses be exempted from the competitive bidding procedures dictated by the Government Procurement Code.

Beyond its obvious economic implications from global tariff cuts and disciplines on the use of NTBs, enactment of the Trade Agreements Act of 1979 demonstrated the apparent success of the two key procedural innovations in U.S. trade policymaking contained in the Trade Act of 1974, the legislative fast-track mechanism and the private sector advisory committee structure. It also offered one more example of the legislative pattern of compromise and trade-off inherent in the executive-legislative relationship over trade. And it may have represented the apex of the various trade policy themes apparent throughout this second era of U.S. trade policy: the executive-led partnership between the two branches in the development and implementation of U.S. trade policy, the domination of trade policy elites in the policy process, strong endorsement of an open multilateral trading system, and bipartisanship in the treatment of U.S. trade policy and law.

3

ATMOSPHERICS: TRADE POLICY DEVELOPMENTS IN THE 1980S

Double, double toil and trouble;
Fire burn and cauldron bubble.
—William Shakespeare, *Macbeth*

In June 1980, the United Auto Workers (UAW) filed a petition under Section 201 of the Trade Act, claiming that increased imports were a substantial cause of serious injury to the U.S. automobile industry. They were later joined in the petition by the Ford Motor Company. It was a year in which the industry lost over $4 billion, laid off a quarter-million workers, and faced import penetration of over 34 percent. Almost seventy years after Henry Ford pioneered mass production technology, this vanguard of U.S. industry was in deep trouble.

That autumn, presidential candidates Jimmy Carter and Ronald Reagan both pledged to aid the beleaguered auto industry. The Carter administration, cognizant of midwestern electoral politics, called on the ITC to hand down its injury determination in advance of the election. The commission refused, and on November 10, by a vote of 3–2, voted "no injury" in the auto case. Most observers were stunned, for while the ITC had acknowledged that the industry was in dire straits, it concluded that the ongoing recession constituted a cause of injury greater than or equal to that of imports.[1]

Early in 1981, the newly installed Reagan administration quickly found itself confronted by growing congressional pressure to limit auto

---

[1] It is interesting to note that in spite of this outcome, the lame duck administration still courted, but then quietly rejected, an offer by the Japanese Ministry of International Trade and Industry (MITI) to limit imports of passenger vehicles to the United States. This was a problem, the White House and U.S. Trade Representative Reubin O'D. Askew finally concluded, better left to their successors.

imports. Included in the mix was an auto import quota bill introduced by Senators John C. Danforth (R-Mo.) and Lloyd Bentsen (D-Tex.), the new chairman and ranking Democrat, respectively, of the Senate Finance Subcommittee on International Trade. The debate that ensued in the new Reagan cabinet was furious, divisive, and ended in a stalemate that pitted economic purists against political pragmatists. The Japanese, meanwhile, were growing anxious about the threat of congressional action. They simply wanted someone in a position of authority to suggest a level against which their government could impose a voluntary export restraint (VER). That spring, the new U.S. Trade Representative, William E. Brock, was dispatched to Tokyo with instructions to consult with the Japanese on the situation in the Congress. Brock was not supposed to negotiate a restraint arrangement, but by May, the administration was able to "acquiesce" in a Japanese-initiated proposal.

Events surrounding the imposition of Japan's auto export restraint offer a glimpse of developments that buffeted U.S. trade policy throughout the 1980s: the relative decline in America's dominance in the world economy, the resurgence of Congress as the action-forcing player in interbranch management of trade, and the search for trade solutions to the trade symptoms of problems not necessarily caused by trade. By 1980, the Tokyo Round MTN was over and the Trade Agreements Act was law. Congress and the executive were expected to move into their respective oversight and implementing modes, with an anticipated post-agreement lull in U.S. trade politics. In fact, the 1980s proved to be one of the most active decades in the history of U.S. trade policy.

The period between 1980 and 1986 was marked by great volatility in the economic, political, and structural forces influencing U.S. trade policy. Economic developments, in particular, were characterized by previously unheard of statistical extremes. The high inflation rates that had plagued the nation in the late 1970s made way for higher interest rates as the Federal Reserve tightened the money supply; the economy went into a deep recession; and tax cuts enacted at the beginning of the decade, while fueling consumer demand and the emergence from recession, also contributed to a dramatic growth in the federal budget deficit. Related to and concurrent with these phenomena was a dramatic increase in the value of the dollar relative to other currencies, comparatively slower growth rates in the economies of the United States' principal trading partners, and a debt crisis in Latin America. Taken together, the result precipitated a massive increase in the U.S. trade deficit.

The distribution of pain within the U.S. economy from these developments was decidedly uneven, with a particularly heavy impact on the traded goods sector. A growing anxiety about U.S. international economic dominance and the health and future of America's manufacturing base began to pervade the trade debate, challenging many of the basic assumptions underlying the nation's open trade bias. The credibility of U.S. trade statutes was increasingly called into question, as an assertive Congress sought to compensate for perceived administration reluctance to act.

There follows a brief examination of the forces influencing U.S. trade policy in the 1980s. It is followed by an exploration of several distinct events during the decade, illustrating how these forces came together to set the stage for what would become the Omnibus Trade and Competitiveness Act of 1988. While U.S. trade policy and legislation enacted during this period still reflected the dominant forces and themes of the second era in U.S. trade policy—a large and influential U.S. economy, market-oriented policymakers, relative bipartisanship in trade politics, and executive dominance of the policy process—the period was marked by evidence of a growing dissatisfaction with U.S. policy principles and the advent of several seemingly countervailing trade policy trends. Some of these trends clearly had their roots in the 1970s and earlier, but their emergence became particularly apparent as the legislative initiatives of the decade moved toward enactment.

FORCES IN U.S. TRADE POLICY: GROWING VOLATILITY

Shifts in the forces influencing U.S. trade policy that evolved through the 1980s began with a decline in the strength of the U.S. economy relative to that of its trading partners. This was accompanied, particularly in the second half of the decade, by an increasing number of policymakers questioning the administration's perceived blind adherence to laissez-faire economics. Where the administration saw competitive adjustment to market forces, others saw only economic Darwinism. Congressional frustration with and disdain for the executive in the wake of the post-Vietnam/post-Watergate era, prompting a general congressional reassertion of prerogative, was also evident to a degree in the trade realm. Finally, a growing number of traditionally free-trade-oriented constituencies began to exhibit more concern with import competition than with the development of export markets, and lobbied their politicians accordingly.

The Economics

Developments of most significance in terms of forces influencing U.S. trade policy appeared in the realm of economics. The U.S. economic scene during the period was a study in extremes, and nowhere was this more evident than in the nation's trade account. Until 1971, U.S. merchandise trade had been at or near balance for close to three-quarters of a century. The U.S. merchandise trade deficit of $4 billion in 1971 had grown to $35 billion by 1981, and reached a staggering $170 billion in 1987. During the period between 1981 and 1987, U.S. imports rose 55 percent from $273 billion to $424 billion, while U.S. exports edged up only 6 percent from $239 billion to $254 billion.

More significant than the aggregate statistics, however, was the dramatic shift in composition within the U.S. trade account. By 1982, U.S. trade in manufactured goods had also moved into a deficit position that reached over $100 billion by 1985. Gone were the days when energy and raw material imports made up the bulk of any U.S. trade imbalance, as the influx of increasingly sophisticated value-added products reached massive proportions. Similarly, the double-digit farm trade surplus that the U.S. had enjoyed up until 1982 had, by 1985, also experienced its first dip into a deficit position lasting several months. Sectors of the U.S. economy that had never encountered foreign competition in their home market or major challengers in export markets, found themselves facing both for the first time.

Related to the changing composition of the U.S. trade balance were similar dramatic shifts in various bilateral balances. The $11 billion trade surplus the U.S. enjoyed with the EC in 1981 had, by 1986, become a $26 billion deficit. U.S. trade with its largest trading partner, Canada, also showed $13 billion gap in 1986, as did a $5 billion imbalance with Mexico. A $7 billion deficit with four newly industrialized countries (NICs) in East Asia in 1981 had ballooned to $30 billion by 1986, with Taiwan claiming some $16 billion, and Hong Kong, Korea, and Singapore accounting for the remainder. Finally, with respect to Japan, source of the United States' most visible bilateral deficit, the $59 billion gap in 1986 represented over one-third of the U.S. total, and far exceeded the U.S. worldwide imbalance only five years earlier. Most of these developments could be accounted for by the trade-distortive strength of the U.S. dollar relative to other currencies that acted like a subsidy on U.S. imports and a comparable tax on U.S. exports. U.S. post-recession economic growth relative to that of its trading partners and the LDC debt crisis served to compound the impact.

The Trade Politics

Closely related to the economics of trade in the 1980s were developments in U.S. trade politics. In this regard, the volatility and unevenness of the economic contortions of the period were probably just as influential as the aggregate statistics themselves. Overall, the balance of pressure from constituencies interested in trade appeared to shift from a predominantly free-trade stance to one supportive of protective intervention.

Interest group trade politics had during previous decades generally been characterized by intense, but fairly narrow, pressure from a few import-sensitive constituencies, such as textiles/apparel[2] and steel, in favor of protection in the writing and administration of U.S. trade statutes. This pressure had usually been offset, however, by a broader coalition of export-oriented businesses, multinational corporations, and farm groups that the executive could count on to weigh in against protectionist legislation and in support of major trade-liberalizing initiatives. But by the middle 1980s, a number of traditional exporters in business and agriculture had grown frustrated with their losing battle against the dollar's inhibiting impact on their exports and with the Reagan administration's perceived failure to respond to the crisis.

Over the longer term, the response of many in industry to these economic developments would be to accelerate their outsourcing and globalization of production, ultimately intensifying their stake in an open U.S. market. In the near term, however, most faced losses in sales revenue and went about belt-tightening by laying off workers. As a result, while the U.S. unemployment rate dropped from its 1982 recession high of 9.7 percent to less than 7 percent by 1986, there was little expectation of the high-wage jobs lost in the manufacturing sector being replaced. Because many of these industries still had an important stake in export markets, most remained opposed to undertaking or supporting import-protective initiatives, often for fear of foreign retaliation. In the face of potentially immobilizing splits over trade in their traditional industry associations, however, many gravitated towards support for a more forceful U.S. approach to foreign barrier reduction—both as a trade initiative all members could support and as a means to further their long-term export objectives.

In the case of agriculture, which had emerged as the backbone of the free-trade movement in the post-war period, developments in the 1980s and the latent impact of several events in the 1970s seemed to have a similarly dampening effect on its willingness to pursue actively an open U.S. trade policy.[3] These developments included global overproduction

---

[2] Subsequent references to the "textile" industry in this book (and in common usage) will be used to encompass the entire coalition that lobbied this sector's trade interests, including textile and apparel producers, cotton growers, the Amalgamated Clothing and Textile Workers Union, and the International Ladies Garment Workers Union.

[3] With the exception of sectors such as dairy and sugar, which had long demanded and received import protection, most U.S. agricultural commodities were still highly

in various farm commodities, domestic price support levels and a high dollar that reduced their competitiveness abroad, lost market share due to the self-imposed soybean embargo of 1973 and the Soviet grain embargo of 1979, and growing competition for declining U.S. price-support dollars. They were compounded by the failure of the United States to convince the EC to moderate its protective variable levy system and its growing use of export subsidies to dump excess commodities abroad. Not only did these contribute to a severe recession in the farm economy and in America's farm trade surplus, the resulting disillusionment with trade and preoccupation with other matters meant that the farm lobby could no longer be relied upon to consistently weigh in against protectionist initiatives.

At the same time that this disintegration of the traditional free-trade coalition was taking place, the sectoral scope of import-impacted industries was also expanding, as manufacturers higher and higher up the technology scale began to face many of the same challenges as their more traditionally import-sensitive counterparts. No longer did the textile, footwear, and steel industries stand in relative isolation in their complaints about jobs lost to imports and in their efforts to use the trade remedy statutes and/or their political clout to seek relief from imports. By the mid-1980s they had plenty of potential company, as industries as varied as machine tools, wood shakes and shingles, auto parts, and chemicals, along with other labor-intensive light industry and parts of heavy industry, began to face the threat of serious import competition for the first time and concluded that preservation of their domestic market had to be their overriding trade policy objective.

The shift in focus was most evident in the high technology sector, where companies that had ceded the consumer electronics market to foreign competition in the 1970s were joined by, for example, merchant semiconductor producers in efforts to slow the erosion of their remaining U.S. and world market shares. And in more heavily unionized segments of the economy, management and labor practiced what textiles and steel had learned years before—namely, that joint support for import restrictions can provide an important unifying objective in the face of hard economic times.

For organized labor, layoffs in the automobile and other major blue-collar industries only compounded concerns about reduced employment in sectors historically dominated by the union movement. As a result,

---

dependent on exports to bolster prices and reduce domestic production surpluses. By the 1980s, for example, soybean producers were exporting over half of their output to foreign markets.

the unions came to focus virtually all of their trade attention and political muscle on legislation, such as sectoral quota or domestic content measures, designed to protect unionized constituencies from imports. With respect to exports, most of the unions were far more concerned about preventing the further opening of the U.S. market than in any nebulous export-related employment to be derived from market-liberalizing trade agreements. This motivation was reinforced by the administration's efforts throughout the decade to eliminate funding for the TAA program and by organized labor's assumption that growth in export-related employment would likely occur in industries not represented by a unionized work force.

While union trade activities were affected by the overall decline in organized labor's influence throughout the period, the unions still benefitted from their ability to mobilize strong grassroots support for their trade initiatives and for the politicians who backed them. While organized labor's position on trade had placed it at odds with many of its Democratic party allies on this issue during the 1970s, developments in the 1980s offered some promise of a reunion. The emergence of the "Atari Democrats," for example, in the early 1980s exemplified efforts of such politicians to maintain an open trade—but pro-employment—stance in the face of mounting political pressure. Through support of the emerging high technology sector in such places as Silicon Valley, they saw the potential for a shift in U.S. manufacturing employment into higher value-added sectors. The movement faltered, however, as the sector encountered trade problems of its own and with the move to offshore production by the company from which the group derived its name. By 1986, the debate had been overtaken by concern about overall U.S. industrial competitiveness, as exemplified by articles like "The Hollow Corporation," a widely read *Business Week* cover story devoted to the decline in U.S. manufacturing.[4]

Although a number of the more influential participants in U.S. trade politics appeared to gravitate away from staunch advocacy of free trade in the 1980s, the period also saw the emergence of some previously less active constituencies with a stake in an open trading system. These included service sector exporters and intellectual property rights (IPR) holders seeking expanded disciplines in global trade rules, along with various foreign export, U.S. import, and consumer interests concerned with the impact of potential U.S. market closure.

During the course of the 1980s, several key service sector firms be-

---

[4] Norman Jonas and other staff writers, "The Hollow Corporation" and related articles, *Business Week*, March 3, 1986, 57–85.

came active participants in U.S. trade policymaking. The impact of technology and the globalization of market activities presented new opportunities for financial, telecommunications, information, and insurance services, and while many U.S. providers already had years of experience in the international marketplace, they often found their growth hampered by foreign government interference and lacked the protection of international rules. In the early 1980s, these interests helped persuade the Reagan administration to place services high on its agenda for new global trade talks. For the most part, however, these firms remained far less influential than their industrial counterparts with respect to Congress. Part of this was attributable to the perception that service sector jobs were lower paying than their manufacturing counterparts; part was simply due to the great diversity of trade-related interests represented within the sector.

Toward the end of the Tokyo Round, a group of intellectual property rights holders also came into the trade picture. They arrived too late to have much of an impact on the MTN and suffered from the perception that their anticounterfeiting movement was designed primarily to protect the profits of foreign name brand watches, cameras, and perfumes. With the expansion of the group to include major U.S. exporters in the chemical and entertainment industries, however, its cause took on more of an employment and export revenue aura. As a result, by the mid-1980s, it had garnered an impressive measure of congressional and executive branch support for the development and enforcement of intellectual property rights protection abroad and the denial of entry to counterfeit goods at home.

With respect to the role of consumers in U.S. trade policy, their interests generally fell into three categories: retailers and importers, ultimate consumers, and industrial users. While they shared a common interest in an open U.S. market, they had rarely had much of an impact on U.S. trade policy. This began to change with respect to the role of industrial users in the 1980s.[5] Such industries, which generally import materials

---

[5] While importers and suppliers of imports had a history of involvement in AD/CVD, escape clause, and customs law cases, their success in the political arena had been more limited. Importers and retailers organized to fight textile, footwear, and auto import restrictions in the mid-1980s, but had far less impact than their U.S. producer allies who could cite a threat to their exports from retaliatory action. Although foreign exporters would often help to bankroll importer efforts, the groups still suffered from the perception in Congress that they were protecting profit margins at the expense of American jobs.

The ultimate consumer, as purchaser of goods for personal use, probably had the most to lose in the "free trade" versus "protectionism" debate during this period, but was the

for processing in the United States, had the political advantage of representing domestic manufacturers and the ability to cite U.S. employment considerations in their representations. Although the diversity of their interests precluded the formation of a cohesive user lobby, individual companies and sectors were able to have an impact on certain policy decisions.[6]

The last group involved in the trade debate worth noting for its role in the 1980s was the media. Although without a direct stake in the debate's outcome, the press was just as active and often more influential than those with something tangible to gain or lose. As noted by Douglass Cater in *The Fourth Branch of Government*:

> The reporter is the recorder of government but he is also a participant. He operates in a system in which power is divided. He as much as anyone, and more than a great many, helps to shape the course of government. . . . He can illumine policy and notably assist in giving it sharpness and clarity; just as easily, he can prematurely expose policy and, as with an undeveloped film, cause its destruction.[7]

Politicians may not always agree with what they read in the press, but they seem to have a sense that "the public" and other policymakers

---

least active and had the least influence. Moreover, most formal consumer organizations had such close financial and working ties to organized labor that trade issues rarely appeared on their agendas. In fact, in 1982, the Consumer Federation of America went so far as to support domestic content legislation that would have severely restricted imports of cars and raised car prices.

[6] Active lobbying by copper fabricators against copper import restrictions in 1985, for example, had an impact on the president's denial of a unanimous ITC recommendation under Section 201 for import relief. By contrast, Caterpillar Tractor had failed a year earlier to convince the president not to place additional restrictions on imported steel. In this regard, it is worth noting that many industrial users of products subject to import protection in the 1980s decided not to oppose their domestic suppliers in trade cases. In another case involving steel import restrictions, for example, not only did the auto industry fail to oppose import restrictions, but one company, Chrysler, actively supported the industry's petition.

Patterns of relationships between industries and their suppliers over trade issues differed by sector. In some cases, users who might have benefitted from cheaper inputs wanted import protection of their own, outweighing the desire to produce more competitively priced products. Similarly, export-capable supplier industries generally supported import restrictions for their customers, believing that their own potential gain from exports could not outweigh the loss of their largest domestic buyers. This user-supplier dilemma was particularly acute in high technology sector, where much of the foreign competition was vertically integrated while its U.S. competition was not.

[7] Douglass Cater, *The Fourth Branch of Government* (New York: Random House, 1959), 7.

both read and are swayed by it. In this regard, the influence of the print
media among Washington policymakers in the 1980s was far more
pronounced than could ever be explained by how voters absorbed news.
Studies showing that most Americans derive their news from television
contrast sharply with statistics for the nation's capital, where newspa-
pers are the dominant news medium and where the *Washington Post*
far outpaces any and all other sources.[8]

One explanation for congressional dependence on the *Post* is simply
that it is the primary source for everyone *else* in the Washington policy
arena. This is particularly significant with respect to editorials. In 1986,
the *National Journal* suggested that "the *Post*, along with *The New
York Times* and *The Wall Street Journal*, play a special role in Washington, described by some as bulletin boards for the elite. . . . The secret
of editorials' influence," the article stated, "is that their readership,
while small, is precisely the right one."[9] As a result, members of Congress, executive branch officials, and the interest groups lobbying them
all made a special effort to court editorial opinion in support of their
positions on trade in the 1980s.

As a general matter, press coverage of international trade tended to
have a distinct free-trade bias, often surpassing that of executive branch
positions. In many ways, the media in the 1980s was one of the last
great bastions of the liberal trade philosophy. This was particularly true
with respect to editorial writers where, for example, of 386 editorials
appearing on international trade and related economic matters between
October 1986 and September 1988, opinions were three times more
likely to be critical than positive, with some form of the word "protec-

---

[8] A study reported in the *Washington Journalism Review* in 1987, for example, found
that the *Post* garnered almost three times the attention from senior congressional staff
and members on a daily basis than any other source of news. This was followed by the
CBS Evening News, the *New York Times*, and *The Wall Street Journal*. Michael J.
Robinson and Maura E. Clancy, "King of the Hill," *Washington Journalism Review*,
July-August 1987. A similar study of "opinion leaders" conducted by a private research
organization in 1988 found that over 90 percent of all Washington-based government
officials read the *Post*, compared to congressional readership of *The Wall Street Journal*
and the *New York Times* of 77 and 68 percent, respectively. Other media sources in the
60–70 percent range were *Time*, *Newsweek*, the *NBC Nightly News*, the *CBS Evening
News*, and ABC's *World News Tonight*. The policy weekly *National Journal* also garnered a strong 58 percent readership on the Hill. Readership of *Congressional Quarterly*,
a Hill staple, was not tested in the study. The *Journal of Commerce* which, largely
through government trade agency press clips, had become an important source for Washington trade staffers, was also not noted. "Opinion Leaders: A National Survey on
Important Issues and Media Influence" (New York: Marketing Projects Group, Inc.,
1988).

[9] Burt Solomon, "The Editorial 'We'," *National Journal*, August 2, 1986, 1882.

tion" ("protectionist," "protectionism," and so forth) appearing in over half of them.[10]

EVENTS IN U.S. TRADE POLICY:
EXECUTIVE-LEGISLATIVE DISSONANCE

Evidence of the volatility of influences on U.S. trade policy in the 1980s was particularly apparent in the arena of executive-legislative relations. It was a period of congressional discontent over executive branch handling of trade matters, ranging from alienation of the trade policy elite over the interpretation of U.S. trade law to the executive's perceived failure to respond convincingly to major constituency trade problems. Congress looked to the executive to take an active stance to deflect growing pressure from constituencies, and was disappointed by the stream of free-trade rhetoric emanating from the White House.

For those members of Congress normally involved in trade matters, there was a further sense that the consultative process had broken down; that the executive was notifying congressional and private sector advisory committees after action was taken, rather than engaging them in a dialogue in advance. For its part, the administration saw an insatiably protectionist Congress behaving in a manner fully consistent with its post–Smoot-Hawley stereotype image. To the extent executive trade officials were acting in the trade arena, they felt they were not getting sufficient credit from the Congress for doing so. The resulting disjunction between the two branches was evident throughout the period leading up to the 1988 act.

Credibility Issues

The seeds of interbranch discontent were evident as early as 1980. Developments in the automobile Section 201 case under the Carter administration, and several subsequent Reagan administration denials of relief under the same statute, left Congress concerned about the credibility of the import relief statutes. If such obviously troubled industries could not gain relief through administrative processes, members of Congress could hardly steer other constituents in the same direction.[11]

---

[10] Drawn from a study by the author on "Trade and the Media," presented at the George Washington University in November 1988. The study employed content analysis to analyze all editorials on international trade and related international economic matters appearing in the *Washington Post*, the *New York Times*, and *The Wall Street Journal* between October 1986 and September 1988.

[11] The Reagan administration did, in fact, take a number of trade-restrictive actions during this period. However, with the exception of Harley-Davidson, the last remaining

This credibility problem was compounded by two other developments toward the end of the Carter years, visible primarily to the trade elite, but compelling nonetheless. The first was the discovery of a previously undisclosed side agreement by Tokyo Round negotiators, essentially conceding the GATT-inconsistency of the 1971 Domestic International Sales Corporation (DISC) tax law. The second event was an agreement negotiated with Pakistan that, for foreign policy reasons, granted it an injury test under U.S. countervailing duty law without gaining a firm commitment in exchange on export subsidy disciplines. With respect to the DISC, discovery of the side deal meant that the Congress had been misled by U.S. negotiators, and was now faced with a negative GATT panel finding and the prospect of having to change the law. In the case of the Pakistan agreement, the trade committees saw a precedent under the new 1979 act contrary to their intent and executive branch commitments, and evidence that foreign policy interests continued to take precedence over trade policy principles.

Congressional concerns over the new administration's approach to trade emerged very shortly after Reagan took office. In a 1982 countervailing duty case involving toy balloon imports, for example, the Department of Commerce tried to apply an injury test to imports from Mexico which, from the perspective of congressional trade experts (and eventually the courts), was in contravention of the antisubsidy commitments policy associated with the 1979 act. The perception that the administration was committed to a unilateral free trade stance was reinforced by its handling of a previously obscure provision of U.S. copyright law known as the "manufacturing clause." In place since before the turn of the century, this provision effectively banned the importation of works by U.S. authors not printed in the United States or Canada. Early in 1981, the Judiciary Committees of both chambers had approved a multiyear extension of the clause. The bill was vetoed by the president on the grounds that it was protectionist, and became the sub-

---

U.S. motorcycle producer that gained relief under Section 201 in 1983, the recipients of import protection appeared to be limited to those able to apply sufficient political pressure to force the administration to act. The tightening of textile import quotas, for example, took place in the absence of any formal remedy process in U.S. trade law, and was seen to have come about by virtue of commitments made in a September 3, 1980 letter from candidate Reagan to Senator Strom Thurmond (R-S.C.), pledging to link import growth under the MFA to that in the domestic market. Voluntary restraints negotiated on steel imports in 1984 ultimately required new statutory authority to implement, because rather than accepting an ITC injury determination under Section 201, the administration chose to justify its actions on the basis of foreign "unfair trade practices."

ject of Reagan's first defeat in a veto override.[12] It was a confrontation generated by senators rarely involved in U.S. trade policy and led by Senate Republicans who were otherwise highly supportive of administration initiatives. Moreover, when the administration approached Finance and Ways and Means Committee members for assistance, they found little sympathy—not because the members cared about the provision's protective impact, but because they objected to the unilateral elimination of any U.S. trade barrier that might instead be exchanged for greater market access for U.S. exports.

Of even more concern to the Finance and Ways and Means Committees during this period was a major turf battle over trade that developed between the Department of Commerce and the Office of the U.S. Trade Representative (USTR), and the perception of a concerted effort on the part of the administration to undermine the position of the USTR. Shortly after assuming office, White House Chief of Staff Edwin Meese had attempted to fold the USTR into Commerce. While the effort failed by virtue of the office's statutory standing and the ensuing congressional outcry, the administration still went on to create a Commerce-led interagency cabinet council that effectively downgraded the USTR-chaired Trade Policy Committee (TPC).[13] Finally, adding to congressional trade elite disquiet over executive branch treatment of the USTR and the interbranch consultative process, was concern about politicization of the private sector advisory committee structure. Appointments to the committees mandated by the 1974 Trade Act seemed increasingly based on partisan political affiliation, rather than on the ability of the appointees to represent industry interests on trade matters.

Split Priorities and the 1984 Act

The differences that developed between Congress and the Reagan administration over trade, however, went well beyond these more process-

---

[12] During the confrontation over the manufacturing clause, the provision was briefly allowed to lapse. Although it had been in effect long before the GATT, once reinstated by the override, the provision could now be treated as a new trade barrier and found in contravention of U.S. GATT obligations. The manufacturing clause expired in 1986 and was not extended.

[13] This problem was compounded by several highly publicized confrontations between Commerce and USTR over trade matters and signaled to the congressional overseers that USTR William E. Brock would not enjoy the backing they considered necessary for an effective trade envoy. The White House treatment of Brock hit members especially hard, not just because of its implications for the office they considered the lead U.S. government trade agency, but also because Brock was well liked as a former senator and member of the Finance Committee.

related matters and into the realm of U.S. trade policy priorities. Early in its tenure, the administration began to focus on launching a new MTN round, with heavy emphasis on trade in services. This was in contrast to steadily growing congressional concerns over trade in manufactures, particularly with Japan, and over European agricultural export subsidies. As a result, Congress refused to act on an executive branch request for extension of the 1979 act's residual tariff-cutting authority, for fear it would be used to begin the negotiations. Administration objectives for a new round were further hampered in 1982 by a GATT ministerial meeting that fell apart over the issue of agricultural subsidies.

Meanwhile, forward movement in Congress of textile quota legislation and an automobile domestic content bill (aimed at slowing the industry's outsourcing of parts and forcing the Japanese to produce cars in the United States), only served to reinforce negative stereotypes. Other members of Congress, often as a means of responding to or deflecting constituent pressure for such import remedies, were drawn to proposals for trade reciprocity legislation, designed to use access to the U.S. market as leverage to eliminate foreign barriers to U.S. exports. But, these proposals, too, were uniformly attacked by the executive branch as protectionist.[14]

In spite of these growing differences, enactment of the Trade and Tariff Act of 1984 left the era's basic balance between executive and legislative roles in trade policymaking largely intact. It was a law consistent with the post-1934 legislative formula in that in exchange for trade-liberalizing provisions needed by the executive, Congress attained enactment of several of its own favored provisions.

Accompanying the administration-requested renewal of the expiring GSP program and authority to enter into a bilateral free-trade agreement (FTA) with Israel, congressionally initiated provisions were enacted to prompt a more activist administration trade stance. These took the form of provisions drawn from trade reciprocity bills put forward by Senators Danforth, Bentsen, and others. They required the USTR to enumerate major foreign barriers to U.S. exports in an annual "National Trade Estimates" (NTE) report, and amended Section 301 to provide authority for formal executive branch self-initiation of cases against such barriers.

---

[14] This split over trade priorities was also exacerbated by the sense that the administration's other major trade-related initiatives seemed to reflect foreign policy objectives rather than a desire to improve the U.S. position in world trade. These included the use of trade sanctions against Nicaragua, export controls applied to the Soviet Yamal pipeline, and efforts to grant unilaterally duty-free status to imports from Micronesia (Compact of Free Association) and various Central American and Caribbean nations (Caribbean Basin Initiative).

While neither provision was really necessary for the intended action to occur, together they represented an unmistakable signal by Congress of its preferred executive branch approach to U.S. trade policy. With respect to authority to negotiate bilateral FTAs, the Congress required that both tariff and nontariff portions of the negotiated agreements be returned to it for approval under fast-track procedures, and added a Ways and Means and Finance Committees preclearance condition for the executive to access the fast-track process for FTAs with any country other than Israel.

Other provisions in the 1984 act included product-specific authority for the elimination of U.S. semiconductor tariffs (in connection with a reciprocal agreement with Japan that was sought by both the U.S. industry and the administration) and additional and more specific causes of action under Section 301, including foreign barriers to U.S. investment, failure to protect U.S. intellectual property rights, and the denial of "fair and equitable" market access. The new law also contained some modifications to the GSP program, a relatively minor change in Section 201 (in response to a failed footwear case), the addition of a cumulation provision to the AD/CVD laws, authority for the administration to limit imports of steel under a recently negotiated VRA, and a hotly debated sectoral reciprocity provision involving wine.

Not only did the 1984 act fit the traditional legislative formula, but the process of its enactment offered evidence that the fundamentals of elite control in the executive-legislative relationship in trade were still intact. The House had originally passed a bill containing a number of routine tariff suspension measures which was then used by the Senate Finance Committee as a revenue vehicle for trade policy initiatives. When the bill, still considered fairly mild by even administration standards, reached the Senate floor, however, it immediately became the target for amendments. These were primarily trade-limiting in nature and were opposed by both the administration and Finance Committee floor managers.

During the course of Senate floor action, the managers were able to defeat several of the amendments. Several others, however, were accepted without recorded votes to avoid losses by the committee that might have made the bill vulnerable to potentially more dangerous sectoral quota provisions. When the newly amended bill arrived back in the House, its leadership bowed to member pressure and returned the legislation to the floor for even more amendments. But once the bill reached the House-Senate conference committee—controlled by senior members of the Ways and Means and Finance Committees—the members worked quickly and closely with USTR Brock to drop virtually all of the most disputed add-ons. The result was a signable bill containing those provisions each wanted most.[15]

The president signed the 1984 act into law shortly before the election. Trade failed to emerge as a major political issue in the campaign that year, in spite of the efforts of Democratic presidential candidate Walter Mondale to make it one.[16] Yet, the latent congressional and business frustration over Reagan administration trade policy remained, festered, and ultimately reappeared with the arrival of the 99th Congress (1985–1986).

Approaching Critical Mass

During the course of the 99th Congress, trade appeared ready to surface as a significant political issue. In fact, the level of government and private sector attention and activity in trade probably rivaled or exceeded that during the 100th Congress (1987–1988) that saw the enactment of the Omnibus Trade and Competitiveness Act. It was a time of advanced political temperature readings in U.S. trade politics; of frenetic activity, few results, and a high destabilizing potential.

The U.S. trade deficit was rising to historic levels with few nonlegislative outlets for release of the frustration that had been building in Congress. Although "unfairness" in the international trading system was no more prevalent at this time than at any other during the era, the tolerance of American politicians for it seemed to plummet. They were inundated by complaints about the high dollar and its impact on U.S. exports and import-sensitive industries, with the message coming as loudly from sectors normally in the forefront of the free-trade movement as from industries from which the politicians had come to expect it. While the size of the U.S. trade deficit was a factor, its composition was even more so. Industries that had never before experienced foreign competition in their home markets or faced an erosion in their overseas market share, brought their trade problems to the attention of politicians who had rarely given trade issues much thought. The level of congressional frus-

---

[15] Brock's role throughout this process was particularly important. Although the rest of the administration generally avoided involvement with the bill, the committees were still prepared to work with Brock and accept his written and/or oral commitments on certain issues instead of writing them into statutory language. Approximately thirty-four letters containing commitments of intent on the part of the administration were signed by the USTR during this period.

[16] These efforts had centered around a message designed to articulate fears about Japanese manufactured imports, a decline in U.S. competitiveness, and the limited promise of a service sector-based U.S. economy. They were combined into a call for economic nationalism and the need to avoid American workers "sweeping up around Japanese computers."

tration and its response to such pressure was compounded by the administration's stance, where through much of 1985 it persisted in a "macho" approach that equated the dollar's strength with that of the country, and in labeling any effort to address its trade manifestations as "protectionist."

This was particularly frustrating to Republicans and their major corporate constituents who could not understand why an ostensibly pro-business administration could be so deaf to their concerns. Congress had no direct means to deal with the value of the dollar in currency markets beyond steady admonitions to the president and the Federal Reserve. Ultimately, in the absence of control over the source of the problem, active executive branch application of statutory escape valves, or a broad policy consensus for action, the trade manifestations of the strong dollar prompted a steady growth in frustration, punctuated by periodic congressional actions to let off steam.

By 1985, congressional impatience with the status quo reached a boiling point. The administration's inattention or unwillingness to work with Senate Republicans to bring down the federal budget deficit, considered a key component of the high dollar/high trade deficit situation, created a fundamental rift between them and the White House that would affect trade and other economic issues alike. The split was cemented in May 1985, when the Republican majority in the Senate attempted to fashion a responsible budget package of its own, fought, and eventually lost a bruising battle with Reagan and House Speaker Thomas P. O'Neill (D-Mass.) over its enactment.[17] The result was enactment later in the year of the more mechanistic Gramm-Rudman-Hollings budget formula, and a level of resentment among Senate Republicans over administration economic policies that lingered for the balance of the Reagan term.

In trade, legislative events resembling spontaneous combustion occurred on several occasions during the 99th Congress, along with the steady movement forward of a number of congressionally generated trade bills. While the executive and its congressional allies consistently opposed and managed to prevent any of the measures from being en-

---

[17] The proposal was an ambitious effort to control all aspects of deficit growth, including entitlements. Its dramatic approval in the wee hours of the morning by a one-vote margin, with Senator Pete Wilson (R-Calif.) being wheeled in from hospital on a gurney and only one Democrat voting in favor, contributed to Republican senators' euphoria over having accomplished something of importance. Unfortunately for them, the proposal was immediately denounced by Democrats and the president. Many Republican legislators still attribute their subsequent loss of the Senate in 1986 to this vote and to Reagan's failure to support the measure.

acted into law at the time, the administration's delay in shifting from a reactive to a leadership mode on trade and the dollar came too late for it to regain the initiative. Examples signaling the approach of a critical mass in congressional frustration occurred in the Senate in early 1985 and then again in the spring of 1986 involving, respectively, trade with Japan and negotiation of a U.S.-Canada bilateral FTA.

Congressional impatience probably reached its apex during the summer of 1985, as the introduction of import surcharge legislation and the forward movement of a textile quota bill coincided with evidence that trade might be reemerging as a significant issue in electoral politics. Shortly thereafter, several omnibus trade measures were also introduced and began to make their way through the legislative process. These ultimately set the stage for legislation in the 100th Congress, as the administration's about-face on the dollar and trade policy that occurred in September 1985 appeared to have come too late to have much impact on congressional momentum.

The first example of spontaneous combustion occurred in March 1985 with Senate passage by a resounding 92–0 vote, of Senate Concurrent Resolution 15 to condition termination of Japanese auto export restraints on increased U.S. exports to Japan and a reduction in the bilateral trade deficit. The resolution itself was not so unusual, since the Congress regularly passes nonbinding resolutions commending or condemning all manner of individuals, nations, and activities. Rather, it was the speed and manner in which the resolution emerged that set it apart, offering a glimpse of tensions in the trade arena that were to characterize the period.

The resolution was first proposed by Senator Danforth in response to reports that the Japanese were about to raise the level of their auto shipments to the U.S. by several million units over the previous VER level. Danforth maintained that if Japan was going to increase its shipments to the United States by some $4 billion a year in this way, the administration should at least try to offset the impact by seeking access to Japan's market for a comparable level of U.S. exports.

The resolution seemed to strike a chord in auto and nonauto state senators alike. Within hours of its presentation, it had cleared the Finance Committee and was on its way to the Senate floor. There, a standard 48-hour layover period was waived and the measure was immediately approved by the entire body. The House followed suit less than a week later by adopting a similar resolution by a vote of 394–19. For an institution known for its slow and ponderous procedures, the speed with which the measure emerged was remarkable. Just as significant, however, was the magnitude of the vote, considering that the measure was generated and propelled exclusively by the Congress and addressed a subject that would normally have been controversial because of its apparent special-interest implications.[18]

All of these developments set the stage for the remainder of the 99th Congress. Congressional efforts to force the administration's hand were largely bipartisan, whether delivered in a partisan or bipartisan manner, making it clear that the fundamental conflict was between the branches of government, not the political parties that controlled them. The administration and many in the press described and dismissed the legislative developments in the 99th Congress as blanket "protectionism," reflecting the post–Smoot-Hawley perception of Congress on trade matters. More astute observers like I. M. Destler, however, perceived a different kind of motivation, namely that of a Congress forced reluctantly to act on trade in the absence of the executive leadership it had come to expect since the Reciprocal Trade Agreements Act.[19]

Both sets of interpretations are supportable by specific examples. A study by the Congressional Research Service (CRS) on trade legislation in 1985, for example, identified 634 separate bills and classified them into five categories.[20] In the "protectionist" category, which included industry-specific tariff and quota measures, the study found 150 bills or 24 percent of the total. A similar number, 126 bills or 20 percent, were identified in the "free-trade" category, including product-specific tariff reductions, adjustment assistance measures, and authorizations for trade-liberalizing agreements. Between the two extremes, the CRS identified three other categories, bills that were "potentially protection-

---

[18] Finance Committee leaders followed passage of the resolution by initiating a more legally binding version of the measure that was swiftly approved in committee and placed on the Senate calendar as S. 1404. The absence of a readily available "revenue vehicle" from the House and disputes over potential amendments that would have linked the increase in U.S. exports to the bilateral trade deficit (rather than just the incremental increase accruing from elimination of the VER), resulted in the bill languishing on the Senate calendar for the remainder of the 99th Congress. S. 1404 later emerged as the conceptual basis for what became known as "Super 301" in the Omnibus Trade and Competitiveness Act of 1988.

[19] Destler, "Protecting Congress or Protecting Trade?" *Foreign Policy* 62 (Spring 1986): 96–107.

[20] Raymond J. Ahearn, with the assistance of Robert Kirk, "Protectionist Legislation in 1985," a study by the Congressional Research Service, Library of Congress, March 31, 1986, 86–632 E. The study employed a broad definition of trade that included measures related to export promotion, trade finance, and foreign policy-related trade sanctions. While the authors concluded that the perception of a rise in "protectionist" legislation in Congress was not clearly borne out by the number of bills introduced (a slight increase over previous Congresses), their legislative categories do offer some insight into the qualitative characteristics of bills being introduced during this period.

ist," "restrictive, nonprotectionist," and "nonprotectionist, nonliberal-izing." These categories dealt as much with legislative intent as with any likely impact from their enactment. Of these, by far the most sig-nificant in terms of the Trade Agreements Program were bills falling in the "potentially protectionist" category. Here the CRS identified seventy-seven bills (12 percent of the total), which included market access measures using access to the U.S. market as leverage, various omnibus bills, and "trade law reform" measures involving amendments to existing trade statutes.

Two significant examples of bills that emerged during the summer of 1985 most readily classified in the "protectionist" category were a tex-tile quota measure and a bill to impose a tariff surcharge on billions of dollars in U.S. imports. Both benefitted from pent-up congressional frustration over trade and both alarmed members of Congress who sought an approach to trade policy that would not automatically be labeled as protectionist.

The textile bill had been introduced in March and for a time that spring, had appeared to be unstoppable. By the time the administration got around to weighing in officially against it, for example, over half the members in both the House and Senate had already signed on as cosponsors. The bill passed the House in October by a vote of 262–159 and, after some modification, the Senate by 60–39. The House then cleared the Senate measure to avoid a formal conference (by 255–161) and sent it along to the president. While the votes for the bill far ex-ceeded those against, the vote margins were insufficient to ensure the two-thirds majority needed to override a presidential veto. This was probably attributable to delays in the legislative process, new adminis-tration trade initiatives that fall, and the emergence of less radical legis-lative alternatives. The bill was vetoed in December, but its supporters held up the override vote until August 1986 when the House failed to override by 276–149. The administration had succeeded in turning back the measure, but had lost votes between final passage of the original bill and the override. Moreover, by that point a number of key Demo-crats who had supported the president's veto were already on record in support of omnibus trade legislation.[21]

---

[21] An interesting analysis of the textile override vote appeared in an article entitled "Textile Override Vote Shows Omnibus Trade Bill May be Unstoppable," in Sam Gil-ston's *Washington Tariff and Trade Letter* of August 11, 1986. It pointed out that while the president has tended to pick up votes in a veto override situation, in this instance the fifteen votes that shifted to opposition of the bill were more than outweighed by the twenty-seven votes that moved the other way. With respect to elite voting patterns, Gilston also pointed out that while Democrats overall voted 82 percent in favor of the

The year also brought with it legislation, introduced in July 1985, that became known as the Gephardt-Bentsen-Rostenkowski import surcharge bill.[22] It required the imposition of a 25 percent surcharge on imports from any country that maintained both a large bilateral trade surplus with the United States and unfair barriers to imports. Although this measure had many fewer supporters than the textile quota measure, it created far more alarm in trade policy circles because of its focus on mandated reductions in bilateral trade deficits and because it had been put forward by well-respected and influential congressional trade leaders.

The measure had been initiated by Rep. Richard Gephardt (D-Mo.), but the fact that the chairman of the Ways and Means Committee and the ranking Democrat on the Senate Finance Committee had lent their names to it meant that it had the ingredients necessary to garner widespread support. In addition to its influential sponsors, the proposal was generic and therefore less susceptible to attack as "protectionist" than a product-specific measure; without being explicit, it was clearly aimed at Japan, the principal foreign target of congressional trade frustrations; and at a time when Congress was struggling to meet the Gramm-Rudman-Hollings budget targets, it promised a new source of revenue. The concern the bill generated resulted in an unusually rapid and vehement press attack, which had both Bentsen and Rostenkowski backing away from the measure in fairly short order. With subsequent revisions, the bill became a stand-alone Gephardt measure and remained a part of the omnibus trade bill debate well into the 100th Congress.

As noted earlier, the summer of 1985 emerged as the most intense and volatile period with respect to trade matters during the 99th Congress. Not only was the import surcharge measure introduced and the textile bill moving forward, but the administration turned down several Section 201 import relief cases. The volatility brought with it a growing element of partisan political maneuvering over trade as Republican and Democratic lawmakers became increasingly suspicious of the other party's motivations. Members from both parties perceived a need for action on trade and the dollar, but while Republicans wanted to distance themselves from the administration without undertaking a frontal as-

---

override, well above the two-thirds needed, the comparable proportion of Democrats on the Ways and Means Committee was less than two-thirds at 63 percent.

[22] Named for its principal sponsors, Congressman Richard Gephardt (D-Mo.), Senator Bentsen, and Rep. Rostenkowski. Later versions of the measure were sponsored solely by Rep. Gephardt, and became known as the "Gephardt bill," the "Gephardt amendment," or, simply "Gephardt."

sault, Democrats saw a potentially valuable political issue and were reluctant to make things easier for their Republican counterparts.

Then in August, a relatively obscure off-year House race for the first district seat in Texas raised the specter of trade becoming a viable partisan issue. The election involved Democrat Jim Chapman, Jr., perceived as the underdog in a traditionally conservative district, beating Republican Edd Hargett, in part because of the latter's apparent lack of concern about the region's trade problems.[23] In fact, more than a month before this election, most of the groups in Congress that would ultimately fashion omnibus trade bills were already at work. As a result of these developments, however, by the time the administration was ready to launch its own trade initiatives, it was hard-pressed to catch up.

The Administration Acts

A dramatic shift in the administration's trade stance took place in the fall of 1985. It involved responses to both exchange rate issues and foreign trade barriers and coincided with James Baker's move from White House Chief of Staff to Secretary of Treasury. On September 22, 1985, finance ministers and central bank heads of the five leading industrialized nations issued the "Plaza Accord," a communique stressing the need for some coordination in economic policies and joint intervention in currency markets to bring down the value of the U.S. dollar relative to other currencies. By November, the dollar had dropped more than 20 percent from its peak in February 1985, offering some anticipated measure of comfort to export-capable and import-sensitive segments of U.S. industry. Its impact on the U.S. trade balance was not expected to be evident for some time.[24]

---

[23] While in retrospect, most political observers agreed that the Republican simply ran a bad race, at the time the result was perceived as evidence that the worst fears of congressional Republicans on trade were being realized. Hargett's comment "I don't know what trade policies have to do with bringing jobs to east Texas," in the face of the recent closure of a local Lone Star Steel plant received considerable press attention. Michael Barone and Grant Ujifusa, *The Almanac of American Politics 1988* (Washington, D.C.: National Journal, 1987), 1138.

[24] This phenomenon is known as the "*J*-curve" effect. A reduction in the value of a country's currency relative to other currencies lowers the cost of its exports and increases the cost of its imports. In the long term, predicted by economists at the time to be 12–18 months, the volume and value of that country's exports should rise, its imports fall, and its trade deficit narrow. In the near term, however, this impact is preceded by the statistical appearance of an even larger trade imbalance as the shift in volume of traded goods catches up with the change in value of those goods. For additional information, see Peter H. Lindert, *International Economics*, 8th ed. (Homewood, Ill.: Richard D. Irwin, 1986), 420.

On September 23, 1985, the president gave a major address that heralded the second key shift in administration trade policy, a focus on "fairness" in trade with respect to foreign barriers to U.S. exports. This meant distinguishing between import protection imposed for purposes of protecting a domestic industry and retaliation or the threat of retaliation as a means to pressure foreign governments to open their markets. Associated with the second policy announcement was a dramatic upsurge in the executive's use of Section 301 as a market access tool, resulting in acceleration of cases against Japan (leather quotas) and the EC (canned fruit), and USTR initiation of new cases against Brazil (informatics), Japan (tobacco products), and Korea (insurance and intellectual property rights). The EC canned fruit case led to U.S. retaliation against subsidized EC pasta exports, EC counter-retaliation, and an eventual settlement of all of these issues. The Japan leather case was settled with limited retaliatory action by the United States and a compensation package of other access concessions by the Japanese (to enable them to keep their quotas intact).[25] The executive branch's more proactive stance probably had some impact in moderating the various trade measures being drafted in the Congress, but it was too little, too late to stop them.

The Seeds of Legislation

The first of the raft of omnibus trade bills that emerged from the 99th Congress was a relatively mild one introduced by House Republicans on October 8, 1985. Prepared under the auspices of their policy committee, the Trade Partnership Act of 1985 gave its sponsors the protective cover of something to be "for" on trade that was not the product of House Democrats. It was given little chance of enactment. On October 17, the House Democratic Trade Task Force announced various measures its members intended to introduce at a later date. These included transfers of presidential decision-making authorities under Section 201 and 301 to the USTR, the addition of foreign "industrial targeting" as a cause of action under Section 301, provisions for the imposition of countervailing duties against imports produced with "subsidized" natu-

---

[25] In another case involving Japan, the administration sought to merge several industry-initiated antidumping cases on semiconductors into one self-initiated case and, by spring of 1986, attempted to settle it and an industry Section 301 case (involving access to the Japanese market) in a negotiated agreement. Other Section 301 cases initiated during this period included one on investment performance requirements in Taiwan (diverting autos produced by Japanese firms onto the export market), and two cases against the EC, involving meat import standards and potential restrictions on U.S. soybean and feedgrain exports (owing to the accession of Spain and Portugal).

ral resources, changes in the trade adjustment assistance program (including a nominal fee on imports to finance it), and a series of provisions related to U.S. export promotion programs. The Democrats further proposed to make authority for a new round of multilateral trade negotiations subject to the prior convening by the administration of an international conference to reform the international monetary system.

Autumn also saw the introduction of the first major bipartisan trade bill, a Republican-led initiative introduced in the Senate on November 20. The bill emerged from a series of meetings called by Majority Leader Robert Dole (R-Ks.) in July at the request of Danforth and other Republicans concerned about the deteriorating U.S. trade picture, growing pressure from constituencies, and fears that the politics of trade were getting out of hand. The process had been opened to staff representing Democrats in October. S. 1860, the Trade Enhancement Act of 1985, was introduced with thirty-three Senate sponsors. Danforth and Senator Daniel Patrick Moynihan (D-N.Y.) were the lead cosponsors of the measure, but then each title was also introduced separately so that other members could take credit for those provisions in which they had the most interest.[26]

As a measure of the partisan tensions developing around the trade issue, sponsorship of S. 1860 was hotly debated within both party caucuses. Democrats signing onto the bill essentially did so against the wishes of Democratic leaders worried about losing partisan advantage over the issue. But Senators Moynihan, Bill Bradley (D-N.J.), Max Baucus (D-Mont.), and others were apparently equally concerned about the negative implications of trade becoming a partisan issue and participated anyway. With respect to the Republicans, a meeting in Dole's office in early November turned into a debate over whether to introduce the bipartisan group's product, which now included several provisions at odds with administration trade policy, or to change it and drop it in with only Republican sponsors. Senators Danforth, John Chafee (R-R.I.), and John Heinz (R-Pa.) insisted that the bill be introduced as drafted and refused to reopen the text to additions or deletions. They contended that a partisan measure was not in the interest of Republicans, that changing the draft now would be seen as an act of bad faith by the Democrats who had bucked their own party leadership, and that

---

[26] Unlike most major bills where members of the majority party generally listed their names first, in this case lead sponsorship for each title alternated between Republicans and Democrats. Of the initial sponsors, twenty-one were Republicans, including Dole, and twelve were Democrats. Twelve of the sponsors were Finance Committee members, although both Packwood and Bentsen, the committee's chairman and ranking Democrat, declined to participate.

separating themselves from administration trade policy was probably both substantively and politically necessary.

The "Dear Colleague" letter inviting members to sponsor the bill described it as offering "realistic responses to the growing problems of foreign unfair trade practices, misalignment of the dollar, and protectionism here and abroad." It contained no product-specific or country-specific provisions so as to avoid a "protectionist" label and to offer a clear alternative to various such bills already pending in the Senate. The bill's seven titles addressed Section 301 foreign barrier and Section 201 escape clause issues, authority for the executive to negotiate a new MTN agreement, and reform of the GSP program to include mandatory graduation of advanced developing countries. It also called for a mechanism to respond to nonmarket economy dumping, amendments to Section 337 to enhance its use in combatting foreign intellectual property rights violations, and changes in procedures under Section 232 national security import relief cases.

The bill's Section 301 and 201 provisions were considered its centerpiece. Under Section 301, executive branch self-initiation of cases was mandated, with priorities based on the trade distorting value of major foreign barriers identified in the annual NTE report. This was accompanied by shorter deadlines, a mandatory response in any case involving the violation of U.S. trade agreements, and the addition of various new causes of action. The bill also transferred Section 301 decision authority from the president to the USTR.

The bill's Section 201 changes were described by its authors as an effort to "revitalize" the statute as a credible source of assistance for industries facing injurious imports. Modifications included expansion of the president's remedy authorities beyond trade restrictive options to include adjustment-related measures and the option for a petitioning industry to submit a plan delineating its own commitments to improve competitiveness should it receive federal assistance. If the ITC found injury and determined the adjustment plan, combined with a remedy, was likely to return the industry to a competitive position, the president would then be required to grant the relief recommended by the ITC or relief substantially equivalent to it. Other than a provision involving nonmarket economy dumping, the bill contained no changes to AD/CVD laws. It did, however, contain multilateral agreement authority mirroring that granted in the 1984 act for bilateral agreements. The bill also contained provisions within the jurisdiction of the Senate Banking Committee, pertaining to exchange rates, developing country debt, and various initiatives to boost U.S. exports.

The Senate bill languished for some time after introduction, as

Finance Committee Chairman Robert Packwood (R-Ore.) declined to schedule hearings on it. The delay disturbed a number of Finance members, who believed the administration to be ignoring congressional trade concerns and pursuing its own agenda with negotiation of a bilateral free-trade agreement with Canada. This contributed in April 1986 to a second major incident of spontaneous combustion. This time, only the president's personal intervention saved the executive from an embarrassing last minute defeat. As it was, the administration's "victory" was barely eked out in a 10–10 vote to shelve a committee resolution disapproving the use of fast-track procedures to implement the Canadian FTA.

Pursuant to the preclearance process established in the 1984 act, the executive had notified the Finance Committee of its intent to negotiate the FTA. The committee then had sixty days in which it could pass a resolution of disapproval. Conventional wisdom had it that the members would use the occasion to express various trade-related gripes, but since most favored the FTA, the resolution of disapproval would be soundly defeated. The largest potential block of negative votes, made up of Packwood and other lumber state senators, had received some administration assurances about their concerns prior to committee action. So, ignoring other warning signs, the chairman waited until less than twenty-four hours before the deadline to hold his markup.

Unlike the incident involving the Japan resolution in 1985, this event was played out in its entirety in the Finance Committee. Moreover, it had very little to do with U.S.-Canada trade relations. Like the events surrounding S. Con. Res. 15, this incident was both spontaneous and entirely member-driven. In this case, in the middle of the markup, the White House and committee members alike were astonished to discover that eleven of the twenty were sufficiently frustrated that they were prepared to vote for the disapproval resolution. "We all thought it was our own personal view," commented Bentsen later, "but found out that everyone felt the same way."[27] And when an urgent presidential call to a staunch Republican free-trader failed to turn his vote, the chairman abruptly adjourned the proceedings.

At that point everyone scrambled. Neither side had a "plan B" and time was running out.[28] Several Senators were quickly summoned to

[27] Glenn Tobin, "U.S.-Canada Free Trade Negotiations," Case Studies, (Cambridge, Massachusetts: John F. Kennedy School of Government, Harvard University, 1987).

[28] Ironically, earlier in the spring, Danforth, Heinz, and Baucus had contemplated using the preclearance process to exert leverage, but had filed the idea as too draconian and bound to fail. While in theory the executive could seek approval for the FTA under

the White House, the president made additional calls, the USTR drafted a presidential letter to address more concerns, and the Republican leader tried to fashion an alternate resolution of approval. On the last day for a vote, the eleven holdouts met together for the first time to consider a course of action. There, the four Republicans and seven Democrats discussed the situation they found themselves in and confronted the implications of following through on their threat. They had stumbled into this power struggle because preclearance was the only available trade leverage over the executive. But it was one thing for individuals to make a statement by voting against the administration; it was quite another to be facing the prospect of actually *winning* the vote.

While frustration with executive handling of trade matters was a common denominator, individual motivations differed widely. Most agreed the administration was ignoring committee trade concerns ("they've stiffed us all year"). Several simply wanted hearings on S. 1860 ("it's pathetic we should have to ask the *president* for permission to hold hearings"). A few were even concerned about the FTA ("commitments we got in writing [on the Israel FTA] didn't amount to a pisshole in the snow"). They were in a quandary. Should they risk messing up U.S.-Canada relations and, conceivably, the future of fast track? Should they cut a deal with the administration? If so, what kind?

Led by Danforth and coached by Senator Russell B. Long (D-La.), they speculated over what they could accomplish without jeopardizing either the fast-track process or their own integrity. They considered simply folding ("are you going to hang tough or be a pussycat," countered one senator). They discussed the "good old days" in executive-legislative trade relations ("get Strauss up here to tell us what to do"). They told stories and shared anecdotes about Hubert Humphrey and Wayne Morse and other members long since gone. And they considered trying to work something out with Clayton Yeutter who had succeeded Brock as USTR, but concluded that he, too, would be unable to deliver ("it's the fellow over him I'm worried about").

By this time, several of the members already had serious reservations about the spotlight they inadvertently found themselves in. Not only did few wish to bring down the fast track or the FTA negotiations, but all had interests in the upcoming tax reform bill. Oil state Democrats had been quietly offered a deal on their favorite tax issue in exchange for backing off, and at least two Republicans had received rather unsubtle leadership threats ("remember excise taxes; you'll need me," one had

---

normal congressional procedures, it was understood that without fast track no agreement could survive the process intact.

been warned). Unfortunately, the members could think of no other leverage to address their frustrations ("I may be wrong," commented one
who favored a firm stance, "but I am sincere").

When, however, they learned that one of their number, Senator
"Spark" Matsunaga (D-Hawaii), had already tentatively conceded his
vote—apparently in exchange for Reagan's comment that he'd "learned
his lesson" and a trip home on Air Force One—they abandoned plans
to seek other side deals ("in this business I don't count on a third-party
beneficiary for a contract," remarked Long). Instead, the ten who remained recalled Ben Franklin's admonition about hanging together and
decided to vote for the resolution of disapproval in block. They would
"lose with honor" on a tie. "At least we got their attention," concluded
Danforth. But by the time hearings on S. 1860 were held and a committee markup commenced it was September, too late to move the process
any farther before pre-election adjournment.

In contrast to the delays in the Senate, the House recommendations
presented by the House Democratic trade task force were, by the spring
of 1986, ready for markup and approval by relevant House committees.
These were combined and introduced in omnibus form on May 9, 1986.
H.R. 4800, the Trade and International Economic Policy Reform Act,
was a major Democratic leadership initiative of House Majority Leader
(and soon-to-be Speaker) Jim Wright (D-Tex.), chairmen of the six
House committees with jurisdiction over its provisions, and several
dozen other Democrats. It contained eight separate titles, and was far
tougher than any other credible trade bill that had been dropped into
the legislative hopper.

A number of the bill's provisions were similar to those contained in
the bipartisan Senate bill, including amendments to Section 301 limiting
executive discretion in responding to foreign violations of trade agreements and the addition of an adjustment plan to the Section 201 escape
clause process. The bill also contained an extension of fast-track implementing authority for multilateral and bilateral nontariff measure agreements and proclamation authority for tariff cuts.

But these more traditional trade provisions were eclipsed by several
others in the bill, the most pronounced being the latest version of the
Gephardt amendment, entitled "Mandatory Negotiations and Action
Regarding Foreign Countries Having Unwarranted Trade Surpluses
with the United States." The provision's authors had by now substituted
for its original import surcharge sanction a multiyear rollback of bilateral trade surpluses with offending countries by 10 percent per year.
Other Section 301 amendments in the House bill involved expanding
causes of action under the statute to include denial of "internationally

recognized worker rights" and "toleration of cartels," along with a provision to offset the impact on U.S. industry of foreign export targeting.

Controversial amendments to existing trade statutes also appeared in the antidumping and countervailing duty area. In addition to the natural resource subsidy provision, these generally involved expansion of the scope of existing AD/CVD law to capture the diversionary impact on the U.S. market from foreign dumping into third country markets, products sold in the U.S. market containing dumped components, and repeated dumping activities by certain foreign producers. To these and other trade measures, including the transfer of various trade authorities from the president to the USTR, H.R. 4800 added provisions from the other committees. These ranged from changes in U.S. export promotion and financing programs to the easing of export controls to the authorization of various job-training programs.

By June, the bill had been approved by the House by a three-to-one margin and sent to the Senate. It was evident, however, that the bill was likely to go no farther, for the attention of Finance and Ways and Means Committee members had already turned to tax reform legislation and time was running out on the Senate floor for action on other major measures.

With the election of 1986, the stage was set for the 100th Congress and the Omnibus Trade and Competitiveness Act of 1988. Congress had seized the initiative in trade during the 1985–1986 period and was not yet prepared to relinquish it. The fact that Congress had done so primarily to fill a perceived vacuum became less important at this point than the fact that years of frustration had built a momentum for its efforts. By then members had invested so much in their own legislative initiatives that they would have been reluctant to abandon them under any circumstances.

The 1980s marked the further evolution to maturity of trends evident in U.S. trade policy since the post-depression era. They also may have witnessed the reemergence of certain forces and themes in trade that had disappeared or lain dormant since their dramatic coming together in the Tariff Act of 1930. Historians may well look back upon the decade of the 1980s and cite it as the decade the momentum for free trade began to run out in the United States. The economic and political forces at work brought with them growing questions about the role and standing of the United States in the world economy, and the credibility and appropriateness of U.S. trade law to deal with the challenges of a rapidly changing economic environment. And trade appeared to be increasingly buffeted by political forces and motivations, a reflection of economic developments and a growing uncertainty about America's future. In 1987, *The Economist* magazine attempted to capture this mood in a thoughtful and provocative cover story entitled, "Whatever Happened to America's Smile." The accompanying editorial noted:

Americans were not born to frown. It does not suit them. The quintessentially American characteristics are cheerfulness, optimism and generosity, a general buoyancy of spirit, a belief that tomorrow will dawn a better day. So it may, but suddenly many Americans seem not so sure. . . . They reckoned their economy to be incomparable; now they find it often outsold by Japan, Western Europe and a string of eager newcomers. They imagined their incomes would for ever rise; now they see them struggling with gravity. . . . They assumed the American Century, born 1941, would endure a hundred years; now, after fewer than 50, they fear it is on the wane.

The frown is not universal; . . . but signs of unease abound. . . . And some of these signs reflect not just bafflement, but sulkiness, defensiveness and pessimism. If these attitudes prevail, America will become a different place, one that allies and antagonists alike will find it harder to live with.[29]

---

[29] "Whatever Happened to America's Smile," *The Economist*, September 12–18, 1987, 11.

4

THE MAKING OF A LAW:
FAST START IN THE HOUSE

The task confronting any observer of Congress—whether journalist, academic, voter, or even spy—resembles that of an anthropologist stumbling into the middle of a tribal village. The natives do bizarre things and speak in strange ways.
—Tribes on the Hill[1]

MOMENTUM

The 100th Congress opened with a veto override. H.R. 1, the Clean Water Act, passed the House on January 8, 1987, by a vote of 406–8. The Senate approved it shortly thereafter, by a vote of 93–6. When Reagan vetoed the bill, as he had pocket-vetoed its predecessor at the close of the 99th Congress, the legislators promptly overrode the veto. Commenting later, the *Congressional Quarterly* noted that "because the override was a certainty from the start, Reagan's veto and Congress' vote to enact the bill anyway were more expressions of attitude than tests of strength."[2] The confrontation illustrated the rift that had developed between Congress and the administration and set the tone for relations in the two years that followed.

The Congress had emerged from the 1986 election with the same frustrations about the executive-legislative relationship as before, but with a dramatically enhanced capability and will to act on them. The Democratic party had regained control of the Senate. Senator Robert

---

[1] J. McIver Weatherford, *Tribes on the Hill* (New York: Rawson, Wade Publishers, Inc., 1981), 20.

[2] Janet Hook, "Reagan Took a Beating on Key Votes in 1987," *Congressional Quarterly*, January 2, 1988, 25. The Clean Water Act (P.L. 100–4) had passed both House and Senate in October 1986, by votes of 408–0 and 96–0, respectively.

C. Byrd (D-W.Va.), with fifty-five Democratic votes in his arsenal,[3] once again assumed the position of majority leader. All Senate committee chairmanships changed hands, and the membership on each committee was adjusted to ensure a Democratic majority. With the retirement of Tip O'Neill, Congressman Jim Wright assumed the position of Speaker of the House. Everyone was very much aware that the next presidential election was just around the corner. Many suspected—and some hoped—that trade would be an issue.

The new Democratic leadership placed trade legislation high on its agenda. In the days following tabulation of election results, any number of political pundits anticipated a renewed activism, if not outright protectionism, in Congress on trade, particularly in view of the new Senate and stated leadership priorities in both bodies. At a mid-December meeting of the moderate-to-conservative Democratic Leadership Council held in Williamsburg, Virginia, both Byrd and Wright were quoted as highlighting trade as a top priority. Wright called passage of a comprehensive trade bill "the first imperative" of the 100th Congress. Byrd agreed, asserting that competitiveness, not protectionism, was the prime focus for their efforts.

Committee leadership changes in the Senate, too, appeared to make the prospect of a trade bill inevitable. Senator Bentsen, with a history of interest and activity in the trade arena, had assumed the chairmanship of the Senate Finance Committee. He confirmed early on that trade would be "the No. 1 priority" for his committee. While considered a trade-moderate, some still recalled his support earlier in the decade for auto import quotas and the original Gephardt-Bentsen-Rostenkowski import surcharge measure. But most pundits predicted he would opt for a middle-of-the-road trade bill, citing his support for renewal of executive branch negotiating authority and initiatives designed to open foreign markets, rather than close that of the United States.

Questions were, however, raised as to whether Bentsen and the new Democratic leader would be on the same wavelength when it came to a trade bill, particularly in view of Byrd's responsiveness to import-sensitive constituencies in West Virginia and the appeal of a potential partisan advantage. The trade interests of other Democratic lawmakers, now in a better position to pursue them, were also noted, including the ascension of Senator Ernest F. Hollings (D-S.C.) to the chairmanship of the Senate Commerce, Science and Transportation Committee. While

---

[3] The ratio of Democrats to Republicans in the Senate changed to 54–46 in March 1987 with the death of Sen. Edward Zorinsky (D-Neb.) and the appointment of a Republican to fill his unexpired term.

not a primary jurisdictional actor in the trade area, the Senator's strong support for textile quota legislation was well known, and he, too, made it clear that trade would be at the top of his list. The potential for a jurisdictional struggle between the Finance and Commerce Committees was also seen as a possibility, given a history of Ways and Means versus Energy and Commerce Committee tensions in the House.

As for the administration, a shift in position was already evident, with Treasury Secretary James Baker signaling the administration's interest in enactment of trade legislation at a conference on trade and third-world debt in early December:

> I am convinced that working in good faith and in a bipartisan way with the new leaders of the 100th Congress—men like Jim Wright, Bob Byrd, Lloyd Bentsen, and Dan Rostenkowski, among others—we can craft responsible legislation that will enhance America's international competitiveness without resorting to protectionism."[4]

He delivered the same message privately to Byrd and Wright, as well as to Rostenkowski, early in the new year, indicating the willingness of the White House to work with them. Senator Dole, now Senate Republican Leader, also commented on the pressure for action on the trade deficit, and endorsed the concept of a bill in the new Congress.

A number of considerations came into play with respect to the administration's decision to engage the Congress over trade legislation at this time. It was clear that the 100th Congress was serious about moving forward on a trade bill; that the new Democratic leadership was prepared, if not eager, for a confrontation over trade with the White House; and that loss of Republican control in the Senate meant the administration could not count on the process being blocked in that body. It was also clear that without the enactment of new authority for the president to engage in trade negotiations, the administration-endorsed launch of the GATT Uruguay Round initiative in September 1986 was doomed to failure.

In addition to these factors giving an impetus to forward movement in the legislative process, there were also several developments pointing to a moderate improvement in the atmosphere for engagement in the debate. Above all, it appeared that the white-hot fury that had characterized congressional attitudes about administration trade policy in the mid-1980s was beginning to dissipate. This was attributable to improve-

---

[4] From the text of "Remarks by Secretary of the Treasury James A. Baker, III to the U.S. Congressional Summit on Trade and Debt," New York, December 4, 1986.

ments in the domestic economy and to initial evidence of the impact of administration trade-related initiatives since 1985.

The domestic economy was, by then, in its fifth year of recovery from the 1982 recession, and was marked by a steady decline in the civilian unemployment rate, from a high of 9.7 percent in 1982, dropping to 7 percent in 1986, and approaching 6 percent by 1987. On the international front, the statistical impact of the dollar's decline since 1985 had yet to be realized, as the U.S. trade deficit climbed steadily to its record high in 1987. However, as U.S. imports grew progressively more expensive and U.S. exports more price competitive, an easing of pressure on the trade-impacted segments of the economy was already being felt.[5]

Finally, the administration's increasingly activist approach to U.S. trade policy was beginning to have a political impact. In his December speech, Secretary Baker had pointed to the administration's "aggressive" attack on unfair trade practices and specifically noted that Reagan had been "the first President to initiate Section 301 cases." In early January, the USTR had announced a dramatic reduction in the duty-free benefits enjoyed by several advanced developing nations—including Taiwan, Korea, and Hong Kong—under the GSP program. These initiatives continued well into the spring, enabling the administration to mark the shift in legislative activity on trade from committee to the House floor with an eleven-page release detailing the results of presidential trade initiatives since September 1985. Among the activities highlighted in the document were actions taken in eleven self-initiated Section 301 cases and the announcement of the first significant imposition of trade sanctions against Japan, valued at $300 million, in response to its failure to implement a 1986 semiconductor agreement.

H.R. 3 INTRODUCED

The House got off to a quick start with its trade bill. At the Williamsburg conference in December, Wright had already served notice that H.R. 4800 from the previous Congress would be the starting point for its 100th Congress initiative. Presumably, Wright saw the old House bill as the fastest way to get the process moving and to lay down the marker of congressional initiative and control. That the plan enabled

---

[5] The near-term statistical worsening in the U.S. trade imbalance that followed the dollar's decline was normal in the context of the "*J*-curve" effect. However, in this case a reduction in the U.S. trade deficit did not become readily apparent until nearly three years after the dollar began to fall in early 1985, in sharp contrast to the 12 to 18 months that had been predicted by economists.

Wright to dominate the internal House process, as well, could only have contributed to its appeal. Objections to framing House legislative efforts in the context of the old bill came from several quarters and for a variety of reasons. Rostenkowski was concerned that, by starting with a bill so widely condemned as protectionist by the press and the administration, perceptions of congressional intent and subsequent efforts to enact serious legislation would be severely hampered. For its part, the administration was anxious to avoid having Congress stake out specific positions until the president could come forward with his own legislative proposals.

Nevertheless, on January 6, 1987, Congress' first day back, the Trade and International Economic Policy Reform Act of 1987, numbered H.R. 3, was introduced in the House. It was 470 printed pages and virtually identical to H.R. 4800. With the help of Wright and his whip team, the bill went in with 180 co-sponsors, all Democrats. At Wright's insistence, Congressman Gephardt's name led the list, followed by various subcommittee and committee chairmen, prime sponsors of the earlier bill, and others listed in alphabetical order. The bill was immediately referred by the House parliamentarian to the six committees of jurisdiction.

Wright's plan, laid out to his chairmen in January, was to put together a comprehensive bill with input from a wide range of House committees. While the single largest portion of the bill would belong to the Ways and Means Committee, the bill as a whole would be under the control of the House Democratic leadership, rather than that of Rostenkowski. Wright asked that all committees report out their bills by April 6 to enable the staff to meld them together over the Easter recess and to have a product ready for the resolution of major outstanding issues by members and the Rules Committee by April 22. House floor action was expected to occur the week of April 28.

Meanwhile, House Republicans, recognizing the inevitable, tried to position themselves to influence the proceedings. House Minority Leader Robert H. Michel (R-Ill.) indicated to Wright that the Republicans were prepared to take him up on his stated pledge of bipartisanship. To Reagan, Michel strongly suggested that the executive move quickly to propose and support a more narrowly focused trade bill. He was convinced that in order for the administration to avoid having to play a purely defensive role later on, it needed to exert some influence at the earliest possible stages of the legislative process. Moreover, Michel knew that his House Republicans needed a serious trade bill to support and could no longer be called upon to consistently oppose every Democratic measure that came before them.

In the end, although the president used his State of the Union address to stress his support for "free and fair trade" and to promise submission of "comprehensive proposals to enhance our competitiveness,"[6] it was not until February 19 that the package finally appeared. Rather than the more narrowly focused trade bill that had been advocated by Michel, however, the administration chose to submit a 1,600-page Trade, Employment, and Productivity Act, with the bulk of its provisions geared to competitiveness rather than trade issues. Not only did it arrive too late to influence the trade bills that would form the basis for House and Senate action, but it was so all-encompassing that many in Congress simply wrote it off as a grab bag of previous initiatives on which Congress had refused to act.

The broad scope of the bill was evident from its referral to ten different committees in the House, four more than had received H.R. 3. Some speculated that this approach had been adopted by the White House to slow the legislation by tying up Congress in jurisdictional knots. Others suggested that both the administration and congressional Democrats felt compelled to wrap their trade bills in "competitiveness" packaging to avoid being accused of protectionist intent. In the trade area, most of the administration's proposals were designed to enhance executive branch trade authorities, in sharp contrast to congressional proposals intent on circumscribing them. This led the *Congressional Quarterly* to conclude that the "President's trade package provided more of a counterpoint than a counteroffer to existing Democratic plans."[7]

WAYS AND MEANS COMMITTEE ACTION

The Ways and Means Committee commenced its legislative activities with a document, based on the text of H.R. 4800, that it fully intended to overhaul. This time when his committee acted on the trade bill, Rostenkowski had decided, they were going to lay the groundwork for a law. His strategic roadmap was clear: if he addressed his key members' interests, kept the bill bipartisan, adopted language different from that expected in the Senate, and produced a text that would not immediately be labeled "protectionist" by the press, then he could get the measure through the House and still have enough maneuvering room in the House-Senate conference to achieve a signable bill. Rostenkowski was well aware that his plan had vulnerabilities. In particular, he knew that

---

[6] Ronald Reagan, "Text of an Address by the President on the States of the Union," a press release (Washington, D.C.: The White House, January 27, 1987).

[7] John Cranford, "Trade Bill: Options Aired, Markup Postponed," *Congressional Quarterly*, March 7, 1987, 433.

the process dictated by the leadership left him with very little control outside his own committee over decisions on two make-or-break issues for the administration and the press, a textile quota amendment and the Gephardt proposal. And he had virtually no control over what would appear in the remainder of the omnibus measure. Decisions on these issues would likely come down to determinations by Wright and the House Rules Committee.

Hearings on H.R. 3 were held in early February by the Ways and Means Trade Subcommittee, chaired by Congressman Sam Gibbons (D-Fla.). In the meantime, Rostenkowski, Gibbons, and their staffs worked to put together the document on which the initial subcommittee markup would be based. On March 3, in an appearance at the National Press Club, the outlines of Rostenkowski's approach emerged.[8]

Speaking to a packed audience of press, lobbyists, and their government guests, Rostenkowski laid out his strategic and conceptual frame of reference for the legislation. His tone was aggressive, but conciliatory. He stressed bipartisanship, and said that while disagreements could be expected, "all the players—including the President, Democrats and Republicans, business and labor—must accept compromise." He stated his objective was a trade "blueprint that future presidents, of either party, can follow," asserting that "good trade policy is good trade politics—for both parties."

Addressing the substance of the proposed legislation, Rostenkowski made it clear that he did not view a trade bill as a panacea. He did assert that it would, in conjunction with budget deficit reduction and other improvements to U.S. competitiveness, make a substantial contribution to U.S. economic interests. "Stripped of the complexities," he declared, "the trade issue involves two simple elements—whether other nations can be convinced to allow American goods to enter as freely as we allow their products to enter the United States, and whether American industry can become more competitive in a more open international market."

The only two legislative specifics addressed by the chairman in his presentation related to the Gephardt bill and the management of federal decision making in trade. He expressed strong support for the "principle" involved in the Gephardt language, but made it clear that he would accept "reasonable modifications" to its text. Calling for "parity" in

---

[8] Sources for quotes that follow: Dan Rostenkowski, "Text of remarks by Ways and Means Committee Chairman Dan Rostenkowski for delivery at a National Press Club lunch," March 3, 1987, Washington, D.C.; Cranford, "Trade Bill: Options Aired," 433; and notes taken by author.

trade with other industrial nations, and citing trade barriers in Germany, Japan, Taiwan, and Korea, Rostenkowski painted a picture of a tough, but moderate market access bill. "I am not," he said in response to a question, "trying to write legislation to please [AFL-CIO president] Lane Kirkland; I'm trying to write legislation that will be signed by the president."

While his message on the Gephardt bill may have sounded somewhat conciliatory to the administration, his demand for consolidation of executive branch decision making on trade in the "special trade representative" was not. Although he did not elaborate, his message was unmistakable: "we need one person who will articulate our policy, provide our answers and take the heat. . . . Our bill will strengthen . . . the [USTR's] position by transferring to him many powers now scattered throughout the federal bureaucracy."

On Wednesday, March 11, the Subcommittee on Trade began its markup of legislation, employing a co-chairman's draft that Rostenkowski and Gibbons had unveiled that day. The text, a substitute for the language in H.R. 4800, made a number of important changes to the original, including the modification of language considered to violate existing trade agreements and the addition of a few statutory changes requested by the administration. As the chairman put it later, "I chased away all the things that were visibly objectionable, not just to the administration but to the business community . . . trying to retain the posture of everybody (giving) a little."[9]

Most important for purposes of outside observers, however, was the absence of the controversial Gephardt language that had given the original bill its "protectionist" label. In its place, was a substitute provision that lacked a mandatory deficit reduction target and offered the president an expanded option for negotiated settlements. While provisions remained that were of significant concern to the administration and the more free-trade oriented members and interest groups, the absence of the Gephardt language alone had the effect of dramatically shifting perceptions about the bill.

Rostenkowski had floated the draft by a several members over the weekend, having carefully identified in advance those he could expect to count on to back it in markup. The chairman knew that he would need the strong support of at least half of the subcommittee's Democrats and most of its Republicans to isolate the handful of Democrats from

---

[9] Dan Rostenkowski, "The Evolution of a U.S. Trade Bill: Rostenkowski Explains the Paths Taken by Controversial Legislation on Capitol Hill," interview by reporters and editors, *Washington Post*, March 22, 1987.

whom he expected the more draconian amendments. Chairman Gibbons' backing was vital, and both he and the Republicans were pleased by the modifications that brought the bill into closer conformity with administration objectives. Three other Democrats, Tom Downey of New York, Robert Matsui of California, and Don Pease of Ohio, each received calls from Rostenkowski with his personal commitment to include provisions they wanted in exchange for their support of the draft and votes to defend it against "unfriendly" amendments in committee. All three wanted a bill that would be perceived as pro-business and accepted compromise provisions on their issues involving, respectively, film copyrights, telecommunications trade, and worker rights. Only Pease was not willing to commit to opposing the Gephardt amendment.

For the four remaining Democrats on the subcommittee, Rostenkowski added a few AD/CVD law amendments, but was not prepared to include their more controversial proposals. Congressman Bill Frenzel (R-Minn.) also received a call from the chairman, asking him to consider the draft in terms of a strategy for getting a bill signed into law. Frenzel agreed to look at it, recognizing that without Republican support, Rostenkowski would have little alternative but to accept the language being pushed by his hard-liners and to rely on party-line votes to move the bill.

The week before the markup, Rostenkowski had made a point of calling Gephardt to discuss substitute formulations for his amendment. In particular, the chairman suggested shifting the provision's focus from one on bilateral balances to one on barriers and dispatched subcommittee Staff Director Rufus Yerxa to Gephardt's home over the weekend with a copy of the new language.

Gephardt, already in the middle of his campaign for the Democratic party presidential nomination, had just returned from a trip to Dixville Notch, New Hampshire, the site of the first votes cast in the New Hampshire primary. After an hour's discussion, during which Gephardt came across fairly receptive to the proposal, he promised to consider it and to run it by his advisors. The absence of any word from Gephardt on Monday was taken by the staff to mean the compromise would fly. However, on Wednesday morning, just before the chairmen were to present their draft bill to the subcommittee for markup, Gephardt telephoned Rostenkowski's office and informed the staff that he was not prepared to accept the substitute. Gephardt's advisors, particularly those representing the UAW, were simply opposed to considering any form of compromise.

Rostenkowski immediately announced a delay in the markup and had staff develop yet another—somewhat tougher—proposal. This one would have mandated dollar-for-dollar retaliation against foreign barriers. But it, too, was rejected by Gephardt, who expressed his intention to offer the original bill as an amendment in full committee later in the markup process.

As a member of the Trade Subcommittee, Rostenkowski participated in its deliberations. He made a point, however, of letting Gibbons manage the process with the expectation that he would then take a proprietary interest in its outcome. The markup, held primarily behind closed doors, took two and a half days. It resulted in relatively few changes to the chairmen's draft, reflecting the careful attention paid by the authors to what would and would not satisfy a majority of committee members. The new member-approved text of H.R. 3 was voice voted out of subcommittee, without dissent, and sent along to the full committee for the next stage in the deliberative process. The swift endorsement of the draft did not necessarily reflect unanimous approval of its content, but rather a desire on the part of the participants to move the process forward. The more controversial amendments would simply be deferred to the full committee session to follow.

Committee Republicans were pleased with the direction the bill was taking and the extent to which they were being allowed to participate. Frenzel, a committed free-trader and the committee's main advocate of administration positions on the bill, assumed that by supporting the bill's forward movement at that point, he would be in a better position to contribute further changes later on. "I voted for the process," he said later, "rather than the pristine beauty of every word in that bill."[10] By contrast, Chairman Gibbons was decidedly effusive about the progress being made, noting "We're on the way to a good trade bill, a really good trade bill, one that has the potential of being historic in nature."[11]

Other House Democrats, however, were not as reassured by the Ways and Means Committee's actions. A number of the hard-liners, including Wright, perceived the panel moving the bill away from the strong statement on trade they had originally intended. Congressman John D. Dingell (D-Mich.), chairman of the Energy and Commerce Committee, for example, told a U.S. Chamber of Commerce group that he considered the bill moving through Ways and Means as far too weak.[12] Still, at that point in time, the general consensus in the House and among

---

[10] John Cranford, "Trade Legislation Passes First Hurdle in House," *Congressional Quarterly*, March 14, 1987, 468.

[11] Ibid.

[12] John Cranford, "Conflicts Sharpen as House Trade Bill Advances," *Congressional Quarterly*, March 21, 1987, 519.

the leadership was that at least the process was moving forward. All participants were well aware that the bigger battles had yet to be joined.

This attitude was shared by many in the administration, as well, as evident in a letter sent by USTR Yeutter to Rostenkowski and Gibbons at the conclusion of the subcommittee's action. The March 18 letter contained the first detailed administration comments on trade measures being considered by the Congress. Its tone was meant to be encouraging, commending the members for the "constructive, bipartisan basis on which the Subcommittee's markup proceeded" and calling the revised bill a "substantial improvement over H.R. 3." However, the letter concluded with a paragraph and a seven-page attachment that appeared to its recipients to take issue with virtually every provision in the bill:

> If the following provisions are not either eliminated or substantially improved, I would find it extremely difficult to recommend that the President sign any trade bill including them: transfers of Presidential authority; worker rights provisions; mandatory retaliation in Section 301 generally and as a mechanism for dealing with bilateral trade surpluses; mandatory exchange rate negotiations; Trade Adjustment Assistance (TAA) earmarking of funds, automatic certification, and the nature and scope of TAA entitlements; amendments to the countervailing duty law's tests for domestic subsidies; diversionary input dumping; private right of antidumping action; and sectoral schemes (telecommunications and intellectual property rights).[13]

This apparent inconsistency in the executive branch response was illustrative of the difficulties facing administration staff negotiators. In spite of the high level decision that had been made to "work with" the Congress on trade legislation, subcabinet officials had no authority to go beyond the stringent trade positions reflected in the president's bill. As a result, while there was extensive interaction between committee and administration (primarily USTR and Commerce) staff throughout the various stages involved in drafting the bill, the executive branch participants were precluded from proposing or accepting compromise language and were therefore limited to providing detailed critiques of the committee bill. Still, this standoff offered certain advantages to both parties. The administration could avoid outright compromise too early in the process, and Rostenkowski could test the level of concern expressed by executive branch advisors with respect to each of the bill's provisions—and begin to position his bill accordingly.

---

[13] United States Trade Representative Clayton Yeutter, Letter to the Honorable Dan Rostenkowski and the Honorable Sam Gibbons, U.S. House of Representatives, March 18, 1987.

Rostenkowski defended his strategy on the trade bill in a lengthy and wide-ranging discussion with *Washington Post* reporters and editors shortly before completion of full committee markup. The interview, published almost verbatim on March 22, 1987, offered a remarkably candid glimpse into the chairman's thinking:

On the Gephardt amendment:

I can pass a bill in the House with the original Gephardt measure because we've done it before. [But] It's members saying "Don't make me vote on Gephardt. Jesus, don't make me vote on Gephardt." . . . [What] that legislator . . . means [is] he's going to vote for Gephardt, but he doesn't want to. . . . [The House members] want a trade bill, but they don't want [a] protectionist label around them. And they're all afraid, you know, of the atmosphere of Smoot-Hawley. . . .

On administration concerns:

I said to them, "Look, I'm not writing this bill for you. I'm writing this bill so I can pass the House of Representatives." There are certainly going to be some things that my Democrats won't like and my Republicans don't like and certainly you won't like. But to tell me that the bill has got to be perfect when it comes out of the committee so that the opposition to it is not as vigorous on the House floor is baloney.

On a presidential veto:

[You] are gonna see this president, who will tell you "I have my pen under my pillow, I will veto anything," you are gonna see him become a politician and that politician will sign legislation if there's a groundswell for it in trade. The palm tree bends and so does the politician, and this president will bend.[14]

That week, the full Ways and Means Committee was to meet and to finalize its part of the bill. It was becoming obvious, however, that the legislation's future prospects could rest almost entirely with the House Rules Committee. At stake was the decision on the number and type of amendments allowed to be offered to the bill on the House floor.

Members of the Rules Committee are appointed by the Speaker and are, therefore, generally subject to his control. While the "rule" governing House floor consideration of a bill is an issue of importance with respect to any piece of legislation, it can be a matter of life and death

---

[14] Rostenkowski, "Evolution of a Bill."

for tax, trade, appropriations, and budget measures. These bills traditionally receive "modified," "modified-open," or "modified-closed" rules (as distinct from "open" or "closed"), because of their complex and technical nature. As a result, the rules approved for such legislation usually limit amendments to those that are germane, and those enjoying widespread member support.

When it came to the trade bill, the outcome of the Rules Committee decision was by no means certain. This was the case not only by virtue of the complexity and controversy surrounding the bill, but also because the Speaker's motivation differed somewhat from that of the committee chairman. Rostenkowski, in his March 22 interview with the *Washington Post*, expressed his concerns about it as follows:

> I always worry about what happens to me in rules, because I have no control over there and they don't like me. You know, you walk in a room and it's very quiet, you know they're talking about you. . . . If we took a bill to the floor [without a rule limiting amendments] with no holds barred, you'd see protectionist legislation like you'd never want to see.

And on the related issue of Wright's motivation:

> Maybe it is that I'm very nervous, but he is not as strong in saying "get a bill and I don't care where labor is" as he was in December. It's, "Well jeez, Danny, we could . . . very well pass 4800, and so what if he [the president] vetoes it." I don't want that. I don't want to work my tail off with the ultimate idea of having [the bill vetoed].[15]

While Rostenkowski could be fairly confident that Wright and the committee would chose a rule that precluded a Smoot-Hawley-type melee generating hundreds of product-specific amendments, he was far less sanguine about their treatment of textile quota legislation and the Gephardt amendment. Both had cleared the House in the past, but each had the potential to be the "killer" amendment on this legislative vehicle.

The pending textile, fabric, and footwear quota bill was similar to the one approved by the Congress in 1985, the one that was subsequently vetoed and the veto upheld in the House. Unlike the Gephardt amendment, which stood little chance in the Senate, the textile measure—if attached in the House—would almost certainly be attached in identical form in the Senate bill. This would have eliminated any flexibility to modify or drop the provision in the upcoming House-Senate

---

[15] Ibid.

conference, making its inclusion in the final product, and another sustained veto, virtually inevitable.

Therefore, with Wright's concurrence, Rostenkowski attempted to work out a deal with the textile bill's sponsors to keep it from being added to his legislation, either in committee or on the floor. He was aided by an emerging consensus that all major product-specific provisions should be kept off the bill for strategic reasons—to protect members against interest group demands to add them, to prevent a few items from snowballing into many, and to reduce the ability of critics to compare the bill to the Smoot-Hawley Tariff Act. Ultimately, the principal advocates of the textile measure—Rep. Ed Jenkins (D-Ga.), a Ways and Means member, and Rep. Butler Derrick (D-S.C.), who served on the House Rules Committee—accepted commitments by Rostenkowski and Gibbons to hold hearings on the bill and to allow a floor vote later in the year.

Rostenkowski considered the Gephardt amendment to be a more manageable problem. His preference was to have a strong, but sanitized, version of the provision in the bill that Ways and Means reported to the House. If Gephardt and his labor allies supported it, so much the better. What he wanted to avoid, however, was taking a bill to the floor that contained the original Gephardt language, and having to defend it against Republicans, the administration, and the press. An amendment "imposed" on him by the will of the House would be less likely to result in a blanket condemnation of the entire bill and could be dealt with later in conference.

As it turned out, Gephardt decided not to seek a compromise in committee or to offer his amendment in that venue. Instead, he opted to stage his fight on the House floor, with an amendment to toughen the language in the Ways and Means bill. As the *Congressional Quarterly* so aptly characterized motivations behind their respective decisions: "Gephardt cannot afford the embarrassment of losing a vote on the centerpiece of his trade strategy, and Rostenkowski cannot send a bill to the floor without Republican support."[16]

The remainder of the full Ways and Means Committee markup, held in closed executive session, went pretty much according to script, although not without a few points of contention. Once again, the final product closely resembled the original chairmen's mark, moving it away from contentious provisions anticipated in the Senate bill, and moving it that much closer in the direction of a signable document.

[16] Cranford, "Conflicts Sharpen as House Trade Bill Advances," *Congressional Quarterly*, March 21, 1987, 519.

THE COMMITTEE BILL

Rostenkowski began the committee markup by playing to his free-traders, the press, and the administration by taking up authority for the negotiation and implementation of trade agreements.[17] This was the provision that would ultimately determine the president's willingness to swallow everything else the bill would contain, and the members knew it.

Negotiating Authority

Negotiating authority approved by Ways and Means was as generous as any the executive might have hoped for. It was more generous than that granted in 1984 for bilateral FTA negotiations and, in some ways, even surpassed that contained in the Trade Act of 1974. It provided for nontariff agreement implementing authority under fast-track procedures for three years. An automatic two-year extension was conditioned on a progress report, USTR consultations and justification, and failure of the Finance or Ways and Means to disapprove it. Proclamation authority for tariff agreements was granted for a period of six years, limited to 60 percent cuts only on those items where the ITC or USTR found a greater reduction would have a "probable significant adverse economic effect on the domestic industry."[18] Tariffs on all other items could, therefore, theoretically be eliminated. For new bilateral trade agreements, the committee agreed to extend existing authority for six years.

Other parameters for use of the authority included a link between committee-stated negotiating objectives and negotiated results, and an array of consultation requirements designed to ensure that executive branch negotiators sought congressional and private sector input on an ongoing basis. In this regard, the consultation and advisory committee processes already specified by law were expanded to include develop-

---

[17] To avoid unnecessary repetition, provisions considered by this author to have been of particular importance to the Ways and Means Committee are described in some detail in this section. Provisions of importance to the Senate Finance Committee that also appeared in the House bill are summarized in this section and then discussed in more detail in Chapter 5. Sources of information on the Ways and Means Committee markup include: Congress, House, Committee on Ways and Means, *Trade and International Economic Policy Reform Act of 1987: Report of the Committee on Ways and Means to accompany H.R. 3*, 100th Cong., 1st sess., 1987, Report 100–40, Part 1; Ways and Means staff, interviews by author, March-April 1987; Cranford, "Conflicts Sharpen," 519; and Cranford, "Panels Take Aim," 554–557.

[18] Congress, *Report of the Committee on Ways and Means to accompany H.R. 3*, Report 100–40, 45.

ment of U.S. government trade policy as well as negotiation of trade agreements.

The committee also added generic authority for the president to reduce tariffs to compensate trading partners in the event any new U.S. import restrictions were found inconsistent with the GATT. This was accompanied by language to specifically authorize the implementation of two outstanding items on the administration's agenda. The first was access to fast-track procedures to convert the entire U.S. tariff classification system to a new "Harmonized System." The second was tariff proclamation authority needed to implement a settlement reached between the United States and the European Community involving a long-standing dispute over citrus and pasta products.

Not surprisingly, members representing import-sensitive constituencies viewed these developments with some alarm, seeing the potential for massive cuts in tariffs and quotas enjoyed by constituencies even now clamoring for more import-restrictive assistance. But the committee held the line, recognizing the very real prospect of a single product exemption snowballing into a long list of items removed from the negotiating table. For this reason, for example, the members turned down two modifications proposed by Rep. Jenkins on behalf of the textile and apparel industries. The first would have removed the sector entirely from the scope of negotiations; the second would have subjected any agreed tariff reductions to fast-track congressional approval. These amendments were considered by Chairman Gibbons to be the most serious that the group would face during markup because their adoption would have torpedoed any hope for administration or Republican cooperation on the bill.

Transfers of Authority

H.R. 4800 had contained a provision delegating to the U.S. Trade Representative the president's determination of whether a foreign practice was actionable under Section 301. It was only with Rostenkowski's National Press Club appearance and expansion of the concept in H.R. 3, however, that such an innocuous and "inside-the-beltway" provision became an issue at all.

The interest of Ways and Means and Finance Committee members in executive branch trade decision making went well beyond the academic. They believed that without a White House-backed USTR with sole responsibility for the coordination and negotiation of U.S. trade policy, "agency shopping" by foreign governments and weak lowest-common-denominator trade decisions would remain a problem. Congress had removed trade policy from the State Department's control in

1962 and had forced the transfer of AD/CVD law decisions from Treasury in 1979, concerned the two agencies would always have other, higher priorities. And while the USTR-Commerce turf battles of the early 1980s appeared to have subsided, a new Treasury-led Economic Policy Council (EPC) would no doubt continue to undermine the USTR-chaired Trade Policy Committee and perpetuate the confusion. Moreover, while Ways and Means and Finance had some jurisdictional control over the Department of Treasury, it had very little over Commerce and none over State, Agriculture, and the alphabet soup of White House agencies. In the case of the USTR, the committees retained sole jurisdiction, including over the agency's annual authorization, and could count on more responsiveness and fewer turf fights with other committees.

Rostenkowski's concern over the issue had grown in the months preceding the markup due to the mixed signals he was getting from different officials in the administration on the trade bill. Not only was there no official with a clear mandate to deal, but he was increasingly suspicious of agency opposition to bill provisions on jurisdictional rather than policy grounds. Finally, if *he* needed a single official who could speak for the president on trade with whom to negotiate, surely such a single point of authority made sense for U.S. trade policy.

The approach contained in the Ways and Means Committee bill, essentially downgrading trade decision-making authority by transferring it from the president to his trade representative, served the members' purposes in several other ways, as well. Not only would other agencies find it awkward to overturn USTR decisions by "kicking them upstairs," but by lowering the level of the official making trade determinations, there was some hope of depoliticizing them. Were the USTR to find a foreign country to be "unfair" and take retaliatory action, it would appear far less confrontational in the context of U.S. foreign policy interests than that same act on the part of a president. If the decisions were considered less confrontational, perhaps there would be more of them and the basic enforcement of U.S. trade law would proceed as Congress had intended.

In the end, the bill's original delegation to the USTR of authority to determine the existence of an unfair trade practice under Section 301 was expanded to encompass decisions on whether and how to respond to certain foreign practices involving trade agreement violations. And while the committee agreed that the decisions identified in Congressman J. J. Pickle's (D-Tex.) highly disputed amendment were to be "subject to the direction of the President," the language still met with exceptional administration wrath.

Other transfers of presidential authority to the USTR approved by the committee during markup of H.R. 3 involved provision of import relief under Section 201 and Section 406 (nonmarket economy) escape clause cases, Section 337 intellectual property rights cases, and the GSP program. All decisions and activities required by the Rostenkowski substitute for the Gephardt bill were also vested in the USTR. Finally, so as to leave no one in doubt of congressional intent, the committee made it clear that henceforth the USTR was to have "primary responsibility for developing and coordinating implementation of international trade policy, international trade negotiations, and trade policy guidance."[19]

Later, during the House-Senate conference on the bill, Rostenkowski commented on the amount of attention the transfer of authority issue was getting from the administration. "God, you can't do that to the president," he quoted one cabinet official as saying. "I'm not trying to do that to the president," said Rostenkowski, "I'm trying to do it to you! . . . [But] I can't understand why they so worry about the STR having so much authority. . . . I mean if he doesn't like the guy, he fires 'em."

Unfair Trade Practices

Section 301. Since the introduction of reciprocity legislation in the early 1980s, Section 301 had in many ways become the central focus for the entire debate over U.S. trade policy. Enacted in 1974 and modified in 1979 and 1984, it was the principal statutory vehicle for U.S. industry to challenge perceived unfair trade practices. Simply put, the statute laid out a mechanism under which U.S. interests could assert that a foreign "act, policy or practice" was in violation of a trade agreement to which the U.S. was a party, or was "unjustifiable, unreasonable or discriminatory and burdens or restricts U.S. commerce." If the president determined that action was appropriate to enforce U.S. rights or respond to the practice, he was instructed to take "all appropriate and feasible action."[20]

Several changes to Section 301 were adopted by the Ways and Means Committee, many of which had first appeared in S. 1860 in the previous Congress. Principal among these changes was a differentiation between enforcement of U.S. rights under trade agreements and responses to other foreign practices affecting U.S. trade. Here the committee agreed that action against an agreement violation should be mandatory, but added a significant loophole in cases where retaliation was considered

---

[19] Congress, *Report of the Committee on Ways and Means to accompany H.R. 3,* Report 100–40, 23.
[20] Section 301, *Trade Act of 1974,* as amended; 19 USC 2411.

likely to run contrary to the "national economic interest." Retaliation against all other actionable foreign practices were left to the president's discretion. This committee compromise, combined with its transfer of decision making to the USTR, established Congress' desire for action, but still left the same "out" that existed, and was regularly used, in the Section 201 escape clause statute. The focus on U.S. "economic" interests (as distinct from more broadly defined "national" or "public" interests, for example) also reflected the strong conviction of the members that the executive branch still placed too high a priority on noneconomic relative to economic considerations in trade policymaking.

The committee also added several new "causes of action" to expand the scope of cases to be considered under the statute. Foreign practices that would become explicitly actionable under the Ways and Means modifications to Section 301 included foreign government toleration of anticompetitive activities and the denial of "worker rights," with the latter defined to include the rights of association and collective bargaining, a minimum age for working children, and, depending on the country's level of economic development, minimum wage, hours of work, and occupational safety and health standards.[21] Both causes of action were placed in the "discretionary" part of the law. A final addition to the actionable causes under Section 301 came in a provision on the treatment of "export targeting," focused on Japan and defined by the committee to refer to "any government plan or scheme . . . bestowed on a specific enterprise, industry, or group thereof the effect of which is to assist [it] . . . to become more competitive in the export of a class or kind of merchandise."[22] Options for action to respond to such cases were expanded to include U.S. government efforts to improve the U.S. industry's international competitive position.

Intellectual property rights. The committee created a parallel mechanism for self-initiation of Section 301-type cases involving "priority foreign countries" with a record of failure to protect intellectual property rights. This program eventually became known as "Special 301," and was championed by the entertainment industry. Determinations under this program would be made on an annual basis, linked to the publication of the National Trade Estimates report, with initiated cases subject to a shorter time frame than under regular Section 301.

---

[21] Congress, *Report of the Committee on Ways and Means to accompany H.R. 3*, Report 100–40, 365. This worker rights provision was slightly weaker than the one in H.R. 4800 in that a country's level of development and its efforts to improve worker conditions were now to be taken into account.
[22] Ibid.

Excessive and unwarranted trade surpluses. By this point in the process, Rostenkowski's substitute for the Gephardt bill and Gephardt's
latest version of his own language were in many ways identical. Principal differences lay in a handful of provisions involving the mandated
remedies and the level of implementing flexibility provided to the executive branch. Both the Gephardt and the Ways and Means language drew
extensively on concepts and language contained in Section 301. Both
were fairly mechanistic in approach, parting company over Gephardt's
heavy focus on bilateral trade imbalances and the committee's primary
focus on the trade barriers presumed to cause them.

Both the Gephardt and Ways and Means provisions required the ITC
to make annual determinations about whether any major U.S. trading
partner was an "excessive trade surplus country," based on specific
numerical threshold values. Both then gave the USTR fifteen days in
which to determine whether these countries also maintained a pattern
of unfair trade practices. At that point, the USTR had 180 days (Rostenkowski's bill added a 60-day extension) to negotiate with each of the
designated "excessive and unwarranted trade surplus countries" an "arrangement" that eliminated the practices or their adverse impact on
U.S. commerce (Gephardt) or that substantially reduced them (Rostenkowski). Both bills required the USTR to estimate the commercial value
of each of the practices so that U.S. firms could be assured (Gephardt)
or given a reasonable opportunity (Rostenkowski) of improving their
bilateral trade with the country by an equal amount.

In the absence of an arrangement, the USTR was required to act
against all of the identified unfair trade practices, with the level of retaliation set equivalent to the previously estimated amount (Gephardt) or
the value of their "burden or restriction on U.S. commerce" (Rostenkowski). In the most dramatic difference between the two bills, the
Gephardt language then imposed an additional "surplus reduction requirement," mandating action to reduce the bilateral trade imbalance
between the U.S. and the designated countries by 10 percent per year
until 1991.

Under both bills, the USTR could avoid retaliatory action if he determined, for example, that it would cause "substantial harm" (Gephardt)
or "adversely affect" (Rostenkowski) the national economic interest of
the United States. However, use of such a waiver required congressional
notification and could be overturned by a joint resolution of disapproval. In practical terms, both bills were designed to target Japan,
Taiwan, and South Korea, that together had accounted for approximately half of the U.S. trade deficit the previous year. Other countries
meeting the quantitative criteria, such as Germany and Brazil, would

probably not be affected—the former by virtue of its relatively open market, the latter because of its balance of payments problems.[23]

Gephardt had, by this time, informed the panel that he intended to take his battle to the House floor. Clearly, the UAW-sponsored "call Rosty" advertisements being run on Chicago radio stations had not achieved their intended purpose.[24] And while the Rostenkowski substitute was certainly not supported by the administration, the more free-trade-oriented members of the committee, or the original Gephardt proponents, it still drew the panel's acquiescence as a defensible alternative for the floor.

Antidumping/Countervailing Duty Laws

A wide array of extremely complex and controversial provisions were included in this part of the committee bill. With a few exceptions, most set out to tighten existing antidumping and countervailing law by broadening relevant definitions and by further circumscribing executive branch flexibility to interpret the law.

Provisions in U.S. law pertaining to products dumped by foreign producers or subsidized by their governments into the U.S. market dated back to 1890. Since then, however, the definitions of what constituted a dumped or subsidized product, and the means of calculating margins, had been progressively modified. By the 1980s, any product sold in the United States at "less than fair value," identified by a price less than that in the producer's home market, a third-country export market, or the estimated cost of production, was considered unfairly traded. In response to a petition, the U.S. Department of Commerce would assess whether and to what extent dumping and/or subsidization had occurred and the ITC would determine whether or not the domestic industry had been injured as a result. Antidumping or countervailing duties are collected at the border in the amount of the estimated margin of dumping or subsidization.

With enactment of the Trade Agreements Act of 1979, the AD/CVD laws had become as close to nondiscretionary as any trade statutes on the books. Means of calculation were prescribed, time limits imposed, and imposition of antidumping or countervailing duties made manda-

---

[23] Both provisions granted waivers for debtor nations. Both also required the Secretary of Treasury to determine whether any of the offending countries were maintaining currencies at artificially low levels relative to the dollar. If a more appropriate currency alignment could not be attained through negotiation, the secretary was authorized to impose an exchange-rate-equalization tax in response.

[24] The "call Rosty" punch line mirrored Rostenkowski's own suggestion a year earlier made on national television in connection with tax reform legislation.

tory in the absence of negotiated settlements ("suspension agreements"). Proscriptions in U.S. law restricting such unfair trade practices were generally held consistent with the GATT and relevant codes of conduct, including limits on countervailable subsidies to export subsidies, other than when a domestic subsidy was specifically provided to aid an exporting industry.

However, the bulk of American AD/CVD law, while generic in nature, had been written by or with the U.S. steel and other heavy industry in mind. As a result, groups advocating changes during this period tended to fall into two categories: high technology (primarily electronic) industries, whose short product life-cycles, reliance on profits to fund subsequent product generations, and use of multiple component inputs were not perceived to be adequately served by existing law; and industries or agricultural interests that had used the laws in the past in failed attempts to gain the desired level of relief. While the language changes being proposed were also generic, it was clear they had been written with several industries and countries, including Japan, in mind.

Opponents of the provisions were prevailed upon by Rostenkowski to leave the changes in the bill, both to placate their committee proponents and for the purpose of having something later with which to bargain away objectionable provisions in the Senate bill. The chairman did, however, instruct his staff and private sector supporters of the measures to try working them out with the administration and other opponents in advance. But while the staff-drafted modifications seemed to meet the strongest objections of USTR and Commerce officials, at that point in the process it was simply not in the administration's interest to acquiesce in specific language.

Judicial remedy for dumping. Among the most controversial of the provisions was a proposal by Rep. Frank J. Guarini (D-N.J.) to amend the moribund 1916 Dumping Act and to provide a private right of action for dumping cases. Most appealing to potential plaintiffs (and most horrifying to GATT supporters) was the prospect of court-awarded damages and of injunctive relief on the basis of a presumption of guilt that could halt imports for the duration of a case.

In the end, the committee watered the provision down substantially, agreeing to repeal the 1916 act's criminal penalties and to delete a treble damages option. It did, however retain a rebuttable presumption of "intent to injure" in multiple offender cases involving foreign manufacturers found to have been dumping more than three times in a ten-year period. Ways and Means opponents knew that a proposal similar to the original Guarini measure, championed by Senator Arlen Specter (R-Pa.), had been defeated by the Senate in the past. They hoped the amendment would meet with the same fate again on H.R. 3, leaving the House version further negotiable for purposes of the upcoming House-Senate conference.

Multiple offenders. This provision was aimed at several vertically integrated high technology producers, particularly in Japan, that were considered the main culprits of predatory dumping. It established procedures for monitoring imports from manufacturers found to have dumped repeatedly in the past. If monitoring offered evidence of further dumping, the Commerce Department could initiate expedited antidumping proceedings. As with the 1916 act provision, the measure had been weakened significantly from the original.

Natural resource subsidies. This provision made countervailable certain finished exports benefitting from domestic (as distinct from export) subsidies on a resource input. Originally proposed by Rep. Gibbons, it was softened with his consent during markup. For this purpose, the staff worked with interested lobbyists to narrow the scope of the language to the holding of a Court of International Trade case on the "general availability" of resource subsidies.[25] Fertilizer or cement imports produced with natural gas were considered likely targets of the provision, which was still strongly opposed by the administration.

Diversionary input dumping. Also referred to as "downstream dumping," this provision involved the use by a foreign manufacturer of an input that had previously been found to have been dumped. The provision, affecting primarily the steel and electronics industries, was to enable domestic manufacturers to bring cases against foreign competitors able to lower costs by incorporating inputs that were elsewhere subject to antidumping duties. The bill also provided for the monitoring of such "downstream products" to assist in identifying the diversionary impact of significant antidumping or countervailing duties on major inputs of parts or materials.

Anticircumvention. Related to the diversionary input language, these proposals were designed to prevent the use of minor product changes to evade outstanding antidumping and countervailing duty orders. Circumvention of outstanding orders through minor alterations and processing in third countries had become of concern to various U.S. producers. Both this and the diversionary dumping provision had been strongly championed by Rep. Martin A. (Marty) Russo (D-Ill.), but were somewhat weaker than their predecessors in H.R. 4800.

[25] In *Cabot Corp.* v. *United States*, 620 F. Supp. 722 (C.I.T. 4 October 1985), the court found the Commerce Department to have employed an unduly narrow interpretation of the concepts of "specificity" and "general availability."

Injury determinations. The committee bill contained several modifications to the "material injury" standard applied by the ITC in AD/CVD cases.[26] These included direction to the ITC to restrict its analysis of injury to the health of only the domestic production facilities of the U.S. industry. In "threat of injury" cases, the ITC was to consider new factors in its determination, including diversion of exports into the U.S. market. In assessing whether imports from a particular country were injurious, the ITC was directed to cumulate the impact of exports from virtually all countries subject to antidumping or countervailing duty investigations.

Other provisions. A variety of other—equally or more arcane—changes in the AD/CVD laws were also contained in the House bill. These included a countervailing duty provision applicable to nonmarket economy countries, various changes pertaining to the treatment of agricultural products, the compensation of injured U.S. producers with collected antidumping duties, and a prohibition on the exemption of U.S. government purchases from antidumping or countervailing duties.[27]

One change was also incorporated in the Ways and Means bill that had the potential of loosening the law in rare instances. This provision authorized the ITC, under certain circumstances, to exclude from injury and remedy determinations imports into "geographically isolated markets."

Escape Clause/Trade Adjustment Assistance

Section 201. Beyond the transfer of decision-making authority to the USTR, the House bill made relatively minor changes to the Section 201 escape clause, the basic statutory remedy available to industries injured by imports. At the time, if a domestic industry could prove to the ITC that increased imports were a "substantial" cause of "serious injury"

---

[26] Since the Tokyo Round and Trade Agreements Act of 1979, proof of injury has been required in all CVD cases involving a GATT Subsidies Code signatory. The "material injury" threshold is lower than that required in Section 201 cases, and is defined in law as "a harm which is not inconsequential, immaterial or unimportant." John Greenwald, an author of the standard, has suggested that the definition was chosen "precisely because it says nothing at all." A definition was needed for Tokyo Round implementing legislation that was acceptable to both domestic industry and key U.S. trading partners. The compromise language was clarified through use of detailed guidance for the ITC determination. (John D. Greenwald, "Material Injury," *Federal Bar News & Journal*, 29/1 [January 1982]: 38–40).

[27] This provision was in response to General Services Administration (GSA) importation—without the payment of antidumping duties—of titanium sponge for a defense stockpile.

(or a threat thereof), and if the ITC recommended relief, the president could impose whatever protective import restrictions he considered appropriate.

Ways and Means Committee modifications to the definition of injury were designed to make it easier for firms to apply in "threat" cases. With regard to remedies, the USTR was instructed to provide some form of import relief unless the costs of providing such relief was said to outweigh the benefits. The bill also required the ITC to recommend an import remedy in any case involving injury, thereby eliminating TAA as a substitute for (as distinct from supplement to) the list of import relief options available to it. In addition, the ITC recommendation to the USTR would have to estimate the effect of the proposed relief on consumers, other sectors of the economy, and on taxpayers, communities, and workers.

The Ways and Means bill went on to allow petitioners to submit proposed industry adjustment plans to the government, but did not make them mandatory. The bill also made a number of other changes to the statute involving remedy options, treatment of perishable commodities, and provision of emergency relief.

Trade Adjustment Assistance. Whether or not import relief were granted under Section 201, the bill granted automatic eligibility for the petitioners to Trade Adjustment Assistance. The TAA program, itself, was also modified by restricting the use of its limited funds to the payment of worker retraining and to supplement the wages of workers who accept lower-paying jobs. A new system of vouchers for displaced workers was added in a disputed amendment by Rep. Pease, at an estimated cost of $60 million.

Other Trade Law Provisions

In addition to the major provisions of trade law noted above, the Ways and Means bill contained a great many other measures of varying length and importance. Among the more significant trade provisions were the following:

Telecommunications trade. Although all parties had agreed to avoid major product-specific provisions, both House and Senate bills made an exception in the case of telecommunications. This provision, introduced by Rep. Robert Matsui (D-Calif.), was the Ways and Means version of a bill first introduced in the Senate in 1984. It mandated negotiations and action to offset the perceived negative trade implications of the breakup of AT&T and U.S. telecommunications deregulation in the early 1980s.

Intellectual property rights. In addition to transferring decision-making authority to the USTR, the committee made several other changes to Section 337 of the Tariff Act of 1930. As noted earlier, Section 337 was now used primarily to obtain exclusion orders for goods violating U.S. intellectual property rights. The most important of the committee's changes was the elimination of the requirement to show injury from such imports.

Customs fraud. Designed to tighten and accelerate enforcement of U.S. customs law, Ways and Means added to the bill a "scofflaw" penalty provision. Ultimately one of the bill's more controversial provisions, it imposed a ban on the importation of goods by anyone found to have violated U.S. customs law on more than three occasions during the previous seven-year period.

National security import relief. Section 232 of the Trade Expansion Act of 1962 contained a relatively loose procedure for an industry to seek relief from imports determined to threaten U.S. national security. The committee proposed to add strict time limits to the law for the Commerce Department's investigation and recommendation to the president, and for the president's decision. These changes were primarily in response to a machine tool case that had been "pending" for close to three years without resolution.

Nonmarket economy imports. Section 406 of the Trade Act of 1974 is the rarely used nonmarket economy counterpart to the Section 201 escape clause. In addition to changing the statute's application of the statute from "communist" to "nonmarket economy" countries, the committee made several minor adjustments designed to lower the injury threshold.

Sugar duty drawback. This provision called for a refund of import duties and fees paid under Section 22 of the Agricultural Adjustment Act for sugar imported between November 1977 and March 1985, provided that the sugar was processed and reexported prior to October 1991. Like many of the noncontroversial tariff suspension bills, this provision was essentially a private relief act. Unlike most such measures, however, the sugar drawback provision turned out to involve a potential drain on the U.S. treasury of over $200 million.[28]

Miscellaneous Tariff and Customs Provisions

Minor tariff measures are often the bread and butter of congressional trade committee activities in years when no major trade negotiation is

---

[28] Three companies would apparently have benefited from the provision by an estimated $200–300 million. Bob Packwood, "Additional Views of Sen. Bob Packwood," Congress, Senate, Committee on Finance, *Omnibus Trade Act of 1987: Report of the Committee on Finance on S. 490*, 100th Cong., 1st sess., 1987, Report 100–71, 261.

at hand. In the absence of permanent presidential tariff authority, it is left to Congress to enact the dozens of miscellaneous tariff law changes sought by individual constituents. As a general rule, only noncontroversial tariff suspensions, eliminations, or reclassifications are contained in these measures, usually involving imported products for which there are no domestic substitutes. Tariff increases are rarely, if ever, included, although an occasional tariff reclassification has the same effect. The popularity of these seemingly mundane bills among members is attributable to their "real world" value to constituents that, unlike trade policy language, can readily be measured in dollar savings.

The House had approved a miscellaneous tariff bill in the 99th Congress on which the Senate had failed to act. This represented a pattern that was a great source of frustration to Ways and Means, attributable in part to the Constitution's revenue origination clause and the Senate's hoarding of House revenue bills as vehicles for other trade and tax matters, and in part to the Senate's inability to invoke a closed rule on trade measures. Because both trade committees preferred temporary tariff suspensions to eliminations—hoping they could be made permanent in a future reciprocal exchange—many often expired before Congress got around to extending them.

In all, the House bill contained seventy-five miscellaneous tariff and customs provisions, incorporating those approved during the 99th Congress. Examples included elimination of the tariff on hatters' fur, reclassification and retroactive reduction of the duty on "extracorporeal shock wave lithotripters," and a long list of duty suspensions on various chemicals, such as "1-(4-(1,1-Dimethylethyl)Phenyl)-4-(Hydroxydiphenylmethyl-1-Piperidinyl)-1-Butanone"!

The Ways and Means bill, as amended, was reported out of committee on March 25, by a vote of 34–2, with only two Republicans dissenting. Members also approved a Rostenkowski-drafted resolution calling on the Rules Committee to disallow amendments by granting a closed rule on the bill.

Consistent with the chairman's goal and expectations, the bill was characterized by press and pundits alike as moderate. That evening, for example, *ABC News* stressed the bill's unfair trade practice provisions, airing the story in conjunction with one on the revival of Harley-Davidson and its unprecedented request to terminate the import relief it was receiving under Section 201. Virtually all press reports noted that the committee had managed to avoid including the Gephardt language. Congressman Frenzel, who voted for the bill, was slightly less generous: "I personally had to cough, and spit, and sputter, and swallow hard at the Committee on Ways and Means bill, and finally voted 'aye' not for the product but for the process."[29] In fact, for Frenzel and the administration, the Ways and Means bill represented a potentially significant strategic achievement: Having focused their efforts during markup on diluting controversial provisions that were also expected to appear in the Senate bill, they had helped Rostenkowski steer the process into one promising maximum flexibility in conference.

Others, however, were not so pleased. Upon seeing the Ways and Means product, lobbyists for various interest groups were astonished by the degree to which their provisions had been watered down. Commented one steel industry association executive, "When Danny Rostenkowski's litmus test is 'can Bill Frenzel live with it,' you know something's wrong." Recognizing that their opportunities to further toughen the bill in the House were limited, most of the lobbyists now turned their attention to the Senate.

HOUSE FLOOR ACTION

Virtually all of the bills that were to be incorporated in H.R. 3 had been reported out of relevant committees by the first week in April. These included the various titles reported by Ways and Means, along with those of the Energy and Commerce, Foreign Affairs, Banking, Education and Labor, and Agriculture Committees. Also reported were bills from the Small Business, Merchant Marine, Transportation, and Judiciary Committees, which were to be added during the course of Rules Committee deliberations. By final passage on the House floor, H.R. 3 contained thirteen separate titles, comprising over 900 printed pages. Of these, the first two titles and roughly one-third of the text had originated in the Committee on Ways and Means.

As might have been expected, provisions reported by other committees varied in both substance and degree of controversy. The House Energy and Commerce Committee, for example, reported its own provisions pertaining to Section 301, dumping, and telecommunications trade, along with anti-bribery (Foreign Corrupt Practices Act) and countertrade language considered to be under the jurisdiction of the Foreign Affairs Committee. This led to a fairly standard refrain from various committees suggesting that Energy and Commerce was using the trade bill to "poach" on everyone else's turf.[30]

---

[29] Congress, House, *Congressional Record* (April 30, 1987), vol. 133, no. 68, H2979.

[30] It was this tendency that had once prompted Rep. Frenzel to remark to a USTR staffer that Chairman Dingell had the "third largest law firm in Washington, D.C.," referring to the number of lawyers and parliamentary experts on committee staff appar-

In addition to these potentially duplicative provisions, the Energy and Commerce Committee had added, by a vote of 21–20, a highly contentious amendment by Congressman John Bryant (D-Tex.) requiring that foreign ownership in a U.S. business in excess of 5 percent be reported to the Securities and Exchange Commission (SEC). This and other information required in cases involving more than 25 percent ownership, was to be provided by both public and privately held firms, and was to be made available to the general public. The committee measure also included a provision requiring the Commerce Department to study the national security implications of foreign takeovers of U.S. firms. This provision, sponsored by Rep. James J. Florio (D-N.J.), had originally been introduced in response to the failed attempt by Fujitsu Inc. of Japan to buy Fairchild Semiconductor Corporation.

The Foreign Affairs Committee issued provisions relating to both export controls and export promotion, including expansion of the ban on the export of Alaskan North Slope crude oil to other U.S.-produced oil and refined petroleum products.

The Banking Committee included language mandating international negotiations on exchange rates; third world debt issues, including establishment of a new (unfunded) refinancing facility; and the creation of a Council on Industrial Competitiveness, to be composed of representatives of government, business, labor, and academia.

The House Judiciary Committee reported out patent, trademark, and other language pertaining to the protection of intellectual property rights.

The Government Operations Committee adopted a provision amending the Buy American Act to preclude U.S. government purchases of goods from any country whose government was found to discriminate against U.S. exports.

Finally, the Agriculture Committee, in the context of several export promotion measures, extended the Export Enhancement Program (EEP), under which the Department of Agriculture could use surplus government-owned commodities to subsidize U.S. farm exports and counter European farm subsidies.

The House committees had been warned to avoid adopting measures that would require substantial funding outlays, in keeping with an April 1 Budget Committee resolution designed to limit the bill's budget impact. In spite of these efforts, however, the administration still calculated the bill's revenue impact at more than $3 billion over a three-year pe-

---

ently dedicated to ensuring that legislation on the widest possible range of topics was directed to that committee.

riod. The most costly of the provisions turned out to be $501 million in new educational grant programs and $980 million for worker retraining, both products of the Education and Labor Committee.

Normally, it would have been left to the Rules Committee to referee jurisdictional disputes arising from the various bills. In this case, however, Wright turned to staffer Peter Robinson to take on resolving committee differences, meld overlapping or conflicting provisions, and forge the "leadership substitute" that would be incorporated in the rule governing House floor action on H.R. 3. Robinson, a trained parliamentarian, developed his own working rules for dealing with the various committee provisions. First, the committees would be encouraged to resolve their own differences. Failing that, Robinson would recommend the Speaker accept the version reported by the committee with predominant jurisdiction. In the few instances where jurisdiction was shared, the leadership would make a judgment call or try to forge a compromise. Any committee objecting to the leadership substitute could always seek Rules Committee approval to offer a floor amendment. For the Ways and Means Committee, this process resulted in their bill staying largely intact. In the case of the telecommunications trade language, however, the Energy and Commerce Committee could legitimately claim some jurisdiction, so a compromise was grudgingly worked out between the two committee staffs and incorporated in the substitute.

All of these preparations notwithstanding, by the time H.R. 3 reached the House floor, the only major focus of public attention was a provision *not* contained in it—namely, the Gephardt amendment. Throughout the consideration of H.R. 3, the amendment would obscure virtually all other provisions in the House bill.

On April 27, the House Rules Committee reported out its resolution governing floor action on the omnibus measure. H. Res. 151 provided for general debate of seven and one-half hours, allotted in one-hour or thirty-minute segments, and equally divided between the chairmen and ranking minority members of each committee of jurisdiction. Action would culminate with a twenty-minute period for final statements equally divided and controlled by each party.

Upon adoption by the House of the modified-open rule, the leadership substitute would become the new text of H.R. 3. The rule waived all points of order (procedural motions) against the bill and specified the few amendments allowed to be offered. These included one amendment in the nature of a substitute for the bill, to be offered by Minority Leader Michel (the so-called Republican substitute); three amendments to Title I (the Ways and Means bill), including the Gephardt language; eleven amendments to other sections of the bill; and a handful of technical corrections. Each amendment was allotted thirty or forty minutes of debate, with a few exceptions, including the Gephardt and Michel amendments, which were each allocated ninety minutes. Finally, the rule provided for one motion to recommit (return the bill to committee) by the minority leader prior to final passage.

Early in the afternoon of April 28, the House opened debate on the bill. That day, members approved the rule (326–83) and completed all general debate. Consideration of amendments to H.R. 3 started with adoption of two relatively noncontroversial additions to the Ways and Means title. The first added certain reciprocity criteria to its trade agreement negotiating objectives; the second, offered by Rules Committee Chairman Claude Pepper (D-Fla.), stressed enforcement of restrictions on imports from Cuba. Both passed with over 390 votes in their favor.

The third amendment placed before the House was that of Congressman Gephardt. As a technical matter, the amendment was a complete substitute for Section 126 of the Ways and Means bill, and was generally perceived and characterized as such. As a practical matter, the most significant difference between the two lay with the Gephardt amendment's mandated 10 percent rollback in bilateral imbalances. But by then the vote had become one as much of symbolism as of substance. The battle had been shaping up for weeks. In an unusual departure from the normal course of business, it pitted the Speaker of the House against his chairman of jurisdiction, with Wright apparently determined to pull out all the stops on Gephardt's behalf. Not all members of the House Democratic leadership supported the Speaker on the Gephardt amendment, however. Majority Leader Thomas S. Foley (D-Wash.), in keeping with his own trade philosophy and the substantial export interests of his Pacific Northwest constituents, opposed the measure. Other prominent Democrats with a history of interest in U.S. trade policy, such as Congressmen Gibbons and Don Bonker (D-Wash.), also spoke out against it. Both Wright and Rostenkowski tried to downplay any personal animosities. In addition to the Speaker and Democratic Whip Tony L. Coelho (D-Calif.), Gephardt was backed by organized labor and a business coalition led by Chrysler's Lee Iacocca. Rostenkowski's coalition included several key trade associations, major multinationals, mainstream agricultural interests, and importers.

To develop his business coalition, Iacocca relied heavily on his firm's supplier network and a variety of like-minded CEOs. In a letter to each member of the House ("The Gephardt Trade Amendment: What it Does . . . and Doesn't . . . Do"), he supplied a long list of the amendment's supporters, including steel producers USX and LTV, textile producer Milliken, major multinationals Motorola and Allied-

Signal, Ford Motor Company, and various auto parts suppliers. In addition, participating in a "Global Market Amendment" press conference attended by Gephardt on April 15, were the AFL-CIO and the UAW, along with more peripheral groups like the American Agriculture Movement, the National Farmers Union, and the National Consumers League.

The opposing business group was patterned loosely after the coalition that had backed tax reform legislation with Rostenkowski in 1986, and involved seventy-five companies and trade associations. These included the four largest exporting firms in the United States, Boeing, IBM, GE, and Caterpillar; along with prominent umbrella business groups such as the U.S. Chamber of Commerce, the National Association of Manufacturers (NAM), and the Emergency Committee for American Trade (ECAT). Retailers such as Kmart, major farm organizations like the American Farm Bureau and the National Grange, and associations representing soybean, wheat, and livestock producers joined the coalition as well.

Each side met regularly, developed and revised headcounts, identified the undecided or wavering, organized grassroots lobbying campaigns, worked the press, and peppered House members with letters, calls, and position papers. Above all, each needed to make sure that no member considered this a throwaway vote, a vote without downside risk or accountability, as had been the case a year earlier by virtue of the amendment's doomed legislative vehicle. As one ECAT official noted: "It's an effort, quite frankly, to tell members that it's not a cheap vote . . . [otherwise] they will think that it's a freebie."[31]

Supporters of the Gephardt amendment tried their best to defend it in the media. In an April 20 Op-Ed in the *Washington Post*, Gephardt focused on foreign barriers to U.S. exports and framed his approach as a rejection of the status quo. He wrote:

> Some claim that this provision is protectionist, or that it ties the president's hands. Nothing could be further from the truth. We are simply trying to put a tool in the president's hands and ask him to use it to pry open foreign markets in support of the world's free trading system.[32]

But most editorial writers disagreed, calling the Gephardt amendment "destructive," "protectionist," and comparing it to the Smoot-Hawley

[31] Robert McNeill, quoted in John Cranford, "Confrontation Likely Over Trade Amendment," *Congressional Quarterly*, April 11, 1987, 678.
[32] Richard A. Gephardt, "The New World of Foreign Trade," *Washington Post*, April 20, 1987.

Tariff Act, leading one AFL-CIO official to accuse opponents of using a "McCarthyite brush" against the amendment.[33]

As the vote approached, even the White House got involved, as cabinet officers and the president made calls to selected members to seek their opposition to the amendment. In a "Dear Colleague" letter to each House member on April 22, Rostenkowski strongly defended the committee language, noting the similarities between it and the Gephardt bill and stressing the dollar-for-dollar retaliation alternative to the more mechanistic deficit reduction formula. He cautioned that foreign countries might be tempted to apply such a formula to U.S. exports in the future, and he reminded his colleagues of the amendment's implications for the bill as a whole, predicting:

> The Gephardt amendment will surely provoke a veto that Congress will not be able to override. This could torpedo trade legislation altogether and kill the many needed reforms in H.R. 3. This will merely serve to strengthen Japan's view that Congress is interested in sending unenforceable messages rather than actually enacting a tough trade bill.

Gephardt controlled the forty-five minutes on behalf of amendment proponents; Rostenkowski and the ranking Republican on his committee, the time of the opposition. Contributing to the drama of the moment and to the unusual spectacle of a full chamber during a debate was a quorum call taken immediately prior to the closing statements.

As debates over intensely felt differences go, this one was conducted in the best tradition of congressional collegiality. Both Gephardt and Rostenkowski received highly unusual (and technically out of order) standing ovations from the members upon conclusion of their remarks. In fact, because both sides were defending virtually identical provisions—but for the deficit rollback—it evolved into a debate between those who wanted to be tough on trade and those who claimed to be tougher. Gephardt cited the need for presidential accountability; Rostenkowski, the need for a law. References to Japan figured prominently in both of their statements, as they had in the remarks of many throughout consideration of the bill. Neither congressman dwelt on the substance of the amendment, acknowledging that members no doubt had already had their fill.

---

[33] Cranford, "Confrontation Likely," 678; quoting Bill Cunningham, an AFL-CIO lobbyist and former Ways and Means Committee staffer. Quoted commentaries are drawn from editorials in the *Washington Post* (April 29, 1987), the *New York Times* (April 29, 1987), and *The Wall Street Journal* (April 28, 1987).

As the debate drew to a close, Gephardt summed up his remarks by stating that the amendment was "about whether you want to maintain the status quo in trade policy or whether you want change" and calling for a new trade policy "based on behavior and action, and not on words."[34] Rostenkowski, characterized it differently: "The Gephardt amendment is too draconian to be effective," he said, asserting that the committee bill "changes the current practice of inaction, but . . . with a surgical knife, rather than a meat ax." Moreover, he went on, "I would rather see us pass a bill that is so tough the Japanese can't ignore it, but so fair the President has no choice but to sign it."[35]

Then it was time for the vote. Wright, Coelho, and their whip team worked the floor. Gibbons, Frenzel, and others of Rostenkowski's colleagues did as well. But the chairman seemed to hold back, letting other members approach him rather than the reverse. When asked, he reiterated his closing statement calling on members to be guided by their consciences and common sense, and committing not to hold grudges against members who disagreed with his position. This led Pease, standing with Rostenkowski on the floor, to wryly suggest that the chairman's promise not to hold grudges had probably cost him forty votes. But Rostenkowski's approach remained consistent with the one he had adopted once he realized the Speaker was going to make the amendment a leadership initiative. If nothing else, it served to set him apart from the more heavy-handed approach adopted by Wright.

With most members already in the chamber, the vote went quickly. And it was close. By the time the 15-minute clock had run out, the vote was tied at 209–209. Several more votes came in, with Wright—in his second vote as Speaker that year—casting the 218th vote in favor. With only 214 voting against it, the amendment carried. Although it had received fewer votes than its tougher counterpart a year earlier, this was really the high watermark for the Gephardt bill; now it was moving on a serious vehicle.

Of votes for the amendment, 201 were Democrats and only 17 were Republican, in contrast to the 44 Republicans who had voted against a motion to strike the amendment the year before. Voting in opposition were 55 Democrats (in contrast to 7 the previous year) and 159 Republicans. There were several reasons for these reversals. Rostenkowski, for example, had voted for a tougher version of the measure the previous year and had sponsored the original with Gephardt and Bentsen in 1985. This time, however, he and other members had a sense they were

[34] Congress, *Congressional Record* (April 29, 1987), H2788–89.
[35] Ibid., H2789.

writing a law, not simply making a statement or sending a signal to the White House or trading partners. This time, too, all had been bombarded by months of negative input on the bill, which had acquired an irrevocable image as the epitome of protectionism. Finally, this time, they had a tough alternative in the bill to vote *for*.

In the wake of the vote on the Gephardt amendment, all others seemed anticlimactic. That same day, two administration-supported amendments were approved to the agriculture title. One deleted a $300 million dairy price support provision, the second eliminated a country-of-origin meat labeling requirement. An amendment by Republicans on the Banking Committee to change Banking title provisions related to negotiation of a "competitive exchange rate," LDC-debt restructuring, and the competitiveness council failed by a vote of 187–239.

On April 30, the House completed action on H.R. 3 with the approval of amendments involving Soviet slave labor and lace gloves. It also approved an amendment by conservative Republicans to suspend MFN treatment of Romania and a Pease amendment to require a competitiveness impact statement with administration and congressional budget proposals. Voted down were all Republican amendments to strike or modify language considered most objectionable by the administration, including the foreign investment registration and "Buy America" provisions. The first was rejected by a vote of 190–230; the second by a division vote (involving a headcount of members present on the floor) of 8 ayes to 17 noes.

Finally, Minority Leader Michel offered his substitute that would have retained all of H.R. 3 with the exception of the Bryant language, the "Buy America" provision, the banking title, and the Gephardt amendment. In his remarks, Michel commended Wright for involving Republicans in the bill's development, singling out the "Flagship" Ways and Means Committee for its "truly . . . bipartisan approach."[36] He also noted that while he wanted a bill that could be signed into law, he was still prepared to leave intact a great many provisions opposed by the administration.[37] Indeed, roughly half the issues raised in a final six-page letter to members from twelve administration cabinet or cabinet-level officials would have been left intact by the Michel amendment. By this time, however, it was clear that H.R. 3 would shortly be

---

[36] Congress, *Congressional Record* (April 30, 1987), H2964.

[37] In a commentary later before the Society of Government Economists, Raymond J. Ahearn, a Congressional Research Service international trade specialist, suggested that what the Michel amendment really signified was that "900 out of 1000 provisions in the bill were really bipartisan. . . . "

approved by a substantial margin, and the amendment fell by a vote of 156–268.

The vote in support of final passage of H.R. 3 was an unusually strong one for a controversial bill, a relatively bipartisan 290–137. Forty-three Republicans joined all but six Democrats in voting "aye," many freed to support the bill by virtue of their previous vote in support of the Michel substitute: In voting on the substitute, Republicans had voted both on the substance of the bill and with their party's leader. Once that amendment had failed (as everyone knew it would), they then could cite a final vote for H.R. 3 as a statement of support for enactment of trade legislation in general. Nominally, the two-to-one margin on final passage was enough to override a veto, but members and astute observers knew that much could and would change in the bill before it emerged from conference.

As Rostenkowski had predicted, the press commentary on H.R. 3 dwelt primarily on the Gephardt language, reinstating the "protectionist" label he and others had wanted to avoid. The label stayed with the House bill through the remainder of the legislative process, overshadowing any of its more moderate components. Moreover, it was the Gephardt amendment and the perception of it that helped to obscure somewhat the fact that there was firm bipartisan support for a fairly tough trade bill. In fact, the vote on final passage of H.R. 3 fell just shy of that on the 1986 trade bill (295–115), a bill most assumed would move no farther in the legislative process.

Most private sector interests, while divided on Gephardt, were sufficiently supportive of the legislation to want to see it move forward to the next stage in the process. Organized labor, which had made the Gephardt amendment one of its key votes of the year, was particularly relieved, knowing the House bill was its best shot for getting the provision into conference.[38]

Free-trade advocates like Gibbons and Frenzel—one voting for and one voting against final passage—both expressed varying degrees of support for the bill. Frenzel cited provisions likely to provoke a veto, but went out of his way to be positive about the bill's future:

---

[38] Rostenkowski, in his March 22, 1987, *Post* interview described organized labor's attitude about the Gephardt amendment as follows: "I met with labor on three occasions. They were in cement in the beginning up to their ankles, then up to their knees. They just weren't going to move, and I suggested to them that, 'You've got your posture, I've got my job, I'm gonna put a bill together that I can develop and send to the House and hope get approved. . . . It was, 'God, if we can't do it in the House, where can we do it?' "

I am going to urge Members on both sides to forget the bad stuff in the bill temporarily. Members do not have to repudiate the good bipartisan work that made up the basis for this bill. Somewhere along the line still we may be able to put it back together again and the process move on. There is enormous incentive on both sides of the aisle for protectionists and free traders alike to get a bill that can be enacted and can be signed into law.[39]

Echoed Gibbons:

I am a free trader. I have no apologies for that. I hope my colleagues will vote for this bill. It is a tough one to vote for, but this is a bicameral organization and there is hope that we can work out an acceptable bill before we are at the end of all of this.[40]

The ball was now in the Senate's court.

---

[39] Congress, *Congressional Record* (April 30, 1987), H2979.
[40] Ibid.

5

MANAGED CHAOS IN THE SENATE

Thomas Jefferson once asked George Washington why he supported a two-chamber Congress. "Why did you pour that coffee into your saucer?" asked Washington of Jefferson. "To cool it," responded Jefferson. "Even so," remarked Washington, "we pour legislation into the Senatorial saucer to cool it."[1]

THE SENATE WRITES A TRADE BILL

With the 1986 election came a new U.S. Senate. The Democrats had regained control and with it the ability to establish priorities, set the agenda, and dominate floor and committee activities. They would, however, have to work with the administration and/or the Republican minority if they wished to see that agenda become law, for their 55–45 majority was nowhere near the 67 votes necessary to ensure a veto override. Such cooperation would not be necessary if the objective was simply to score political points. For Senate Republicans, loss of the Senate meant that the burden to regularly deliver a majority for the administration—with or without Senate Democrats—had eased. But to get something tangible accomplished, working with the Democratic leadership was now a must.

Early commitments by Majority Leader Byrd and Finance Chairman Bentsen had made movement of a trade bill inevitable. But while the Senate's principal trade committee shared many of the same objectives as its House counterpart, it had to operate in a very different environment, one more often characterized by unwritten—than by written—rules. As a result, the outcome was less predictable from the start and a process that had taken four months in the House took almost twice as long in the Senate.

---

[1] Adapted from Walter J. Oleszek, "Members and Their Constituencies," *Congressional Research Service Review*, 9, no. 5 (May 1988): 29.

This was Bentsen's first opportunity to chair the committee and to claim the mantle held by its legendary previous Democratic chairman, Russell Long, who had retired at the end of the previous Congress. In the 100th Congress, Finance would have a total of eleven Democrats and nine Republicans. Two of the new committee members, Senators Donald W. Riegle (D-Mich.) and John D. ("Jay") Rockefeller IV (D-W.Va.), represented states with a high proportion of import-sensitive industries; the third new member, Thomas A. Daschle (D-S.Dak.), and both Republicans leaving the committee represented farm constituencies. Spark Matsunaga, considered a trade-liberal on all issues but sugar, was appointed the new chairman of the International Trade Subcommittee; John Danforth became its ranking Republican member.

Bentsen had previously served as ranking member of the Trade Subcommittee, and was considered an active and informed participant in its deliberations. A latecomer to sponsorship of what became the 1984 Trade and Tariff Act, he eventually assumed the lead with Senator Danforth, on those provisions requiring administration compilation of annual foreign barrier lists. In 1985 he had been a sponsor of the original import surcharge bill and had declined to sponsor the Republican-led bipartisan trade bill. But he had studiously avoided any involvement with the Gephardt provision since and in 1986 had been among the block of ten Finance members seeking to use the disapproval vote on fast-track authority as leverage over administration trade policy. Observers speculated that he would likely take a moderate approach to trade as committee chair, and, in view of his longstanding interest in the topic, probably raise most trade activities to the full committee level.

Unlike his Ways and Means counterpart, Bentsen had the option of beginning from scratch to formulate a trade bill. He immediately tasked his Chief Counsel for International Trade, Jeff Lang, with gathering Finance Committee and member trade staff to develop a bill that could become law. Most of the staffers attending the sessions that began in December 1986 had been involved in writing the multiprovision bipartisan bill introduced in 1985 and were inclined to use it as their point of departure. All agreed it would be preferable to act on the bill knowing which House provisions they would face in conference, but knew the timing of the markup was up to the chairman. With regard to issues of interest to the administration, Bentsen had already decided to include presidential negotiating authority without waiting for the administration to ask for it. More important, however, was his decision to go with a bipartisan bill and his willingness to accommodate certain Republican trade objectives to achieve one.

The staff met frequently during the days that followed and thrashed out the issues of most interest to their senators. Among these were presidential authority to implement trade agreements and the limitations that might be placed on its use, issues of mandatory initiation and retaliation in Section 301 cases involving barriers to U.S. exports, and whether or not to require industries seeking import relief under Section 201 to also commit to adjustment-related activities. Consensus emerged over the need to include a revitalized TAA program, time limits for action in national security import cases, Bentsen's proposal to strengthen the role of the interagency Trade Policy Committee, and improved protection for intellectual property rights. There was less agreement on whether to include telecommunications trade legislation (because it was sectoral) or anything to do with trade reorganization. And most wanted to avoid the numerous amendments to the AD/CVD laws being circulated around the Hill by several interest groups, both because of their complexity ("this stuff fries the Senators' brains . . .") and because of the controversy surrounding them. Senator John Heinz's longtime trade staffer, Bill Reinsch, disagreed and warned that his Senator fully intended to offer such provisions for inclusion in the final product.

Shortly after the 100th Congress convened in January 1987, the Finance Committee began a series of hearings on "Mastering the World Economy."[2] It consisted of seven sessions of invited witnesses, beginning with former trade representative Robert Strauss on the topic of "building consensus relationships between Congress and the Executive Branch on trade policy." Other witnesses in the series included several prominent corporate executives, most of whom also chaired major business organizations; presidents of the AFL-CIO, the UAW, and the United Steelworkers; and several economists on the role of developing countries and third world debt.[3] Secretary of Treasury Baker and USTR Yeutter were the sole witnesses appearing on February 19, the final day of the series.

Any Finance Committee hearing on trade that included Bob Strauss

---

[2] The title for the hearings was drawn from Albert Bressand, "Mastering the 'World-economy,'" *Foreign Affairs* 64, no. 4 (Spring 1986): 745.

[3] The corporate witnesses (and groups they represented) included John Young of Hewlett-Packard (President's Commission on Industrial Competitiveness), Edmund T. Pratt, Jr. of Pfizer (ECAT), James D. Robinson III of American Express (Business Roundtable), Mark Shepard, Jr. of Texas Instruments, Colby H. Chandler of Eastman Kodak, Robert W. Galvin of Motorola, and William Lilley (American Business Conference). The union presidents included Lane Kirkland (AFL-CIO), Owen Bieber (UAW), and Lynn R. Williams (Steelworkers). The remaining expert witnesses were Alan Greenspan of Townsend-Greenspan & Co., Robert D. Hormats of Goldman, Sachs & Co., and Rudiger Dornbush of the Massachusetts Institute of Technology.

was guaranteed to be a success. Considered by both Democrats and Republicans to have been the most effective trade representative to have served in the post, the members regarded Strauss' tenure during the Tokyo Round MTN to have set the standard for committee-executive relations. Exchanges with him at this hearing helped to crystalize member thinking on several key issues: In response to questions raised by Senators Bentsen and Chafee on the relative importance of fast track implementing authority, Strauss gave it a "10" on a scale of 1 to 10. "There is no question in my mind that it must be passed if you hope to have a successful negotiation," he said.[4] When Bentsen suggested that Congress should not be expected to "surrender our constitutional rights by providing the administration with fast track" in the absence of a definitive (and congressionally approved) statement of administration policy and intentions, Strauss agreed, but he went on to note that without fast-track authority, trading partners would simply not take the negotiations seriously. Describing the perspective of a European or Japanese negotiator, he illustrated:

> They are going to amend this thing to death when it gets back. It is going to sit awhile, and nothing will happen. And why should I put this on the table and then have it bit on here, and nibbled on there, and torn apart here, and then you come back and insist that I do this, that and the other. I want to know when we shake hands and walk out of this room, that is what your Congress is going to vote up or down on or I won't go. And the truth of the matter is, people will go 25, 30 percent further if they know you are not going to be coming back and nibbling again and re-trading a traded deal. It is the same old story. If you think it is a final trade, you will give the last dollar. If you think it is going to come back, you will hold back.[5]

The signal to the members was pretty clear. If the administration wanted a negotiation, it needed fast-track authority; if the Congress wanted a trade law, it would have to provide it. Bottom line: without fast track, it probably was not worth writing a bill.

On whether to require the administration to retaliate against foreign trade practices under Section 301, an exchange between Senator Packwood and Strauss elicited the turn of phrase that ultimately was to govern committee thinking on a range of issues involving presidential discretion:

[4] Robert S. Strauss, Senate, "Mastering the World Economy: Hearings," January 13, 1987, 53.
[5] Ibid, 53–54.

Senator Packwood: . . . Do you think we should require mandatory retaliation?

Mr. Strauss: Well, I am a little hesitant to require mandatory retaliation, Senator Packwood. I think 301 could have been used more effectively than it has been. . . . On the other hand, I hate to make it mandatory. I think somewhere in between. . . . A lot of it depends upon the attitude of the man who sits in the White House. . . . I guess "more mandatory" is a bum choice of words—

Senator Packwood: But not compulsory.

Mr. Strauss: But not totally inaccurate. Let me say that.[6]

From that point on, "mandatory but not compulsory" was adopted by members and staff alike to describe the concept, all the staff had to do was figure out how to write it in statute! What they came up with was "mandatory but waivable."

During the weeks that followed, various Finance members and staff would meet informally to discuss the outlines of the Senate bill. Substance and strategy, however, were now largely dictated by the decision to go with a bipartisan bill and by the need to reach the floor with language that could withstand the multitude of amendments likely to be offered to it. Bentsen and his colleagues had decided they wanted a law.

s. 490 INTRODUCED

Several days before the bill's introduction, the chairman circulated a memo to members of the committee, inviting their cosponsorship of a "tough but fair" trade bill and noting that Senator Danforth had agreed to be principal coauthor. Bentsen had already decided to exclude product- or country-specific measures to reduce potential administration and press accusations of protectionism and to reduce the chances of protectionist riders being added on the floor. Like Rostenkowski, Bentsen had to anticipate textile quota language and a Gephardt-type amendment being offered once the bill reached the full Senate. Unlike in the House, Bentsen would not have a Rules Committee and the prospect of a rule to preclude them.

The Omnibus Trade Act of 1987 was introduced in the Senate on February 5 with fifty-seven original cosponsors; twenty-five of them

[6] Ibid., 44–45.

Republicans. Seventeen of the twenty members on the Finance Committee signed on to the measure. Bentsen and Danforth headed the list,
followed immediately by the majority and Republican leaders, Byrd and
Dole. This meant there was strong support for trade legislation, that
this bill would be the Senate trade vehicle, and that for now at least, it
was moving forward in a bipartisan manner. It did not mean the bill
was a consensus document, as more than one sponsor made clear in
remarks accompanying the bill's introduction.

S. 490, slightly over 200 printed pages in length, was introduced in
much the same manner as S. 1860 some eighteen months earlier, both
as a single omnibus measure (referred to Finance) and separately by
title, dividing lead sponsorship between Democrats and Republicans.
Of the separate measures, seven were referred to Finance; one to the
Committee on Agriculture, Nutrition, and Forestry; and one to the
Committee on Governmental Affairs.[7]

As introduced, the first title of the Senate bill contained presidential
authority to negotiate trade agreements, with access to the fast-track
implementing process in two five-year increments. It contained no tariff
proclamation authority, requiring both tariff and nontariff measure
agreements to be enacted through the fast track. In addition, it made
access to the fast-track process contingent on prior congressional approval of a presidential statement of trade policy.

The next title, labeled "Enhancing Competitiveness," addressed the
Section 201 escape clause and Trade Adjustment Assistance. In Section
201 it proposed to differentiate between petitions likely to result in
enhanced competitiveness and those "facilitating the orderly transfer of
resources to alternative uses," a euphemism for "going out of business."
In cases involving a meaningful adjustment plan and a unanimous ITC
vote in favor of relief, the president would essentially be required to
grant such relief. In other cases, the president would have more relief
options than ever from which to choose, but less ability to deny relief
entirely in any case where the ITC had recommended it. The TAA
portion of the bill linked receipt of benefits to retraining and established
a mandatory import fee to fund it.

The third title of the Senate bill concentrated primarily on foreign

---

[7] Unlike the House, where the parliamentarian regularly refers bills jointly to a number
of committees, Senate bills tend to be referred solely to the predominant committee of
jurisdiction. Referrals beyond that are worked out between committee chairmen under
UC agreements, often limiting the time the second committee has to act on the bill.
Should the lead committee refuse to acknowledge another's claim, it risks the other
committee placing a "hold" on the bill, preventing it from being taken up on the floor
by unanimous consent.

practices affecting U.S. exports. It also contained the handful of AD/CVD law changes in the bill. Each of the several provisions addressing the export side of the equation were characterized by their action-forcing nature, and their mandates for setting priorities and achieving tangible results. The provision entitled "Negotiations in Response to Adversarial Trade"[8] was considered either the Senate's alternative to Gephardt or a temporary placeholder—depending on one's expectations for subsequent markup and floor action. It amended the 1984 law's annual National Trade Estimates (NTE) report enumerating foreign barriers with instructions that the president negotiate the elimination of barriers with countries found to be "maintaining a consistent pattern of barriers and market distorting practices," adding, "as in the case of Japan." It then required the president to report on action taken in response to the barriers or on "evidence that the level of United States exports . . . [was now] commensurate with the level . . . reasonably expected to result from the elimination of [such practices]." The provision did not contain sanctions or enforcement language.

The other key components of this title involved amendments to Section 301, including mandatory self-initiation of investigations of practices considered both "significant" and in contravention of U.S. rights under international agreements. This requirement was juxtaposed against other changes mandating retaliation in many such cases. In instances where the foreign practice was found to be "unjustifiable" or to violate a trade agreement, retaliation could only be avoided if the GATT failed to agree that a violation had occurred or if there was an industry-approved settlement offsetting or eliminating the practice. In cases not involving agreement violations, the president could also terminate the investigation, providing he certified to Congress that a satisfactory resolution was not possible and that retaliation would harm the national economic interest.

Remaining titles of the bill addressed intellectual property rights protection and access to foreign technologies, import relief in national security-related cases, executive branch formulation of trade policy, and export promotion of agricultural commodities.

Time had been set aside on the Senate floor for introductory statements by sponsors of the new trade measure. Bentsen opened by stressing the bipartisan nature of the bill and the three-year process by which

---

[8] "Adversarial" was a term taken from an Op-Ed entitled "Japan and Adversarial Trade" by Peter F. Drucker, published in *The Wall Street Journal* on April 1, 1986. At the time, the provision's authors did not know that the word "adversarial" could be translated into Japanese as "enemy" and would, in itself, cause a great deal of consternation.

it had evolved. He suggested it could well be the last such trade bill of the century and noted that world trade needed to grow to enable Americans to "earn their way out of debt." He cited the importance of U.S. leadership in the world trading system, including the use of access to the U.S. market as leverage. His final point, which he called "a practical point of politics," dealt with executive-legislative relations:

> Our President cannot be an effective negotiator without the support of Congress, and Congress cannot support loss of American leadership or the prospect of no growth as the future of this country.
> These will be difficult policies to frame. Since Congress cannot negotiate with foreign governments, we need and we seek the administration's advice and counsel in these matters. . . .
> . . . The bill is tough on foreign market distortions that limit the growth of trade, and it frankly limits the President's discretion to do nothing about trade problems. But it also greatly enhances the President's power to improve the situation, and it gives him the mandate he and the next President will need to make trade talks work.[9]

Senator Danforth, in his opening remarks, suggested that while the sponsors represented diverse constituencies, " . . . we share a common trade philosophy—namely, that a global trading system that is fair and open can only be achieved through a more effective and aggressive American trade policy." He stressed the bill's generic approach, contrasting it with product-specific quota legislation favoring a selected few at the expense of the rest, and the emphasis it placed on restoring the credibility of U.S. trade laws and agreements. "If a referee blows his whistle and never walks off the yardage," said Danforth about Section 301, "pretty soon the game is going to deteriorate—and that is what is happening in trade." On the escape clause he opined, "If industries damaged by imports are told that Section 201 of the Trade Act is not available as a means of gaining temporary GATT-consistent relief from imports, then we cannot be surprised when Congress reacts to rampant protectionism by enacting quota bills for any industry with enough political clout to muster the votes." He concluded by drawing the following link between politics and policy:

> The protectionist demagoguery, free trade dogmatism, and partisan bickering that increasingly dominate our debates over international trade offer no solutions. . . .The polarized nature of the current debate over imports offers us a choice between economic Darwinism at one extreme and the

---

[9] Congress, Senate, *Congressional Record* (February 5, 1987), vol. 133, no. 18, S1852.

proliferation of special interest quota protection at the other. When it comes to fighting foreign barriers . . . we are told the choice is between risking a trade war through massive retaliation and playing the world's sucker.

These are not acceptable alternatives. They are not and cannot be the only available alternatives. The Omnibus Trade Act revitalizes and expands the middle ground. Congress need not use the legislative sledgehammer provided by the Constitution if the President consistently and effectively wields the precision trade tools delegated to him.[10]

Other senators, including the leadership, also weighed in. Senator Dole characterized his sponsorship as support for enactment of a trade bill within the year, but made it clear he had some real reservations about the bill's contents. He also expressed his expectation that the administration would soon come forward with its own competitiveness package. Senator Byrd was far less forthcoming about the role he expected the administration to play in the process, commenting that "the President may veto the legislation, but it will be put there on his desk."[11] And he went on to call for other committees to produce legislation to go into an omnibus bill for which the trade provisions would form the centerpiece.

In the weeks that followed, Finance members and staff tested the reaction to the bill and prepared for hearings and markup on their part. Meetings were held with representatives of the administration, interested private sector groups and their lobbyists; questions were fielded, clarifications sought, and modifications prepared. Introduction of the administration's bill took place the third week in February, but was largely ignored.

Several hearings were held between February and early April on the operation of various trade laws and on comparison between H.R. 3 and S. 490. For the administration, these hearings provided the first and nearly the last opportunity for concentrated input into the Senate's deliberative process. At a hearing on February 19, for example, Secretary Baker and Ambassador Yeutter devoted the bulk of their time to causes of the U.S. trade deficit, the administration's record, and the president's trade bill. They also made a point of stressing the parameters the administration expected to employ in determining its opposition to or support for congressional trade initiatives. In this regard, Baker laid out five key "considerations" that would be applied by the administration to assess pending trade proposals. These included impact on U.S. competitiveness, conformity to international obligations, enhancement of leverage

[10] Ibid., S1879–90.
[11] Ibid., S1898.

in the Uruguay Round and other trade negotiations, avoidance of retaliation against U.S. exports, and avoidance of trading partner mirror legislation that could harm U.S. exports. Therefore, noted Baker:

> Some of the proposals that we have seen run counter to these principles; and, without suggesting an all-inclusive list, I can note that the Administration will resist the following:
> First, that we would impose a general import surcharge. . . .
> Second, we oppose sector-specific protection, such as establishing import quotas for individual products. . . .
> Third, we oppose mandatory retaliation.
> And finally, Mr. Chairman, it comes as no surprise, I know, that we oppose limits on Presidential discretion.[12]

By the time of his appearance on April 2, Yeutter was in a position to get far more specific about the Senate bill, and his assessment—in the form of a detailed thirty-eight-page, section-by-section analysis of S. 490—was almost uniformly negative. He expressed the administration's concern about the bill's negotiating authority, including its pre-clearance requirements and the absence of tariff proclamation language; Section 301 self-initiation and mandatory retaliation provisions; and limits on presidential discretion to deny import relief in Section 201 cases involving industry adjustment plans. The senators in attendance appeared neither surprised nor particularly concerned about the administration's objections. The tone, set by Bentsen, was cordial but made it clear he was intent on writing this law as much for the next president as for the incumbent. On the issue of presidential discretion, for example, Bentsen put it this way:

> I see a dramatic change in the policy of this Administration, much more aggressive trade policy and tougher trade policy; but how do we know that the next Administration won't duplicate what this Administration did in its first four years? . . .
> . . . Ambassador Yeutter, speaking for the Administration argues that trade policy decisions require consideration of foreign relations, national security, foreign economic considerations and, domestic economic, and domestic political considerations. And therefore, the President's discretion must not be limited.
> I argue that historically, and not with this Administration alone, all these other considerations have crowded trade off the agenda. . . .
> The fact is that trade is the handmaiden of all other policy considerations

[12] Congress, Senate, Committee on Finance, *Mastering the World Economy: Hearings before the Committee on Finance*, 100th Cong., 1st sess., February 19, 1987, Senate Hearing 100–6.

of the U.S. Government, and I am convinced it will continue to be so unless we have some limits on the President's discretion.[13]

Yet, for all of the suggestions being put forth by the administration or by interested parties from the private sector, the Senate bill was, and remained, a largely self-generated document. Exceptions to this included miscellaneous tariff bills, many of the proposed changes to the AD/CVD statutes, and intellectual property rights provisions; but for the most part, provisions at the core of the trade policy debate continued to be developed largely within the confines of member and staff groups. Drafts might periodically be discussed with industry or labor representatives, outside trade experts, and administration staff, but as often as not the input sought was largely technical in nature. The senators had fairly well established opinions about what was needed and were comfortable relying on their own counsel and that of staff when it came to basic concepts in the bill. Moreover, as had been the case in Ways and Means deliberations, few thought the bill was being written to solve the trade problems of any specific industry or group. Rather, they perceived their role as reformulating—or at least influencing—the overall direction of U.S. trade policy. This turned the hearing process into more of a public brainstorming session and discussion of policy issues than for specific outside contributions to the content of the bill.

These characteristics of the bill's evolution were particularly evident when it came to the subject of enforcing U.S. rights under trade agreements. Throughout the hearings, foreign barriers to U.S. exports, and the perceived need for aggressive use of Section 301 to combat them, were dominant topics. At the hearing on February 19, for example, Danforth illustrated the perceptions and frustrations shared by most on the committee:

> . . . Nothing really works. Take Japan, as obviously everybody's leading example of the trade problem. . . .
> We negotiate, we harangue, we cry, we sob, we plead, and nothing happens. . . .
> . . . where there is a general principle of mercantilism that pervades the country, . . . you negotiate down one barrier and, as soon as you have gotten that out of the way, you find five more have cropped up to take its place. . . . unless there is a will in the other country to do business fairly, and to give a fair opportunity to other countries to export into their markets . . .
> Now, how is that will created? How is a will created in, say Japan? . . .

[13] Congress, Senate, Committee on Finance, *Comparing Major Trade Bills: Hearings before the Committee on Finance*, 100th Cong., 1st sess., April 2, 1987, Senate Hearing 100–419.

Do they do it because they have had a change of heart? Do they do it because they have had some sort of religious experience? . . .

I think that the reason they would do it is because they believe that there is a down side in not doing it. If they were to believe that somehow it would not be in their self-interest to be protectionist themselves, if they believed that there was a down side in mercantilism, then maybe they would be more reasonable and open up their markets.

Now why do I believe in retaliation, mandatory retaliation, almost automatic retaliation? Why? Because I think that a Japan has to feel that it is their choice. . . . Let them decide. . . . But that decision has to carry with it a down side; that decision has to trigger, automatically, something bad that happens to them. . . .

Now, the reason I think we should rewrite the trade laws is not out of joy of retaliation. . . . But what I do believe is that there must be penalties which are surely imposed on those who don't want to do business with the United States. And if we don't have such penalties, then I fear that nothing happens.[14]

When the same topic was the focus of the committee's hearing on March 17, USTR General Counsel Alan Holmer was there to respond. It was a topic on which there was a general consensus—among members considered "free traders" and "protectionists" alike—that the administration was lacking in its enforcement of the law. Holmer, in addition to defending the administration's record on Section 301, endeavored to make a broader strategic point about the statute:

In considering any amendment to Section 301, I hope that you will ask one key question: Will this amendment help or hurt the ability of U.S. negotiators to pry open a foreign market to U.S. exports? It really comes down to this issue: Is Section 301 an import-relief law, or is it a negotiating tool? . . .

Retaliation really means failure. It may make us feel better temporarily. It may provide import relief for another U.S. industry. But the guy that brought the case, the U.S. industry that brought the case, is generally not going to sell a nickel's more goods in that foreign market simply because we have retaliated. . . .

What you have to have is a credible threat of retaliation. . . .[15]

Ultimately, the debate over executive branch flexibility in the trade bill, particularly with respect to Section 301, came down to the issue of credibility. Few of the statutory changes contemplated by the senators

---

[14] Senate, "Mastering the World Economy: Hearing," February 19, 1987, 114–5.

[15] Congress, Senate, Committee on Finance, *Improving Enforcement of Trade Agreements: Hearing before the Committee on Finance*, 100th Cong., 1st sess, March 17, 1987, Senate Hearing 100–474, 12.

involved activities that could not already be undertaken under existing law. But a lack of trust was evident—even in the most honest and collegial of exchanges:

> Senator Daschle: . . . If we don't have some assurance that someone with your ability and determination is going to use that tool, don't you understand then a little bit better why we are interested in somehow finding a measure by which we can ensure that tool will be used?

> Mr. Holmer: . . . The concern I have is, if you put the 301 program on automatic pilot, . . . the end result is likely to be less success on the part of your negotiator in opening up foreign markets.

> Senator Daschle: But you are telling us you don't want that involvement. You are saying that the kind of influence we are exerting right now may be counterproductive.

> Mr. Holmer: No, this is very productive. The letters that we get from the members here, and the legislative proposals—as long as they don't get enacted. . . .

In the end, the senators approached the issue as one of trade policy; the administration, as a matter of presidential discretion. "Mandatory but not compulsory" had come down to a basic tenant best expressed, perhaps, by Senator Bentsen:

> Predictability is the key word here. We need a trade policy that our trading partners can predict, and I maintain that requires limits on the President's discretion not to act. He needs plenty of discretion on what action to take, but limits have to be placed on his discretion to take no action.[16]

FINANCE COMMITTEE ACTION

The Senate Finance Committee's deliberations on S. 490 began on April 22, with several days of the committee staff walking the members through the contents of the Senate bill and its principal differences with the one pending in the House.[17] The object was to air the various trade policy issues in the bill prior to the more formal amendment process

---

[16] Senate, Committee on Finance, *Comparing Major Trade Bills: Hearings*, April 2, 1987, 11.

[17] Unlike its House counterpart, the Senate Finance Committee traditionally holds all markups at full committee level. In this case, virtually all members of the committee (eighteen of twenty), including its chairman and ranking member, also served on the International Trade Subcommittee.

scheduled for the following week. Deputy USTR Alan Woods represented the administration at the markup, but with the exception of these sessions where he could offer specific criticisms of the bill, executive branch participants were not generally involved in the proceedings. They were available to answer questions at markup or to provide technical drafting advice, but only during sessions on the antidumping and countervailing duty laws were they asked to play any but a perfunctory role. Unlike the Ways and Means Committee proceedings, where the Democratic leadership sought USTR and Commerce Department opinions on a fairly regular basis, to the extent S. 490 was moved in the direction of the administration, as often as not it reflected member policy concerns, rather than change at the behest of the executive.

Thought had been given to delaying the Finance markup until after passage of the House bill. This would have enabled the members to act knowing precisely what they would be facing in conference. But it was already late April and the press of other business meant they had only a short window during which to act. This put the chairman at something of a disadvantage in conducting his markup and had a distinct impact on his approach. Bentsen needed his members to reach consensus as quickly as possible on each issue. Therefore, on such complex provisions as AD/CVD changes, the absence of overwhelming member backing meant the fastest treatment was virtually no treatment at all. And on the core issues, time was better spent working out compromise language to hold the support of his original bipartisan group of backers, than on working with the administration to capture the votes of the three lone Republicans not on the bill. The result was a lot of late night staff work and a relatively smooth markup with frequent bipartisan consensus on amendments.

In fact, H.R. 3 still had a significant influence over the Finance bill. Because the product reported by Ways and Means was perceived and had been characterized in the press as moderate (prior to the adoption of the Gephardt language), the House bill essentially became the floor for protection in the Senate. This was particularly true with respect to House AD/CVD law changes and such issues as worker rights under Section 301. Without an effective "free trade" counterweight in the form of administration-endorsed alternatives, there was a distinct risk that mirror language would be adopted in the Senate, thereby limiting flexibility in conference. It was a situation that Bentsen and his allies were determined to avoid.

For purposes of the Finance markup, the committee staff had prepared a detailed spreadsheet comparing S. 490, H.R. 3 (as reported by Ways and Means), and current law. The document, on 17-by-11 inch paper, numbered 126 pages and described each provision using the minimum necessary legalese. The formal markup began on April 28, and required seven working days until its completion on May 7. During that time, a pattern developed whereby the senators would debate amendments to various sections of the bill each morning; and staff would meet each afternoon and into the night to prepare provisions and issues to be addressed by senators the next day. The staff was expected to reach consensus and resolve all but the most contentious amendments, meeting in smaller groups as necessary to develop compromise language for presentation to the whole.

Because all but the most controversial issues were tentatively worked out in advance through these consensus-building sessions, and because the remaining amendments in dispute were well defined in advance, the markup held few surprises. As each amendment arose, it was described by committee staff; noncontroversial amendments were adopted, controversial ones were debated and voted on in turn. For the most part, the votes were held on the basis of trade policy concepts or the occasional turn of phrase used to describe them. Once adopted, the amendments would be reformulated by staff and the Office of the Legislative Counsel into formal legal text.

In contrast to Rostenkowski who began his markup by presenting the administration and the press with trade agreement authority, Bentsen's agenda was based on the degree of consensus about a given topic. Therefore, the first day of markup was devoted to intellectual property rights and TAA. Amendments to Section 301 consumed the second, third, and part of the fourth days of the markup, after which the committee turned to Section 201. This section of the bill, along with negotiating authority and antidumping/countervailing duty law provisions were completed on the fifth and sixth days, respectively, with most of the AD/CVD decisions adopted in closed session. The last day was devoted to miscellaneous tariff measures and to finalizing action on a handful of touchier issues. Principal provisions in the committee bill and their disposition in markup follow.[18]

Negotiating Authority

The Finance bill provided for both tariff and nontariff measure agreements to have access to the fast-track approval process for a six-year

---

[18] Sources of information on the Finance markup include: Congress, Senate, Committee on Finance, *Omnibus Trade Act of 1987: Report of the Committee on Finance on S. 490*, 100th Cong., 1st sess., 1987, Report 100–71; Congress, Senate, Committee on Finance, Committee Press Releases M-3 through M-9; April 28, 29, 30 and May 1, 5, 6, 7, 1987; and observations by author, March–April 1987.

period. No proclamation authority was provided for tariff cuts, which were to be limited to 50 percent. The committee also layered onto the fast-track process a new series of checks and balances. These included a pre-clearance requirement that the president submit a statement of U.S. trade policy, but omitted an earlier proviso that Congress then approve it. The bill also established several preconditions for entry into trade agreements involving countries with "state trading enterprises,"[19] and the achievement of enforceable agreements that met congressional negotiating objectives. With respect to an otherwise automatic extension of fast-track authority from four to six years, the bill established a "resolution of disapproval" process that could be triggered by one house of Congress concluding that trade negotiations were failing to make sufficient progress.[20] Finally, the committee added a "reverse" fast-track provision providing that at any time the administration failed to consult on U.S. trade policy, Ways and Means and Finance could initiate withdrawal of fast track by resolution of disapproval of both houses.[21]

In addition to specifying various negotiating objectives, mainly related to trade liberalization and the strengthening of GATT rules, the committee mandated negotiations with countries manipulating their currencies or using other measures to prevent adjustments in balance of payments. It also instructed the president to withhold U.S. approval for GATT accession by any country with major state trading enterprises, unless either that country agreed its enterprises would operate based on commercial considerations or the Congress approved (under fast track) a presidential request for that country's accession. Although the markup coincided with China's contemplation of negotiations to rejoin the GATT, the provision was in fact prompted by committee concerns about the future prospect of Soviet accession.

Escape Clause/Trade Adjustment Assistance

Section 201. The escape clause provision in the Senate bill was a substitute for Sections 201–203 of existing law and was designed to

---

[19] This precondition precluded entry into a trade agreement with a country maintaining state trading enterprises unless that country agreed the enterprises would trade in accordance with commercial considerations.

[20] For this purpose, the Ways and Means and Finance Committees were given a six-month window in early 1991 in which to act. The one-house resolution of disapproval would not have been contrary to the Supreme Court's *I.N.S.* v. *Chadha* decision on one-house vetoes since the president would still technically be able to submit trade agreements for congressional approval under regular procedures.

[21] In addition to the "reverse" fast track assurances of improved executive branch consultations, the committee amended Section 135 of the 1974 Trade Act to require that the Advisory Committee on Trade Negotiations also be consulted on trade policy matters.

revitalize the import relief statute by turning it into a tool to facilitate adjustment by U.S. industries unable to meet foreign competition at home. The provision, championed by Heinz and Bentsen, generated the most vehement trade policy debate of the entire markup. It was based on concepts that Heinz and Bill Reinsch had worked on for years in an effort to move the statute beyond its reputation as merely "burial insurance." Like several of the other internally generated provisions of the bill, it had never enjoyed particular industry or labor support.

The bill entailed a major transformation of the statute, shifting the focus from import relief "necessary to prevent or remedy serious injury" to remedies likely to assist the domestic industry in making a positive adjustment to import competition. For this purpose, the bill defined "positive adjustment" to include not only the ability to compete successfully with imports, but also an industry's "orderly transfer of resources to other productive pursuits." To accomplish this objective, the petitioning industry was required to submit a viable adjustment plan to which the ITC was to obtain commitments from relevant segments of the industry, including its workers. The USTR and other executive branch agencies were also encouraged to get involved working with industry and labor on the plan, leading critics to label the entire measure an experiment in "industrial policy."

The committee increased the scope of relief options available to the president beyond import restrictions and TAA to include potential antitrust and regulatory exemptions, but then required he take actions "substantially equivalent" to those recommended by the ITC. And to reduce the chances of the ITC or the president opting for only nonimport remedies, the committee report made it clear that in most cases some form of import relief was expected as part of the package. The provision also limited the ITC commissioners allowed to vote on the form of relief to those who had found injury—a swipe at several Reagan appointees who had chosen to ignore this traditional practice. Waivers available to the president to avoid granting the ITC-recommended remedy included a determination that it would endanger U.S. national security or would be "a substantial cause of serious injury" to a domestic industry consuming the product.[22] Dropped was a provision in existing law that other consumer interests also be considered.

The committee saw the trade-off as a reduction in presidential discretion in exchange for expanded relief options and a higher standard

---

[22] The reference to consuming industries was attributable to the Section 201 case on copper in 1985, where workers for industrial copper users were found to far outnumber copper miners. It was included both for policy reasons and to avoid the Senate bill being labeled a "Trojan Horse" for overturning previously failed cases.

for industry to meet in the first place. "What we have done with our legislation," Bentsen commented at one point, "is to make it a lot tougher to qualify for relief. But we have said, then, if you can prove that you will be world competitive, then we give you more assurance that you are going to be granted some relief—not total, but more assurance."[23] In the same vein, the bill increased the number of years relief could be made available, but then added a monitoring provision that would enable the president to modify or terminate relief if the industry was found not living up to its commitments.

Trade adjustment assistance. In addition to making certification of workers automatic in affirmative 201 cases, the Senate, like the House, established a new "Trade Competitiveness Assistance" program where workers would only be eligible for TAA if they entered training programs to learn new skills. Finance expanded access to the program from workers in industries affected directly by imports to industries supplying essential goods and services to such industries. Oil state Senator David L. Boren (D-Okla.) and Bentsen then further expanded it to cover oil and gas sector workers—previously denied TAA—as well.

Finally, the committee adopted a controversial amendment requiring the program to be funded by a small import fee (of no greater than 1 percent), and made the program an entitlement. Acknowledging that the fee was likely to violate U.S. GATT obligations, the bill called on the president to seek GATT approval and set the fee to go into effect with conclusion of such an agreement or three years from enactment of the new law—whichever came first.

Unfair Trade Practices

Section 301. This provision represented the centerpiece of the Finance Committee's legislative initiative and epitomized the effort to define "mandatory but not compulsory." It was based on Danforth-Moynihan language from S. 1860, modified primarily by a Packwood compromise developed during pre-markup staff sessions.[24] It was a provision that enjoyed the support of members representing the gamut of trade philosophies on the committee.

---

[23] Senate, *Comparing Major Trade Bills: Hearings*, April 2, 1987, 39.

[24] Danforth and Bentsen decided to support the compromise during a private strategy session the afternoon of April 28. They felt the compromise was sufficiently strong and were willing to risk angering a few hard-liners to have Packwood on board. At the same meeting, the two senators also agreed on the need to ease somewhat their fast-track preclearance process, and to ensure that the AD/CVD provisions of the Senate bill remained different from those of the House.

As noted earlier, Sections 301–307 of the Trade Act of 1974, as amended, set out procedures and authorities for the enforcement of U.S. rights under trade agreements and for responses to other foreign practices found to be "unjustifiable, unreasonable, or discriminatory and burdens or restricts U.S. commerce."[25] The Trade and Tariff Act of 1984 had added executive branch self-initiation provisions and had expanded causes of action to include services, intellectual property rights, and foreign direct investment. It had also created the annual National Trade Estimates survey of major foreign barriers to encourage self-initiation.

The markup rendered the Senate provision less stringent than that originally introduced in S. 490, but substantially more restrictive of executive branch activities than the one being contemplated by the House. It reduced severely the president's discretion not to act in Section 301 cases. It tightened deadlines for action, whether settlements or retaliation. And it further expanded the scope of practices that were to be actionable under the statute. Also added to the bill were several provisions establishing processes to ensure the systematic, targeted, and proactive use of the statute through mandatory executive branch initiation of cases.

The Senate provision began by amending the NTE to require assessments of the trade distorting impact of the foreign barriers identified. This was to assist in setting priorities for action, including a requirement that the USTR initiate 301 cases against those practices "the pursuit of which will result in the greatest expansion of U.S. exports, either directly or through the establishment of a precedent beneficial to U.S. exports in general."[26] With respect to the nature of action to be taken, the Senate bill mandated that the president take whatever actions were necessary to enforce all rights and to eliminate or offset any act, policy, or practice the statute defined—and the USTR determined—to be unfair. New deadlines were imposed, with the longest period from initiation to action being nineteen months in cases involving GATT violations taken to dispute settlement or six months after the GATT ruling, whichever was shorter.[27]

The mandatory retaliation provision in the Finance bill also contained a limited number of waivers, but these, too, were more narrowly drawn

---

[25] Section 301(a), *Trade Act of 1974*, as amended; 19 USC 2411.

[26] Senate, Finance, *Omnibus Trade Act: Report*, 78.

[27] The committee reaffirmed its support for GATT dispute resolution in its report, but noted the problem of protracted delays. As a case in point, the committee cited a provision requested by the administration to implement a settlement in the sixteen-year U.S. citrus dispute with the EC. Senate, Finance, *Omnibus Trade Act: Report*, 81.

than their counterparts in the House bill. To avoid retaliation, the president had to negotiate an agreement that fully offset or eliminated the burden or restriction of the damaging practice on U.S. commerce. Otherwise, in trade agreement violation or "unjustifiable"[28] cases, waiver options were limited to a GATT decision contrary to the USTR's finding of illegality, a settlement agreed to by the U.S. industry, or determinations either that action would cause serious harm to U.S. national security or that "enforcement of the rights or the elimination of the unfair practice by the foreign country is impossible and the foreign country has agreed to provide the United States with compensating trade benefits."[29] In the case of "unreasonable" or "discriminatory" practices—namely, those not necessarily involving the violation of an agreement—a slightly looser fifth waiver provision was added. In such cases action could also be avoided if elimination of the practice was "impossible" and the taking of action was determined to be contrary to the national economic interest.

When it came to defining the practices that would be actionable under the statute, Finance added several, including "mercantilist practices" by state trading enterprises, and mandatory technology licensing or other "unfair trade concession" requirements imposed in exchange for market access. Export targeting was included over the objections of one senator who suggested that it was hypocritical when many on the committee obviously wanted the U.S. to engage in the practice. Foreign government toleration of anticompetitive practices was also added, having won the strong endorsement of two senators arguably at opposite ends of the trade spectrum—Riegle because of auto parts and Malcolm Wallop (R-Wyo.) because of soda ash—both cases involving Japanese import restrictions. The committee also included language on worker rights with a slightly higher threshold than that in the House.

Finally, were the new Section 301 requirements to result in U.S. action at odds with its international legal obligations, the bill provided compensation authority. And to avoid having retaliation under 301 create its own constituency for protection, the president was authorized to modify or terminate retaliatory action that had previously been taken.

Adversarial trade. As a result of controversy generated by the "adversarial" title of the original S. 490 provision, this section was renamed "Countries Maintaining a Consistent Pattern of Trade Distortions."

---

[28] The "unjustifiable" criterion in the law had been defined to include violations or inconsistencies with the international legal rights of the United States, not necessarily those in formal trade agreements. Section 301(e), *Trade Act of 1974*; 19 USC 2411.

[29] Ibid., 82.

Otherwise, the language emerged from the markup unchanged from that introduced in February. It generated a lengthy, but inconclusive, discussion in committee where the only real consensus was on delaying action. Bentsen, Danforth, and the others were very concerned about adding anything that would be labeled the Senate's "Gephardt" amendment. Moreover, despite extensive staff-level meetings between Danforth and Riegle staffers, no agreement on an alternative formulation had been reached.

The committee failed to act in spite of a private letter to the chairman from Senator Byrd making it clear he wanted the issue resolved in committee and not left for the floor. The majority leader's concern was that a floor fight on the Gephardt amendment would split his party, make the bill appear partisan, and result in a "protectionist" label being pinned on all Democratic trade initiatives. In fact, in spite of heavy Chrysler and UAW lobbying for a strong provision, not even its proponents really wanted the Gephardt language offered on the Senate floor.[30]

Antidumping/Countervailing Duty Laws

The AD/CVD law issues were not addressed by the committee until after passage of the House bill, by which time Bentsen and Danforth knew they would face language in conference that was already anathema to the administration. At minimum, the Finance leadership wanted to keep the Senate provisions sufficiently different from those approved by Ways and Means to ensure flexibility in conference. In fact, most on the committee believed these laws had been operating fairly well since 1979. This section of the bill was the only major one about which written submissions had been requested in lieu of a formal hearing, and, as it turned out, was the only one addressed by the committee in a closed session.

The chairman knew that Heinz and a few others felt strongly about AD/CVD matters; that there was a small, but enthusiastic coalition of companies and attorneys supporting them; and that the provisions were too complex to risk a major floor fight over amendments professing to stop "unfair trade." So he called an executive session of the committee to gauge the greatest points of controversy and to consider options. In attendance were Commerce Secretary Malcolm Baldrige, Alan Woods

---

[30] Amendment supporters, including Riegle and the labor lobbyists, wanted to avoid a Senate vote on the Gephardt amendment. They were certain it would lose, enabling the Senate conferees to reject the House language in its entirety in conference. Any strong Senate language would keep both provisions alive for negotiation in conference. Without compromise language, Gephardt supporters feared that some senator would feel compelled to offer the amendment as a gesture.

and Alan Holmer from USTR, and ITC General Counsel Lyn Schlitt. Bentsen told them that he needed something to take to conference; he wanted to be responsive to his members, but also wanted language that was both GATT-compatible and different from anything in the Ways and Means bill. He then instructed the committee staff to work with the administration and member staff to formulate and broker a package of acceptable alternatives.

The result was a lengthy series of AD/CVD amendments that were adopted in markup the following morning. Some, such as ones involving Airbus Industrie subsidies, were not in the House bill; others resembling House language had generally been weakened or made entirely discretionary. Also included was Heinz's detailed rewrite of the law governing the treatment of dumping by nonmarket economies.

Other Trade Law Provisions

Telecommunications trade. The Telecommunications Trade Act, a bill originally introduced by Danforth in 1984 and by Danforth and Bentsen jointly in 1985, in many ways resembled a sectoral application of the committee's Section 301 self-initiation language. It was one of a handful of sectoral provisions the Senators decided to risk adding to their bill on the last day of the markup.

The provision provided for USTR identification of foreign practices that denied to U.S. telecommunications firms "competitive opportunities that are substantially equivalent to opportunities available to foreign telecommunications firms in the United States."[31] It then mandated retaliation against any such practices in violation of trade or trade-related agreements, and negotiations to achieve removal of the rest so as to achieve "Substantially Equivalent Competitive Opportunities" (SECO) for U.S. firms abroad.[32]

The provision was based on the premise that U.S. deregulation in the telecommunications sector, particularly the breakup of AT&T in the early 1980s, had inadvertently resulted in the unilateral opening of a new multibillion dollar market for foreign companies in the United States. Moreover, this had occurred in spite of the fact that most foreign PTTs remained government-owned and largely closed to competition from the outside.[33] The amendment's authors saw this as their last

---

[31] Senate, Finance, *Omnibus Trade Act: Report*, 222.

[32] Ibid., 221.

[33] With the exception of Sweden and, to a degree, Japan, the U.S. had failed to get foreign Post, Telephone, and Telegraph (PTT) entities placed under the 1979 GATT Government Procurement Code.

chance to harness the trade impact of deregulation as leverage for U.S. negotiators to gain access for U.S. producers abroad. The amendment was added to the Finance bill without objection.

Intellectual property rights/access to technology. Consistent with Ways and Means Committee action, the bill created a "special 301" track for pursuit of foreign violations of U.S. intellectual property rights and eliminated the injury test required under Section 337 of the Tariff Act of 1930. Other provisions involved monitoring of foreign restrictions on technology transfer and assistance for developing countries to establish intellectual property rights regimes.

National security import relief. Similar to the one in the House bill, this provision, originally proposed by Senator Byrd, sought to rectify problems in the administration of Section 232 of the Trade Expansion Act of 1962. It also provided authority for the president to enforce voluntary restraint arrangements on machine tool imports.

Energy security act. On the last day of markup it became clear why the chairman had refrained from acting earlier on the noncontroversial national security provisions of the bill. It was at this point Senator Bentsen offered a surprise amendment calling for a national energy policy to prevent U.S. dependence on oil imports from exceeding 50 percent of consumption. It required the president to submit annually to Congress estimates of U.S. oil production and consumption, along with a plan to keep imports from going beyond half the expected consumption. The plan would go into effect automatically if not disapproved by a joint resolution of Congress.

The amendment generated a fair amount of consternation in the committee. Members from oil-consuming states had concerns, as did those disinclined to engage in a full-blown debate on energy policy in the context of the trade bill. But it was, after all, the chairman's initiative; maybe it would pick up a few more votes for the bill on the Senate floor. . . . So the amendment was adopted by a vote of 12–8.

Auctioned quotas. Authority for the auctioning of import quota licenses had existed in law since 1979 but had never been used. The theory behind it was to have the U.S. Treasury, rather than foreign license holders, benefit from the monopoly rents created by the import quotas. Opponents, including the administration, asserted the program would provoke retaliation, reduce foreign willingness to accept negotiated restraints, and be a nightmare to administer. There was also concern about creating a constituency for protection based on its revenue-raising implications.

A hotly debated amendment by Senator Max Baucus (D-Mont.) to require such auctioning under a Section 201 pilot program was originally voted down by the committee in a tie vote. The issue was reopened on the last day of markup, and the amendment was adopted in the only party-line vote of Finance deliberations on the bill.

Lamb import quotas. This provision, the most blatantly import-restrictive in the Senate bill, imposed a new system of import quotas on lamb parallel to those applicable to beef under the Meat Import Act of 1979. The vote on the amendment was close, but still demonstrated the parochial appeal of sectoral trade issues. Even Senator Wallop, who had consistently criticized the bill as protectionist, voted with his ranch constituency for the measure.

Sugar duty drawback. In keeping with the committee's long history of supporting the U.S. sugar industry, Finance adopted a Moynihan provision identical to that in the House bill. As with the lamb quota language, the sugar amendment provided one of the few close votes of the markup.

Formulation of U.S. trade policy. The only transfer of presidential authority contained in the Senate bill involved some additional USTR responsibilities under Section 301. The bill did, however, contain a section related to the executive trade policy process. Relevant provisions included elimination of the interagency Trade Policy Committee (TPC) and its replacement with a National Trade Council (as the trade counterpart of the National Security Council), a requirement for trade impact statements by federal government agencies, and the establishment of a National Trade Data Bank (NTDB) of trade and export information for distribution to U.S. industry.

Miscellaneous Tariff and Customs Provisions

The Senate bill contained thirty-nine miscellaneous tariff measures already in H.R. 3 and seventy-two of its own. These included duty-free treatment for the personal effects of athletes in the Tenth Pan American Games and an extension of the tariff suspension on "mixtures of hot red peppers and salt," a Russell Long–era perennial applying to ingredients for Tabasco sauce. The committee also added small, but controversial amendments pertaining to the duty-free importation of ethyl alcohol mixtures from Caribbean Basin countries, and a tariff reclassification of color TV picture tubes designed to help what remained of the domestic television industry.

Finally, the committee narrowly adopted an amendment creating a new administrative procedure for handling noncontroversial tariff suspension bills. It provided for the ITC to receive petitions and to determine whether a proposed tariff suspension would negatively affect any domestic U.S. industry. The ITC would then make recommendations to the president who would be authorized to suspend any duties that would not have an adverse impact on a U.S. interest or generate a revenue loss of more than $100 million. Debate over the provision pitted those concerned about a major new delegation of tariff-cutting authority and loss of potential House revenue vehicles, against those tired of facing unhappy constituents watching their tariff-suspension bills get delayed in the convoluted legislative process.

On May 7, the Senate Committee on Finance approved S. 490, as amended, by a vote of 19–1. The bill emerged with reasonable reviews in the press, primarily because it lacked the Gephardt language and because most of the administration's objections were hard to explain in a fifteen-second "sound bite" or a few columns in a newspaper. Both the *New York Times* and *The Wall Street Journal* characterized it as less stringent than the House bill, with the *Journal* noting that it "generally emphasizes expanding exports and increasing U.S. companies' access to foreign markets, rather than protecting them from imports." The *Washington Post* suggested that while the Senate bill "differs in significant ways from the measure the House passed . . . it is considered equally tough on unfair trade practices by foreign countries."[34]

The members were extremely pleased with the outcome. Most were comfortable with the bill's trade policy themes and believed they had a document that could be defended on the Senate floor. And while no one expected floor action to be quick or easy, S. 490 in its current form would be a good match in conference for the bill that had emerged from the House.

Senator Bentsen, speaking before the National Press Club, described the bill and its future as follows:

> We reported out a tough but fair trade bill that has a ninety-five percent approval rating in the committee. I just wish our numbers were that high in the White House.
>
> . . . And I think we'll win. I think we'll win because the whole purpose of this exercise has been to produce the best possible trade bill *that can become law*, preferably with the President's blessing but—if necessary—over his veto.
>
> . . . The days of free hands and unlimited White House discretion on trade are over. . . . The [bill] . . . does not usurp presidential privilege or seize power that does not belong to us. [But] the Bentsen-Danforth bill . . . does

[34] Jonathan Fuerbringer, "Senate Trade Bill Gains; Not as Harsh as House's," *New York Times*, May 8, 1987; Moncia Langley, "Senate Panel Finishes Work," *The Wall Street Journal*, May 8, 1987; and Stuart Auerbach, "Senate Panel Approves Trade Bill," *Washington Post*, May 8, 1987.

recognize that Congress has a clear constitutional role in the formulation of trade policy.

. . . It takes courage to propose changes in trade policy. Because anyone who questions the current system is immediately branded as a protectionist and a linear descendant of the legislators who brought about Smoot-Hawley and The Great Depression.

. . . Bentsen-Danforth . . . sets out to solve the *problem* of trade by increasing the *volume* of trade.[35]

Senator Packwood put it somewhat differently, suggesting that "a very good" trade bill was "do-able" by combining "the best parts of the Senate bill and the best parts of the House bill."[36] Senator Danforth called the committee bill "strong, yet responsible," but predicted the legislation would be "a high-wire act right to the end."[37]

AN OMNIBUS BILL

By early June, the Democratic leadership had yet to decide on how to proceed with floor action on the bill. One option was to bring up S. 490 and have other committees add their bills as amendments; the other was to meld all the bills into one before going to the Senate floor. Bentsen's clear preference was not to let the other committees slow down the Finance bill. The shorter the elapsed time between markup and the floor, the fewer the "unfriendly" amendments likely to emerge and pick up support. Moreover, with respect to provisions from other committees that might jeopardize enactment of the trade bill, it would be easier to stop them on the floor than to strip them later from an omnibus bill.

Nine Senate committees were expected to contribute to the Senate initiative, and as the weeks progressed, the following trade and competitiveness measures began to emerge:

The Agriculture Committee reported various trade-related measures, including additional funding for the Export Enhancement Program (EEP) to respond to European Community agricultural export subsidies. The committee also adopted a measure to trigger export marketing loan programs for wheat, feedgrains, and soybeans in the absence of

---

[35] "Remarks by Senator Lloyd Bentsen," National Press Club, Washington D.C., May 19, 1987. Emphasis contained in text.

[36] Robert Packwood, as quoted in Stuart Auerbach, "Packwood Says Congress Can Pass 'Very Good' Compromise Trade Bill," *Washington Post*, May 6, 1987.

[37] John Danforth, as quoted in Auerbach, "Senate Panel Approves Trade Bill."

a satisfactory GATT agreement to discipline such export subsidies.[38] However, in an interesting "jurisdictional" message to his members at the opening of markup, committee Chairman Patrick Leahy (D-Vt.) admonished: "There are not now any protectionist import restrictions in this bill. Import restrictions are largely under the jurisdiction of the Finance Committee. . . . I urge my colleagues not to offer any amendments not within the jurisdiction of this Committee. Amendments restricting imports should be held for the floor."[39]

The Banking Committee approved a bill easing certain U.S. export controls and provisions of the Foreign Corrupt Practices Act. It also called for exchange rate negotiations and adopted a Riegle amendment, aimed at Japan, to prevent foreign firms from serving as "primary dealers" of U.S. government securities unless U.S. dealers received similar access abroad.

From the Judiciary Committee came measures to protect U.S. process patents and related property rights language.

After much debate and delay, the Governmental Affairs Committee approved a reorganization of the Department of Commerce and the Office of the USTR, renaming Commerce the "Department of Industry and Technology." It mandated the creation of several new commissions and offices, including a tripartite Council on Economic Competitiveness. And it approved an amendment blocking foreign purchases of U.S. banking and securities institutions in the absence of reciprocal access for U.S. firms.

The Small Business Committee agreed to provisions aimed at increasing exports by small businesses.

The Foreign Relation Committee authorized U.S. participation in the Multilateral Investment Guarantee Agency (MIGA), reported provisions involving multilateral development agencies, and called on the secretary of treasury to negotiate an international debt-management facility.

The Labor and Human Resources Committee agreed to various measures designed to assist workers facing permanent layoff, including the authorization of funding for dislocated workers and worker retraining. By far the most hotly contested of the committee provisions, however,

---

[38] The provision was based on a bill introduced by Senators Danforth, Bentsen, David Pryor (D-Ark.), and Thad Cochran (R-Miss.) that would have triggered the program in time for the 1990 marketing year. The committee added presidential waiver authority and a provision for congressional override by joint resolution. At the time, only cotton and rice had marketing loan programs, which allow farmers to maintain their income levels and still sell at low world market prices.

[39] "Statement of Senator Patrick Leahy, Markup of Agricultural Trade Legislation," press release, May 6, 1987.

was one requiring firms to give advance notice of plans for major layoffs or plant closure. A similar provision had been considered in the House, but because of its perceived controversy, had been left out of the House bill.

Finally, the Senate Commerce Committee, having seen its markup initially stall over the issue of foreign investment in the United States, managed to report out a multiprovision industrial competitiveness bill. On investment, the committee grappled with a provision offered by Senator James J. Exon (D-Neb.) that would have allowed the secretary of commerce to block foreign acquisitions, mergers, or joint ventures that could have a negative impact on U.S. national security or "essential commerce." Danforth, the committee's ranking Republican, worked with Sen. Exon and business community opponents of the provision to formulate compromise language limiting its scope to national security matters. Although still opposed by the administration for its potential "chilling effect" on investment, the compromise measure was adopted by a unanimous vote.

The Commerce bill also proposed to transform the National Bureau of Standards into a National Institute of Technology and to create an Advanced Technology Program to fund research and production modernization efforts. Finally, the committee's Merchant Marine Subcommittee decided to add its own trade provision, empowering the Federal Maritime Commission to conduct Section 301-type investigations and to retaliate against foreign carriers.

Over breakfast on the morning of June 11, Byrd talked strategy with his committee chairmen. He had pretty much decided to have the bills stitched into a single omnibus measure, with each title to be managed on the floor by the relevant chair and ranking member. He asked the chairmen to have staff work out any remaining jurisdictional problems, making use of what became known as the "InterCommittee." This informal group, placed under Bentsen's general control, met regularly at staff levels and evolved as the principal coordinating mechanism for Senate action during evolution of the omnibus bill. Although not tasked with resolving substantive disputes, the group's technical and jurisdictional mandates enabled it to help settle all but the most extreme differences. Operating consistent with the collegial approach required to accomplish almost anything in the Senate, the InterCommittee was later characterized by an amused House observer as "a process for herding cats."

Bentsen used the meeting to describe his committee's markup and to suggest that at least on S. 490, there was a real prospect of garnering a two-thirds vote on final passage. Byrd urged the chairmen "not to trim the sails" of their bills in the hopes of a presidential signature, but did suggest they try to avoid "red flags" that would guarantee a veto. In this regard, Senator Hollings reported that he and the textile industry coalition had decided not to offer their quota bill as an amendment. With respect to the plant closing provision, however, the chairman of the Labor Committee, Senator Edward M. Kennedy (D-Mass.), made clear it would remain in the bill, the concerns expressed by his colleagues notwithstanding.[40]

Battle lines were being drawn over the bill, and the administration knew it had a problem. At a meeting of the Economic Policy Council on May 7, for example, it was already obvious that provisions emerging from committees other than Finance were likely to cause even more difficulties than the trade provisions themselves. When the president met the following day with Packwood and members of the Senate Republican leadership, he reiterated his desire to sign a trade bill and had the White House issue the following warning:

> The bill reported yesterday by the Senate Finance Committee represents an improvement over the original Senate version, but very serious problems remain with several of its provisions.
>
> Other Senate Committees will be reporting their related bills in the days ahead. As the President has said, he would like to get trade legislation from Congress he can sign, but what we have seen to date is not at all encouraging.[41]

At another meeting on June 2, attended by Packwood and Bentsen, the president thanked Bentsen for his work and expressed the hope that they could work together to develop a signable bill. "If you can't work with Bentsen and Rostenkowski . . ." responded Bentsen.

Finally, on June 16, a week before the bill was to reach the floor, the president and his cabinet met with Dole and nine ranking Republicans at the White House. This was followed by an unusual visit to Capitol Hill to join the weekly Republican caucus over lunch. Both occasions were used to criticize the House bill and to rally Republicans for the floor.

---

[40] It is interesting to note that with the exception of the Steelworkers, all of the major unions were prepared to leave the provision out of the bill and to focus on their trade agenda. However, Kennedy and Senator Howard M. Metzenbaum (D-Ohio) informed the union leadership that if they wanted plant closing to move at all that year, it would have to be on this vehicle.

[41] "Statement by the Assistant to the President for Press Relations," Office of the Press Secretary, The White House, May 8, 1987.

The president noted the improvements in the Finance bill, but reiterated the need for help to change remaining problematic provisions. Treasury Secretary Baker, in addition to criticizing automaticity and limits on executive discretion in the trade title, also commented on the LDC debt facility, exchange rate negotiation requirements, and investment restrictions. Secretary Baldrige complimented the Senate on its AD/CVD measures, export control provisions, and amendments to the Foreign Corrupt Practices Act, but criticized its trade reorganization proposal. Ambassador Yeutter opined that a "salvageable" product could be put together in conference on the trade issues, but expressed concerns about Section 201, worker rights, TAA, oil import restrictions, the plant closing measure, and the prospect of Gephardt or "son-of-Gephardt" language being added on the floor. Over lunch, the president also strongly criticized the plant closing measure. He closed by suggesting, "the ghost of Smoot-Hawley seems to be rising again, threatening our economic expansion, our prosperity and our very livelihoods. We must eliminate the worst provisions of both the House and the Senate bills."[42]

SENATE FLOOR ACTION

Although as of June 18, only half of the Senate committees had actually reported their bills to the floor, by the evening of June 24, the omnibus measure was ready and was placed on the calendar as S. 1420. Pursuant to a unanimous consent agreement, Byrd could now call up the bill at any time, subject to consultations with the Republican leader.

On Thursday, June 25, 1987, the Senate turned to consideration of the Omnibus Trade and Competitiveness Act of 1987. It was, by this point, 958 pages long and contained 45 separate titles. With unlimited opportunity for amendment and debate, the Senate spent a total of thirteen days on the bill between June 25 and July 21, including one Saturday and several late nights. It conducted 43 roll call votes and fielded 160 amendments, of which 129 were adopted, 22 were rejected, and 9 withdrawn; dozens of other amendments were filed, but never offered.

While this was not the Senate's first experience with an omnibus bill—omnibus measures on drug policy and the homeless had been considered in 1986 and 1987—it was probably the most ambitious. Virtually every known form of parliamentary motion or maneuver that can

---

[42] "Remarks by the President to Senate Republican Committee Lunch," Office of the Press Secretary, The White House, June 16, 1987.

be used on the Senate floor came into play during consideration of the bill: amendments in the first and second degree, perfecting amendments, tabling motions, motions to reconsider votes, motions to table motions to reconsider votes, motions to request attendance ("bed check" votes), filibusters and votes to invoke cloture, and some successful and many unsuccessful attempts to forge unanimous consent agreements.

Slightly over half (eighty-seven) of the amendments offered pertained to Finance Committee trade issues. Other provisions of the bill, however, were also subject to amendments, with senators using the occasion to engage in lengthy and often acrimonious debates over issues ranging from the federal budget deficit to U.S. "reflagging" of Kuwaiti tankers in the Persian Gulf.

Amendment strategies were generally the same as those employed on other bills. The preferred option for both managers and amendment seekers was to work out compromise language so that the amendment could be accepted without a floor fight and formal roll call vote. This option reduced the risk on both sides and helped managers avoid the appearance of weakness that comes with losing too many motions to table unfriendly amendments. Senators opted to risk a floor vote if they thought they could win or if they felt strongly enough that they were willing to lose. If a controversial amendment looked like it had strong support, managers would sometimes accept it to avoid recording too many losses. This was more often the case with provisions not in the House bill, where in conference—a forum that would probably not include the amendment's author—managers could anticipate being "forced" to drop it. On occasion, a vote would also be used to contribute to a more political agenda, that of forcing senators to go on record on "key votes" later used by interest groups to measure member "ratings" on their issues.

The Senate got off to a very slow start on S. 1420, with nine hours of opening statements. Many of the anticipated trade amendments were either not ready or were being held back by their sponsors for tactical reasons. One important exception was Senator Specter's effort on the first day to amend the 1916 Dumping Act to provide an accessible private right of action. It was an auspicious beginning for the Finance managers, who saw the amendment tabled by a comfortable 69–27 margin.

During the course of Senate consideration of the bill, the managers established a mixed record with respect to provisions mirroring those in H.R. 3. For example, when Senator Tom Harkin (D-Iowa) attempted on the second-to-last day to add the Bryant amendment on inward investment, it was soundly rejected by a vote of 83–11. Knowledge that the House provision already invited a veto, strong private sector opposition, and the fact that the amendment came on a day when members were tired of the bill and voted down everything, contributed to this outcome. Unfortunately for those trying to delete provisions mirroring House language, that was the same day Senator Chafee failed in his attempt to strip the sugar duty drawback provision from the Finance bill. The vote was 49–44 in favor of tabling the Chafee amendment.[43] A final amendment mirroring language in the House involved the withdrawal of Romanian MFN. In this case, several attempts failed to keep the amendment, one of several containing foreign policy-related trade sanctions, off the Senate bill. Other foreign policy measures that were added pertained to Angola, Iranian Silkworm missiles, Afghanistan, Cuba, Panama, South Korea, and state-sponsored terrorism.

Halfway through consideration of the bill, the pace of amendments began to pick up with 119 of the total 160 amendments offered coming up between July 8 and 21. The bulk of the trade amendments also appeared during this time, but most were either tariff suspensions or relatively minor modifications of trade negotiating objectives, AD/CVD provisions, Section 201 and, to a lesser extent, Section 301 provisions.[44] Several amendments were also added with specific reference to Japan on such issues as access to the Japanese market for supercomputers, auto parts, construction, agriculture, and the FSX fighter project. Most came in the form of nonbinding resolutions, with the important exception of an amendment imposing sanctions against Toshiba Corporation of Japan and Kongsberg Vaapenfabrik of Norway in response to an illegal sale of sophisticated machine tools to the Soviet Union. The amendment carried 92–5, after a tabling motion failed by a vote of 19–78.

Contrary to conventional wisdom, press and administration expectations, and Finance member and staff fears, only a limited number of blatantly trade-restrictive amendments appeared and these were, for the most part, kept off the bill. For example, one such amendment, offered

[43] There was a great deal of arm-twisting in the well of the Senate floor during the vote on this provision. The vote to retain it was probably influenced most by the support of Senator Bennett Johnston (D-La.). With Chairman John C. Stennis (D-Miss.) often indisposed, Johnston was considered the de facto chairman of the Appropriations Committee and few were prepared to risk voting against him.

[44] Most of the relatively few trade amendments adopted prior to this period also fell into the "less controversial" category. One exception turned out to be an Exporter Sales Price (ESP) amendment to U.S. antidumping law. This highly technical provision offered by Senator Hollings, would have had the effect of increasing calculated margins of dumping. It was accepted by the managers since they expected to lose on a tabling motion and knew there was no counterpart measure in the House bill.

by Senator Pete Wilson (R-Calif.), would have effectively gutted the fast track process. It was tabled by a vote of 68–9. Commented Danforth staffer Marjorie Chorlins, "that would sure have pulled the rug right out from under this Christmas tree!" In fact, the net effect of the trade amendments added to the bill was probably to weaken, rather than toughen it and to move it in the administration's direction. This was true with respect to Section 201, for example, where although the most significant challenge to the Finance provision failed, its opponents were still able to get the managers to accept slightly more flexible criteria for presidential action.

In the end, by far the most divisive and hotly debated amendments to the bill involved the plant closing language, oil and energy security, and the Finance Committee's Section 201 provision. The amendment expected to cause the most controversy—the Senate's answer to the Gephardt amendment—ultimately caused little more than a ripple.

Everyone knew the fight on plant closing was coming. In the Senate, it had become the main focal point for business and administration opposition. It also prompted the most politically charged confrontations of the entire process. At the outset, the provision's sponsors knew they did not have the votes to defend against an amendment to strike their language from the bill. So while the Senate addressed other parts of S. 1420, the plan's supporters set about progressively tempering the plant closing measure, with each new version containing that change needed to garner the support of yet another senator. Ultimately, Kennedy, Metzenbaum, and their labor allies prevailed. On July 8, Byrd offered a series of amendments to the bill, including the final plant closing measure and enough perfecting and second degree amendments to "load" the amendment tree, thereby preventing opponents from offering other weakening amendments. This left them with the options of filibustering the entire trade bill or moving to strike the provision. A motion to strike offered by Senators Dan Quayle (R-Ind.) and Boren failed by a vote of 40–60. Ten Republicans had voted against the motion; four Democrats had voted for it.

The lines had been drawn on the energy import provision of the Finance bill well in advance of its arrival on the floor. Twenty-nine senators, mainly from industrial or agricultural states, had circulated a letter seeking support to strike the provision. There followed a war of words, exchanged in "Dear Colleague" letters and Op-Eds in the *Washington Post*. Although the provision was stripped from the bill on July 1 in a 55–41 motion to strike by Senator Bradley, oil-state senators still managed to triumph when two weeks later the Senate voted 58–40 to repeal the windfall profits tax on crude oil. Finance would normally have objected to the amendment by Senators Boren and Phil Gramm (R-Tex.), because the committee judiciously tried to avoid mixing trade and tax measures. In this case, whether for substantive reasons or to broaden the base of support for the bill, the chairman and most members supported the amendment.

The long-awaited Packwood amendment on Section 201 generated the most heated debate over U.S. trade policy during the course of Senate consideration of the bill. Pursuant to a unanimous consent agreement limiting the time and precluding second-degree amendments, the Senate debated the amendment for four hours on the evening of July 7. A bipartisan mix of twenty-two senators spoke on the proposal that would have added to the Section 201 language discretion to avoid granting relief in any case where the president determined it was not in the national economic interest. "National economic interest" was defined to include harm to consumers in general and the potential for foreign retaliation against U.S. exports.

Packwood was backed by an impressive coalition that he and his staff had put together that included most major business and agricultural organizations, a number of big multinationals, and retailers and importers. He also had strong support from the administration, bringing with it calls to senators by cabinet officers and the White House chief of staff, and Vice President George Bush, in his capacity as president of the Senate, presiding over the vote.

On the other side, Bentsen had a few colleagues with a strong interest in the provision and relatively little active private sector support. However, his Senate supporters saw the Packwood amendment as a threat to Finance leverage with the House, a symbolic threat to the broader bill, and a matter of principle. The small group of companies, trade associations, and unions that Bentsen, Danforth, and Heinz staffers pulled together had only one interest in common, and that was a desire not to see the Senate bill weakened. None of the coalition members had a direct stake in the outcome of the vote, and while the AFL-CIO put out a written circular on it, most of the lobbying was conducted by the senators and staffers themselves. As it turned out, enough of their colleagues were inclined to back the committee bill that the amendment failed to carry on a vote of forty-one yeas to fifty-five nays.[45]

[45] The vote offered interesting insights into action on the Senate bill in general. Positions were primarily taken on the basis of geography (exporting versus import-sensitive states) and philosophy (the free trade-protectionism continuum or the issue of executive discretion). As to partisan lines, eight Democrats voted for the amendment; eleven Republicans voted against. An example of how one senator grappled with his decision was Sen. Pete Domenici (R-N.M.), who held seven hours' worth of meetings with his staff,

The fight over the Gephardt amendment was the one that never took place. Riegle had introduced it in the Senate the same day S. 490 was introduced and most observers had been waiting nervously for nearly five months for him to offer it on the floor. Meetings between Riegle and Danforth staffers and meetings involving Riegle, his staff, Danforth and his staff, and representatives of the UAW, AFL-CIO, and Chrysler about substantive and strategic options for compromise had been going on since April. Riegle and his allies wanted the strongest possible provision in the Senate bill to ensure the Gephardt measure was considered in conference; they wanted it as specific and as binding as possible, and they knew they needed Republican support to do it.

Danforth strongly opposed the Gephardt language, but still wanted a measure that forced the executive to deal systematically with foreign barriers. As outlined by Danforth in a note to his staff in early April, he wrote:

(1) Mindless, mechanical approach to unfair trade practices is inappropriate.
(2) Systematic policy of ignoring violations of trade agreements/other unfair trade practices undermines the international trading system.
(3) The Administration is receptive to pressure.

Therefore, we need to write a reciprocity bill that puts the Administration under great pressure to address unfair trade practices but gives them enough discretion to avoid an excessively mechanistic approach . . .

Early on, Danforth and Riegle had also recognized that they had a major perception problem. "It's like when the least popular boy in school decides to be your friend," commented Danforth at one point. Not only did they need a provision their colleagues would consider a real alternative to the political pariah the Gephardt amendment had become, they needed for it to have extraordinarily strong bipartisan backing from the start. Danforth therefore asked Dole if he would be willing to cosponsor a "leadership" amendment with Byrd—assuming one could be brokered. Dole agreed to give it a try.[46]

By early July, Danforth staff, working in parallel meetings with staff

---

and then called in Danforth and Packwood staffers to "debate" the issue before making his decision. He ultimately worked out two minor amendments with the managers of the bill to alleviate his concerns and voted against the Packwood amendment.

[46] Bentsen and Packwood were the first ones approached to take the lead on a compromise amendment, but Bentsen had been burned by reaction to the import surcharge bill in 1985 and was not willing to get out in front. Packwood also declined, predicting that whatever they came up with would inevitably be labeled "Son-of-Gephardt" and "trashed" by the *New York Times*.

and advisers to Riegle and Dole, finalized the outlines of a proposal based on several provisions already in law or in the Senate bill. It was to be action-forcing, focus on barriers rather than balances, and contain a means of measuring results; and it was to be sufficiently flexible for the president to avoid having to take draconian action.

Nicknamed "Super 301," the proposal targeted countries in the same manner as the old Adversarial Trade provision—namely, those shown to maintain "a consistent pattern of import barriers and market distorting practices." Section 301 investigations would then be initiated against that country's "major barriers . . . the elimination of which are likely to have the most significant potential to increase U.S. exports." Subsequent action would be consistent with the language and procedures in the Senate bill for Section 301, including its "mandatory but waivable" sanctions. Evidence of results was to be reported annually and contrasted with earlier estimates of the increase in U.S. exports that could have occurred had the barriers not existed in the first place. Finally, Section 301 was amended to provide for the filing of cases by either Finance or Ways and Means in the event they were unhappy with executive handling of the program.

On the afternoon of July 9, the amendment received Dole's conceptual blessing. That evening the formal drafting of the amendment was completed, and there began several hours of wrangling over the details. This ultimately took the form of Danforth mediating over the final words and phrases as he shuttled between two rooms in the Capitol— one occupied by staffers for Riegle, Byrd, Chrysler, the UAW, and the AFL-CIO; the other by staffers representing Dole, Packwood, and the administration. It was past midnight by the time differences had been narrowed to two sentences in the eight-page document and the Senator was able to embarrass the staffers into working out the final compromise. At 1:15 A.M. on July 10, agreement was reached; it was filed later that morning on the Senate floor as a Byrd-Dole-Riegle-Danforth amendment.

The senators and staff spent the morning gathering support for the measure, which was intentionally left short enough to be read in its entirety by the most suspicious of those gathered on the Senate floor. Statements were heard, and questions about the provision were raised and responded to until early afternoon, as all involved went out of their way to describe the provision in the most moderate, conciliatory terms possible. The amendment passed by an overwhelming 87–7.

Late on July 15, the leadership was able to get agreement on a process to unravel the legislative gridlock that had by that time been created by pending amendments on a balanced budget, windfall oil tax, and reflagging. It then propounded a unanimous consent request to limit remaining amendments and to lock in a date and time for final passage. The time agreement invoked cloture on the bill, specified that the vote on final passage would occur no later than 6:00 P.M. on July 21, and limited amendments to a maximum of two per senator from an agreed list of sixty-three. To emphasize the point, Byrd, Dole, Bentsen, and Packwood also made clear that they would not hesitate to move in unison to table any nongermane or particularly controversial amendments. In the end, only thirty-four amendments were actually raised, of which twenty-five had been worked out with the managers in advance.

As action on the trade bill was drawing to a close, the administration and Senate Republicans faced a strategic dilemma. Although the bill still fell far short of addressing the thirty-two-page list of administration objections cited in a June 22 letter to the members, it did contain strongly supported provisions such as trade agreement authority and repeal of the oil windfall profits tax. In addition, several of the amendments added to the bill on the floor had moved it closer to the administration on various other issues.[47] But the fight over plant closing had embittered many Republicans and caused them to question the Democrats' motivations. Moreover, if Republican senators were to vote en masse for the bill, they were concerned it would be interpreted by the Democratic leadership to mean the votes were there to override a presidential veto of any product emerging from conference—regardless of the administration's position.

At the weekly Republican policy lunch on July 14, several senators and administration officials argued in favor of Republicans voting in a block against the bill. At minimum, they argued, at least thirty-four votes were needed against final passage to demonstrate the absence of a veto-proof majority. Danforth and Chafee countered that the bill contained a good many positive elements and had been crafted as a bipartisan product. They warned that a large-scale defection by Republicans at this point could hand the trade issue politically to the Democrats and jeopardize any influence Republicans might have in conference to rid the bill of its most egregious provisions. To this end, they began circulating a letter to their Republican colleagues seeking support for final passage. "At minimum," they wrote, "we urge you to vote 'yes, but . . .' with those of us willing to give the conferees and the administra-

---

[47] In addition to the amendments already noted, the reorganization language had been stripped, the LDC debt facility and treatment of securities dealers provisions had been watered down, and the president's Caribbean Basin Initiative program had been extended twelve years.

tion a chance to turn the measure into a law of which we can all be proud." In the days that followed, they worked the floor and the Republican cloakroom, carrying a statement and seeking Republican signatures. The statement read:

> We are voting in favor of the Omnibus Trade Act, but with profound reservations. The bill contains a great many good provisions and some remarkably bad ones.
>
> Ours is a "yes, but . . ." vote. We wish to see the conferees develop a sound final product that can be signed into law. Failing that, we reserve our rights to vote against the conference report when it comes before the Senate later this year.[48]

When the statement was filed on July 21, sixteen Republicans had signed it. But in many ways, the partisan damage had been done: Bentsen, Byrd, and their colleagues had heard about the Republican caucus and knew the administration was now pushing hard for "no" votes. They were furious, and immediately concluded that the administration would approach conference with a veto strategy—a list of demands and no flexibility—thereby making the need for a veto a self-fulfilling prophecy. This rupture was reflected in statements from both sides on the Senate floor in advance of final passage, and in the vote itself.

On final passage of S. 1420, there was much discussion and debate among Republicans in the well. In the end, there were seventy-one votes in favor of the bill and twenty-seven votes against it. All of the Democrats—including several who, but for the last minute drawing of partisan lines, would have opposed it—voted "yea." Of the nineteen Republicans voting in favor, sixteen had already characterized their votes as "yes, but. . . ." Everyone declared victory. It was time to go to conference.

---

[48] Congress, *Congressional Record* (July 21, 1987), S10311.

6

ATMOSPHERICS: CONTEXT OF A CONFERENCE

The conference committee is many times, in very important matters of legislation, the most important branch of our legislature.
—Senator George Norris[1]

THE HOUSE AND SENATE GO TO CONFERENCE

Decades after Senator Norris compared the House-Senate conference committee to a third house of Congress, his observation still rang true. Conference committees are ad hoc joint committees set up to resolve differences between House- and Senate-passed bills. They represent a critical point in the legislative process because failure to reach agreement on a common text means the legislation dies. The enormous power of conference committees lies with the limited number of participants making decisions that are binding on the entire Congress. With very few exceptions, both chambers must either accept or reject the entire conference package.

Conferees are appointed by the presiding officers of each house, generally upon the recommendation of the relevant committee chairmen who traditionally select the most senior members of the committee. Conference bargaining is an exercise in both "conflict and cooperation,"[2] where conferees are expected to represent their chamber's bill and not their own views—whether a provision was adopted by the committee in markup or later on the floor. Conferees from each house must vote as a single unit, and their final product, known as the conference report or "Statement of Managers," must be "generally supported"

---

[1] George Norris, quoted in David J. Vogler, *The Third House: Conference Committees in the United States Congress* (Evanston: Northwestern University Press, 1971), 3. Norris, of Nebraska, served both as a Representative (1909–1913) and as a Senator (1913–1943).

[2] Vogler, *The Third House*, 90.

by a majority of conferees.[3] To the extent any rules apply to conference proceedings, they impose limits based on the "scope of conference," confining modifications to those provisions in disagreement and precluding the addition of new material. While failure to comply can later be attacked on the floor through the raising of points of order, each house retains the ability to waive all such rules and points of order. Moreover, with the exception of "money" bills, where amounts authorized, appropriated, or taxed offer some reasonable guidelines for scope, the confines of scope can often be difficult to judge.

Assessing which chamber generally "wins" or "loses" in conference is almost impossible. Analyses using "House recedes/Senate recedes" calculations can be misleading because both chambers approach conference with bill strategies to achieve a preferred outcome. For example, provisions may be included for the purpose of trading them away or desired provisions omitted because they are already in the other chamber's bill. Congressional staff are convinced that the "other" house usually prevails in conference!

In the case of H.R. 3, the process of setting up a conference committee to reconcile House and Senate bills was, in itself, a challenge. The time required for Senate passage of its bill had set back a number of time-sensitive activities, including Senate action and the conference on the annual budget reconciliation bill. Leadership plans to complete this measure in August meant that the Ways and Means and Finance Committees needed to mark up legislation, take it to the floor, and go to conference on it before turning to the conference on H.R. 3. Still, the task of identifying and sorting out jurisdiction and selecting conferees—particularly in the House—on a bill as complex as H.R. 3 was going to take some time.

The first, and as it turned out, last formal meeting of the full conference on H.R. 3 took place on August 7, 1987, in the Caucus Room of the House Cannon Office Building. For purposes of this largely ceremonial opening, forty-four Senate conferees had been appointed; House conferees consisted of the three senior-most members from each of eleven committees and Rep. Gephardt, who was included at the Speaker's insistence. The remaining sixty to seventy House conferees were expected to be named in September. By the time the selection of conferees on H.R. 3 was complete, twenty-three congressional committees were rep-

---

[3] Oleszek, *Congressional Procedures,* 207. Prior to the adoption of congressional "sunshine" rules in 1975, all conferences met in secret and published no records of proceedings. Today, conference proceedings can be closed by a majority vote of participants.

resented—nine from the Senate and fourteen from the House—accounting for more than 200 conferees.[4] Work was organized into seventeen separate subconferences determined largely by jurisdiction, with individual conferees appointed to confer on specific titles and, in a number of cases, distinct sections of the bill.[5] The official side-by-side comparison of the two bills was 504 pages long, measured 10-by-15 inches and was over 2 inches thick; it weighed 8 pounds. The first 223 pages went to Subconference #1 and consisted of trade provisions primarily under the jurisdiction of the Committees on Finance and Ways and Means. A few sections claimed by committees beyond Ways and Means resulted in six other House committees in thirteen combinations of conferees also being added to the mix.

Still, as in any conference situation, the number of participants directly involved had now narrowed considerably, with a concomitant increase in the power of each. Subconference chairs and ranking members, specific conferees, committee staffs, and a few personal staffers would come to dominate this stage of the process. Congressional leadership figures took on an oversight role, calling periodic meetings of their chairs and ranking members to mark progress and discuss strategy. Parallel meetings were held more frequently at the staff level. In the Senate, Byrd, Dole, and Bentsen were responsible for overseeing most of these organizational meetings. In the House, it was more often Rostenkowski, who was also chairman of the full conference, and his Trade Subcommittee staff director who took the lead with Wright's people in attendance. Unlike the standard one-issue/two-committee conference where trade-offs were possible throughout a piece of legislation, the atomization of the conference structure precluded compromises across issues and subconferences. This posed a serious potential threat to the conference outcome, and left to the leadership (and Bentsen and Rostenkowski) whatever jaw-boning of subconferences and conferees might be necessary to bring events to a successful close.

The Ways and Means Committee fielded nine Democrats and five Republicans as conferees; the Senate Finance Committee team was split

[4] This was in contrast to conferences on the Trade Expansion Act of 1962 and the Trade Act of 1974, where both consisted solely of seven members each from the Ways and Means and Finance Committees. Stanley Bach, "Conference Committees: Reflecting Change in Congress," *Congressional Research Service (CRS) Review*, June 1988, 27. The conference on H.R. 3 was not, however, the largest on record. Oleszek cites the omnibus budget reconciliation bill in 1981, where over 250 conferees met in 58 subconferences to reconcile nearly 300 issues in disagreement between Senate and House texts. (*Congressional Procedures*, 207).

[5] For example, a separate "mini-conference" on the Bryant amendment was established to which Wright appointed Bryant a conferee.

five-to-four. Bentsen's Democrats, including Matsunaga, Moynihan, Baucus, and Boren were chosen on the basis of seniority—a lineup that just happened to include a second oil-state senator and exclude several members with particularly strong feelings about Section 201 and the Gephardt amendment. Packwood was joined by Senators Chafee, William Roth (R-Del.), and Danforth, members with the most seniority in both the full Finance Committee (excepting Dole) and its Trade Subcommittee. It was also a group that, with the exception of Danforth, was inclined towards a more free-trade agenda. Several of the Finance conferees were also assigned to other parts of the bill by virtue of their seniority on other committees. From his Commerce Committee position, for example, Danforth, along with Sen. Exon emerged as principal Senate negotiators on the Exon-Florio and Bryant amendments.

Rostenkowski's Democratic conferees included all members of his Trade Subcommittee, consisting of Reps. Gibbons, Jenkins, Downey, Pease, Russo, Gephardt, Guarini, and Matsui. Ways and Means' ranking Republican John J. Duncan (R-Tenn.) had with him a similar lineup with Reps. Bill Archer (R-Tex.), Guy Vander Jagt (R-Mich.), Philip M. Crane (R-Ill.), and Bill Frenzel. Throughout the conference, however, it was Rostenkowski's handpicked core group of Gibbons, Downey, Matsui, and a few Republicans who made the bulk of Ways and Means decisions on the bill. Pease was also periodically drawn in, particularly with respect to labor-related issues. In the case of these Democrats, Rostenkowski and Rufus Yerxa made a point in early 1988 of calling on each member individually in his office. The chairman's pitch was simple: "I need your help," he would say; "I want a good bill, not a protectionist one, so tell me what you need and you have my support"—and one by one he exacted the commitments he required. With respect to the Ways and Means Republicans, Alan Holmer was apprised of the chairman's strategy, and it became USTR's responsibility to work with them. In the case of Finance Committee participants, Bentsen's views already reflected those of a number of his members, although he occasionally called on Danforth and a few others for input and to close ranks at critical moments.

The administration had a more difficult time organizing itself for the conference. Various interagency working groups were established under the EPC, with USTR Yeutter responsible for the group on Subconference #1; James Baker, the banking and investment issues; Labor Secretary Brock, the labor and the export promotion and control topics; and Agriculture Secretary Richard Lyng, agriculture. Much of the coordination was left to a subcabinet working group chaired by Holmer and the handful of executive branch agency heads and staffers who worked directly with the subconferences. Yeutter, for example, devoted a great deal of time to the conference. Baker, considered by many to be the pivotal administration actor on the bill, made it clear that his general involvement was conditioned on his Treasury-related issues being resolved first. This, however, was complicated by the fact that the managers of the Subconference #7 investment deliberations (Dingell from House Energy and Commerce, Hollings from Senate Commerce, and William Proxmire [D-Wisc.] from Senate Banking) were not willing to allow executive branch participants to attend their conference sessions.

In a conference situation, personal working relationships can be as important as substance; knowing what to expect from the other side, respect for the other's abilities, and member "bonding," can often be vital to a successful outcome. In the case of Subconference #1, all of the key committee and administration actors already shared several histories. Most had worked together on the 1984 trade bill and had a fairly decent relationship with USTR. More recently, both sets of conferees and James Baker had shared the ups and downs of 1986 tax reform legislation.

In the wake of Senate passage of H.R. 3, the attitudes of those contributing most to conference atmospherics were mixed: There was a cautious optimism among Finance and Ways and Means members about their portions of the bill. Senate Democrats—particularly Bentsen, the Senate's single most important actor on the bill—were still mistrustful of the administration's motives. The administration felt it had won more than it had lost during Senate floor deliberations, but was still smarting from losses over Section 201, sugar duty drawback, and an Exporter Sales Price (ESP) amendment. It came into the conference troubled by House provisions involving Gephardt, AD/CVD, and transfer of authority issues, and the various Senate constraints on discretion in Sections 201, 301, and negotiating authority. But for almost every provision it opposed in one of the bills there was an acceptable alternative in the other, creating the potential for an acceptable outcome. What bothered the executive branch most was issues and strains in relationships outside of Subconference #1, along with a negativism perceived in the attitudes of Byrd and Wright, characterized at one point by Deputy USTR Woods as "what's mine is mine; what's yours is negotiable."

It had, however, by this time become evident that the addition of the windfall profits tax repeal in the Senate had the potential of changing fundamentally the dynamics on the entire bill. Suddenly, there was a provision of equal—if not greater—importance to the administration than authority for a new trade round. Vice President Bush and Secretary Baker had strong Texas ties and perceived the provision's value to the

upcoming presidential race. Speaker Wright was also a Texan, with
more than a passing interest in oil issues; and many wondered how
much Bentsen would be prepared to concede to achieve the provision's
enactment, particularly since his Republican counterpart had helped
engineer the amendment. Rostenkowski might have had a history of
opposing the provision and objections to seeing tax issues on a trade
bill, but he also knew the value of leverage when he saw it.

With the stage set for conference, quiet meetings began to take place
between and among the various executive and legislative branch actors
to consider strategies for saving the trade portion of the bill. In early
August, for example, Danforth spoke with Ken Duberstein, White
House Deputy Chief of Staff, James Baker, and Clayton Yeutter about
a "breakout" strategy for the trade component. They agreed such a
strategy was essential and pondered what, if anything, might persuade
the Democratic leadership to split the measure into two bills and move
the provisions of Subconference #1 separately. Baker suggested a show
of strength, with forty Republicans stating in a letter to Byrd that unless
the conference proceeded on two tracks they would vote to sustain a
veto. Danforth disagreed and opined that forcing the issue this early
would backfire with Byrd and Wright. It would be far preferable, he
asserted, for the administration to work with the conferees, accomplish
as much as possible, and have an agreed trade bill to point to before
issuing an ultimatum. Besides, concluded Danforth, he had made a personal commitment to stick with Bentsen for the duration of the conference. Baker and Yeutter admitted that their real problem was in the
administration and that unless they could show progress to their own
hard-liners, they doubted it would be possible to deliver the administration on anything; perhaps they should float the breakout idea with
Bentsen?

When Danforth met later with Bentsen, both agreed that the "deals-
first-ultimatum-later" strategy was the only one with the slightest
chance of success with the Congress. And in follow-up conversations
involving Baker and Yeutter, Bentsen and Rostenkowski, the Ways and
Means chairman also became intrigued by the idea of a breakout or
"spin-off" strategy, particularly in view of the jurisdictional chaos being
caused by the conference in the House. However, he maintained, unless
a good faith effort was made by the administration to reach an accommodation on Subconference #1 issues, no real progress on the omnibus
bill was possible. The other problem, from the perspective of committee
leaders, was that no strategy could be expected to work unless and until
someone—preferably Jim Baker—took the lead for the executive. When
Danforth had raised this with Baker earlier, the response was that he

could not speak for the whole administration on the bill. But *someone* had to speak for the president, suggested Danforth, or how could they expect conferees to negotiate down to a bottom line without some assurance the deal would go through?

September was the month for quiet meetings, as discussions of strategy merged into discussions of substance. As the principals were emerging at the end of one such session between Baker, Yeutter, and a handful of the Finance conferees, Japanese Ambassador Nabuo Matsunaga happened to walk by a group of journalists hanging around to see if anything "newsworthy" had occurred. "What happened?" asked Matsunaga of *Washington Post* reporter Stuart Auerbach. "Nothing," responded Auerbach. "Nothing?" questioned the Ambassador. "Well," said the reporter after a few moments, "at the opening of a Sumo match, don't the wrestlers stand in the ring, stare at each other, and bump bellies? *That*'s what happened."

The conference was difficult to get off the ground. There was no real sense of urgency and the members, having shifted their attention away from trade, were increasingly involved in partisan debates over budget reconciliation. The House had yet to finalize its conference assignments and, with multiple committees involved in each part of the bill, developing the "House" position on any issue was a real challenge. The side-by-side was not available until early October. And the executive, which had yet to decide on its strategy for the conference, was now preoccupied with concluding FTA negotiations with Canada.

The first meeting of Subconference #1 was scheduled for the morning of Thursday, October 22, 1987. On Monday, October 19, the stock market crashed, dropping 508 points. Policymaker attention was drawn to the crisis, effectively terminating movement on the bill for the balance of the year. Developments on Wall Street had made congressional trade leaders particularly skittish, since market declines the previous week had been attributed in part to worse-than-expected news about the U.S. trade deficit.[6]

Although the initial meeting of the subconference took place as scheduled, Bentsen and Rostenkowski realized the atmosphere was far too

---

[6] That week the Dow Jones industrial average had fallen 235 points, including a plunge of 95 points on October 14, following announcement of the August trade deficit. The $15.7 billion deficit, a slight improvement over July, was still less of an improvement than had been expected. All major newspapers linked the two events, with a few also pointing to the impact of a Ways and Means Committee-passed bill to limit corporate takeovers. The 508-point fall on October 19, and the record 600 million shares traded far exceeded those of Black Tuesday in 1929. Several factors were blamed, including the "twin deficits" of trade and the budget, and computerized program trading.

volatile to take up any controversial topics. Therefore, only "positive" proposals were addressed that day: Some noncontroversial tariff suspension measures were adopted and the administration was tentatively granted fast-track authority for nontariff trade agreements. A two-year extension of this authority beyond May 1991 would go into effect automatically unless the Congress enacted an "extension disapproval resolution" to stop it. Tariff-cutting authority, "reverse" fast track, and other disputed agreement authority issues were not discussed. All other decisions were deferred until further notice.

PARTICIPANTS, OBSERVERS, AND OTHER FORCES

Toward the end of Congress' August 1987 recess, the *National Journal* ran an article by Bruce Stokes entitled "High-Stakes Trading on the Hill."[7] It reflected on the many actors with an interest or investment in the trade bill, noting that "the Reagan Administration, the congressional Democratic leadership, organized labor, the business community, and a number of presidential candidates all have a great deal to gain or lose." Indeed, the motivations of those in a position to influence U.S. trade policy during this period had an important impact on the movement and outcome of the legislation. These actors were, in turn, influenced by other developments, including growing tangles in executive-legislative relations and the economic environment within which the dramas were being played.

Congress and the Executive

In early September, a *Washington Post* editorial commented: "The world's greatest living argument against divided government is reassembling; the president returned on Sunday, and Congress reconvenes tomorrow." It dwelt on the paralysis in government and contained a lengthy list of issues on which neither branch seemed capable of acting. These included the federal budget deficit, appropriations bills, and several highly charged issues from reversal of a 1984 Supreme Court decision on civil rights (*Grove City College* v. *Bell*) to catastrophic health insurance to the Persian Gulf. The "cumbersome" trade bills were also mentioned. The *Post* attributed the general lack of progress to politics: "The Democrats have majorities, but the Republicans have the veto and the filibuster; particularly in the Senate, neither side seems to have the

---

[7] Bruce Stokes, "High-Stakes Trading on the Hill," *National Journal*, August 29, 1987, 2160.

votes to win. . . . The President won't bend, and neither party in Congress seems quite to know what to do about it."[8]

Paralysis and partisanship appeared to be the order of the day in the 100th Congress; relations between the two branches were not much better. And as the 1988 election approached, it was a problem that would get substantially worse. Still, in its end-of-year analysis for 1987, the *Congressional Quarterly* was willing to term the session "productive."[9] Unfortunately, only crisis management and artificially-imposed deadlines had kept things moving.[10]

Between the time of the *Post* editorial and sine die adjournment by Congress on December 22, 1987, the stock market had collapsed and an executive-legislative budget "summit" had reached agreement on a budget package. The package was implemented through a budget reconciliation measure and the bundling of thirteen appropriations bills into a single continuing resolution that was enacted around 3:00 A.M. on the morning of adjournment. Because no regular appropriations measures had been approved by the end of fiscal year 1987, an automatic sequester of federal funds had gone into effect under the Gramm-Rudman-Hollings budget law and four short-term continuing resolutions had to be passed to keep the government from shutting down. A short-term "fix" to extend the limit on the national debt had also been needed until the other money issues had been settled. The budget agreement was hailed by Democrats and the White House, but left a bad taste in the mouths of congressional Republicans who felt they had been cut out of the process.

The first session of the 100th Congress had lasted 351 days, placing it in a tie with the first session of the 80th Congress in 1947 as the twelfth-longest on record. During the session, 7,532 bills and resolutions had been introduced; 204 had become law. President Reagan had vetoed three bills, of which two, involving clean water and highways, became law through veto overrides. The Senate had cast 420 votes

---

[8] Editorial, "Paralysis," *Washington Post*, September 8, 1987.

[9] "The 100th Congress: A Productive First Session," Legislative Summary, *Congressional Quarterly*, December 26, 1987, 3213–3232.

[10] In an editorial marking Congress' departure on recess in August, the *Post* had remarked: "Congress has punctually disappeared on its August vacation, the only deadline it has met all year. . . .They chose a short-term extension [of Treasury borrowing authority] rather than a long-term extension so they would have another artificial crisis to galvanize them when they come back." Editorial, "Wheelspinning," *Washington Post*, August 9, 1987.

during the year; the House had cast 488. Of the Senate's votes in 1987, fully 10 percent had been cast on the trade bill.[11]

Much of what the Congress had touched that year had turned into a partisan brawl, a confrontation with the White House, or both. This was particularly true in the Senate, where the "reflagging" and budget fights on the trade bill joined showdowns over campaign finance reform, "Grove City," catastrophic health insurance, aid for Nicaraguan contras, the nomination of Robert H. Bork to the Supreme Court, and proposed revisions to the War Powers Act. Questions were raised about the ability of the Democratic leadership to lead, and about the willingness of anyone else to follow. And the president had yet to convince the pundits that his political clout had not been diminished by the ongoing Iran-Contra scandal.

Still, little of the partisanship that characterized the 100th Congress seemed to spill over into the trade arena in spite of its potential appeal to the Democratic leadership. With only unpleasant choices to be made with respect to the budget deficit, no money for new initiatives, and tax reform enacted into law only the year before, trade was one of the few economic issues it had left. But with few exceptions, the relative absence of partisanship during action on the trade bill also extended to other trade issues that arose during the two-year period.

The administration had maintained a fairly activist stance on trade during the course of congressional action on the omnibus bill. There was movement (if not resolution) on issues involving Korea (beef, tobacco, and counterfeiting), the EC (Airbus, feed grain exports and Spanish accession to the EC, beef hormones, and the third-country meat directive), Brazil (informatics), and Japan. Moreover, in January 1988, it had suddenly and unilaterally announced a decision to "graduate" several advanced developing countries from the Generalized System of Preferences (GSP) program—something of an irony in view of a major battle fought and won against a similar House amendment to the 1984 act, and the fact that such a mandate had been purposely left out of S. 490 in 1987.[12]

March 1987 marked the most dramatic of the administration's trade

---

[11] Janet Hook and the *Congressional Quarterly* staff, "100th Congress Wraps Up Surprisingly Busy Year," *Congressional Quarterly,* October 29, 1988, 3119.

[12] Two lessons are worth noting from this event: (1) The president enjoys extensive authorities under U.S. trade law to make market-closing decisions that few expect him ever to use. (2) When politicians and their staffers disagree on a trade policy issue, the politicians win. The decision to deny GSP to Hong Kong, Korea, Taiwan, and Singapore was made directly by the cabinet, just as the Senate provision had been proposed by senators. In neither case was the idea supported by staff.

actions; this time with respect to Japan. The decision to retaliate—in the form of 100 percent tariffs on $300 million in Japanese high technology exports—was announced on March 27 and put into effect in mid-April. The move was in response to Japan's failure to comply with a bilateral semiconductor access agreement. It was triggered by a story in the *Washington Post* that quoted a high-level MITI official as suggesting Americans should forget trying to sell supercomputers to the Japanese government or to Japanese universities.[13]

Congress, too, addressed several trade issues not in the omnibus bill during this period. The Senate, for example, had rejected a "buy America" cement amendment to the federal highway bill in January 1987; had restricted access by foreign companies and governments to Strategic Defense Initiative (SDI) research contracts in September; and had failed to delete domestic usage requirements from an Energy Committee bill designed to help the uranium industry. In a measure that went into law with the fiscal year 1988 continuing resolution, both the House and Senate voted to prohibit for one year the granting of federal public works and construction contracts to Japanese firms "in response to Japan's . . . longstanding policy of discriminating against American construction firms."[14] Finally, pursuant to agreements reached between textile quota bill proponents and the chairmen of the Finance and Ways and Means Committees, both chambers held hearings, fought over, and approved textile and apparel quota measures. The bill was sent to the president in September 1988, lacking the votes to override his subsequent veto.

Two administration initiatives requiring congressional action also appeared during the period. The executive succeeded with one and met with a setback in the other. On January 2, 1988, the United States and Canada concluded a bilateral free-trade agreement. Contrary to speculation that Congress might try to hold the implementing legislation hostage to progress on the omnibus trade bill, a deal was brokered by Bentsen and Baker staffers to move the bills in parallel. In an exchange of letters, Byrd, Wright, Bentsen, and Rostenkowski agreed Congress would act on the FTA implementing bill before the end of the session, and Baker and Yeutter committed not to trigger the fast-track clock by submitting it before June 1. The administration also agreed to engage

---

[13] Stuart Auerbach, "Remark Fires U.S. Campaign To Retaliate Against Japan," *Washington Post*, March 26, 1987.

[14] Congress, *Making Further Continuing Appropriations for the Fiscal Year Ending September 30, 1987: Conference Report to accompany H.J. Res. 395*, 100th Cong., 1st sess., December 22 1987, Report 100–498, 1183.

in a consultative process similar to the one used to implement the Tokyo Round agreements in 1979. Hearings began in March in the midst of the omnibus trade bill conference; intra- and inter-branch negotiations over language and the "mock" markups took place in May; and on September 28, 1988, the United States-Canada Free-Trade Agreement Implementation Act of 1988 was enacted into law.

Efforts by the executive to accelerate implementation of the "Harmonized System" did not fare as well. The new customs nomenclature was to go into effect worldwide on January 1, 1988. When the administration and interested private sector groups realized in November 1987 that the United States would not ratify it until much later the following year—if at all—in the omnibus bill, they sought to break the noncontroversial measure out of the bill and move it separately. Committee members were split over the issue, but Bentsen and Rostenkowski dug in their heels, citing the lack of time and the administration's failure to show any real interest in the problem until too late.

During this period, the administration's stance on trade issues was also somewhat affected by several unexpected personnel developments. Secretary Baldrige had died in a riding accident the week following Senate passage of H.R. 3. This meant that one of the administration's few business-oriented activists on export controls, competitiveness, and AD/CVD measures would no longer be contributing to cabinet and conference deliberations. Alan Holmer replaced Deputy USTR Woods, who was named to head the U.S. Agency for International Development (AID). And Labor Secretary Brock resigned to join Senator Dole's presidential campaign.[15]

With respect to trade and electoral politics, the 1988 presidential race had commenced already in 1986, but it was not until the "Super Tuesday" group of primaries on March 8, 1988, that the question of whether trade would be an issue was finally settled. Gephardt, who had made trade an integral and active part of his campaign, had been roundly criticized in the press for doing so. His stance was, however, credited with having contributed to his victory in the Iowa caucuses in February. Democrats Jesse Jackson, former Arizona Governor Bruce Babbitt, Senator Joseph Biden (D-Del.), and Senator Albert Gore (D-Tenn.) also favored various lesser (or less conspicuous) forms of import protective measures, as did Pat Robertson and former Senator Paul Laxalt (R-Nev.), running on the Republican side. Massachusetts Governor Michael Dukakis, Vice President Bush, Senator Dole, Congressman

---

[15] James Baker's move to the Bush campaign did not occur until 1988, two days after Senate passage of the second trade bill.

Jack Kemp (R-N.Y.), former Delaware Governor Pete du Pont, and Alexander Haig were all on record opposing "protectionism."

The trade positions of the candidates had been dissected and discussed in some detail in the press, but with the end of Gephardt's campaign on Super Tuesday and the successful emergence of the Bush and Dukakis candidacies, the issue disappeared once again from the electoral scene.[16] Super Tuesday was portrayed as a victory for free trade, and those in Congress who had not been sure they wanted a trade law or a political issue found that their options had narrowed considerably. In the end, to the extent partisan politics and the biennial "silly season" came to affect later developments in the 1988 act, it was not over a trade issue.[17]

Interests and Interest Groups

Prior to the conference on H.R. 3, the influence of business and labor on the legislation had generally exceeded that of the administration. While this changed somewhat once the conference really got down to business, both groups still maintained a hand in conference developments. It was at this point, too, that a few foreign interests weighed in—with limited result. The press, on the other hand, was an important observer and, in many ways, participant from start to finish.

Industry and services. In contrast with previous major pieces of trade legislation in the post-1934 era, the business community got out in front of the executive branch on the omnibus trade bill. Rather than waiting to see and coalesce behind the administration position on the most contentious substantive issues, this time the business community chose instead to carve out its own set of positions. Wrote Bruce Stokes in the *National Journal:*

> Business also faces a test. Such groups as the U.S. Chamber of Commerce, the National Association of Manufacturers, the Business Roundtable and

[16] Between November 1986 and March 1988, the *Washington Post,* the *New York Times,* and *The Wall Street Journal* ran thirty-seven editorials on the trade positions being taken by the various presidential candidates. At least six editorials were devoted exclusively to the trade stand of Gephardt-as-candidate, including *The Wall Street Journal*'s "President Smoot" (April 28, 1987), with several attacking a television commercial he ran in Iowa about auto imports ("Beggar Thy Hyundai," *The Wall Street Journal,* February 11, 1987 and "Mr. Gephardt's Reckless Driving," *New York Times,* February 13, 1987).

[17] In two related political developments: (1) At the press conference announcing Bentsen as Dukakis' running mate on July 12, a number of his achievements were mentioned; the plant closing measure—not trade—was one of the first. (2) Although the second omnibus trade bill passed Congress on August 3, 1988, it was held back by the Democratic leadership until after the Republican convention to ensure Reagan did not sign it surrounded only by Republicans.

the Emergency Committee for American Trade have favored passage of a nonprotectionist trade bill. This stance set them apart from the Administration and gave them great influence in shaping the current bills. . . . Observers wonder whether business groups will be willing to give up their newfound influence for the sake of a single issue or swallow hard and accept some provisions they do not like.[18]

It was, in fact, these larger business groups that had the most influence over the House and Senate omnibus trade bills. The CEO-level Business Roundtable (BRT) and the Emergency Committee for American Trade (ECAT) both were active players throughout the process, as was the U.S. Chamber of Commerce, that had heretofore seemed incapable of taking a position on anything that was not the administration's. Since the positions taken by these groups usually placed them somewhere between the adamantly free-trade stance of the administration and the tougher, more activist approach of congressional trade leaders, many of the positions ultimately made it into the law. This was in spite of the fact that there was remarkably little in the trade bill of direct interest to the corporations making up the business groups. It was also in contrast to some of the narrower-focus provisions actively promoted by individual firms and smaller interest groups which—if added to the bills in the first place—often fell out in conference.

In 1986, the business community had stuck with the executive in disclaiming any need for trade legislation. Following the election, however, the larger groups had concluded that legislation was inevitable and that they needed to get involved early enough to have an impact. Because it took the administration an inordinately long time to get into the conference with detailed and/or negotiable positions, the conferees turned to the business community as a good source of constructive criticism. In essence, there had been an inversion in traditional roles in the development of trade legislation: Instead of the executive branch drafting a bill and rallying the private sector to lobby it on the Hill, in this case Congress drafted the bill and turned to the business community to help with the administration.

For their part, the major business groups were generally supportive of negotiating authority for a new trade round and of stronger Section 301 language with respect to foreign barriers to U.S. exports. With the exception of a few prominent companies and groups in the services sector or with a direct interest in intellectual property rights protection, however, their interest often appeared based as much on theory as on

---

[18] Stokes, "High-Stakes Trading," 2160.

considerations of profit. When it came to Section 301, for example, the proactive stance of the industry associations belied the ambivalence of most major firms with a toe-hold in a foreign market: When faced with a trade barrier, they were often unwilling to jeopardize their small but real market share to go after the much larger one they could realize if the barrier were removed.

The absence of direct profit implications was not the situation, however, with respect to provisions to liberalize the U.S. export control regime being considered outside the Finance Committee. Neither was it true of specific industries such as oil and gas, for whom the windfall profits tax repeal turned the bill into their principal legislative agenda item for the year, or for individual companies now paying import duties on items whose previous tariff suspensions had expired. Beyond these exceptions, attention paid by the major multinationals to individual provisions was more in the nature of minimizing any unforeseen damage such provisions could have on their vast business interests in the future.

Several developments illustrate the extent to which the more "disinterested" private sector actors achieved their objectives in the trade bill where others did not. Most of the examples relate to what was *not* left in the bill, rather than what was. Partway through the Finance-Ways and Means conference, the conferees began to drop virtually all of the explicitly sectoral provisions in the bill. This approach by members to what had come to be considered "special interest protectionist" provisions was later extended to several narrower, but still generic, sections of the bill, including many of the antidumping and countervailing duty measures. On the other hand, on the broader generic provisions, such as those involving Section 201, it was the major business groups rather than a self-styled "pro-trade" coalition of firms—considered by several conferees to simply represent "special interest free-traders"—to whom the members and staff turned for advice on moderating changes. As long as the administration's motivations about the final product were uncertain, the committee leaders realized that they only had the business community in their corner to lend their efforts legitimacy and to demonstrate desire for a bill that could become law.

The only exceptions to this predominantly successful venture of the business community into the trade bill fray came in those instances where its membership became totally focused on one or another provision of the bill to the virtual exclusion of all else. A case in point was the Gephardt amendment. The almost undivided attention of many business groups to this lightning rod during Ways and Means markup, House floor action, and the early days of the Senate Finance markup explains in part why the Senate bill emerged tougher than that out of

Ways and Means, and why several other provisions they eventually opposed got into the House bill in the first place. These included various Ways and Means AD/CVD measures, and several of the non-trade provisions appearing in other parts of the bill.

However, the biggest private sector defeat in the trade bill came in the form of the plant closing provision, both on the Senate floor and eventually in conference. This was attributable to several factors, including the nature of the business groups involved, political considerations beyond their control, a questionable strategy on the Senate floor, and the totally unexpected shift that took place in the public and press perception of the measure as the bill evolved.

The first of these factors, the nature of the groups themselves, relates as much as anything else to the diversity of issues in the omnibus bill. Whereas the bulk of the bill's provisions were tracked, analyzed, and lobbied by international trade experts from each company or group, the plant closing provision fell squarely within the purview of their respective corporate labor relations counterparts—who were vehement and single-minded in their opposition. Moreover, while many of the major corporations involved had vice presidents in charge of industrial relations, few had comparably placed figures in charge of trade. The BRT position on the provision, for example, was one dictated by its industrial relations task force, not its trade task force. An even more complex intra-organizational situation at the National Association of Manufacturers (NAM) ultimately negated any role its trade group was able to play on the rest of the bill. In fact, with the exception of the NAM and, to a lesser extent, the Chamber, it was primarily a small hard core group of individual firms and the administration that did the most lobbying against the provision.[19]

Ironically, by the time the plant closing provision was finally enacted into law in 1988, organized private sector opposition had all but disappeared. This was in part because most of the *Fortune* 500 corporations had either given up or had acknowledged that their union contracts already contained advance notification clauses for plant closing. Fewer had layoff notice clauses, but in general it was mid-sized companies that were not union organized or lacked a notification policy that were most likely to be affected by the provision. The other reason related to consid-

---

[19] During a meeting of Business Roundtable executives in May 1988, held to discuss the anticipated trade bill veto and override votes, serious consideration was given to parting company with the administration and the rest of the business community to work out a deal with labor on plant closing. They ultimately concluded that Senator Kennedy was unlikely to accept any form of compromise, and decided against taking any action.

erations of corporate image, and evidence in editorials and polling data of an increase in popular perception of the plant closing notification language.

Sometime during the course of the spring and early summer of 1988, the public debate over the plant closing provision changed from one about a "labor" issue (defined in the context of management flexibility, labor-management contract disputes, and the appropriate role of government in regulating business practices) to one about "equity." And no one was more surprised by this development than the proponents of the measure themselves.[20]

Agriculture. Compared to industry and relative to most previous congressional debates on trade, the role played by the agricultural community was notably limited. It was clearly not organized to weigh in on issues that might have been of interest to "agriculture" as a whole, as the fragmentation that had characterized this sector's response to declining funding of commodity programs throughout the 1980s continued. The role of farm groups paled, for example, by comparison with their activities in the spring of 1987, when they were pushing for the United States to finance a wheat sale to the Soviets. Instead, several of the individual commodity groups worked their own issues, while the major umbrella organizations lent their names to a handful of trade provisions (such as the main Senate floor amendment on Section 201) but failed to actively lobby them. In spite of the potentially negative implications to U.S. farm interests of AD/CVD provisions, such as that involving resource subsidies should the Europeans add it to their arsenal of agricultural import restrictions, they seemed prepared to let others handle it.

There was, obviously, a handful of exceptions to this general rule: The major commodity groups certainly followed the developments in the agricultural portions of the bill and, for example, supported the expanded Export Enhancement Program and the marketing loan provision in the Senate bill. But they were apparently comfortable letting the Agriculture Committee water down both. The National Pork Producers pushed hard for an AD/CVD provision that would respond to an ITC finding that had earlier denied that pigs and pork were "like" products. And the National Corn Growers' lobbyists (led by Archer-Daniels-Midland and the Renewable Fuels Association) were actively involved in limiting the scope of an import-related ethanol provision.[21]

---

[20] A senior House Education and Labor Committee staffer later remarked that the committee had purposely left its own plant closing measure off H.R. 3 in 1987 for fear it would jeopardize worker adjustment and other programs that the members and unions wanted in the bill.

[21] It is interesting to note that the active support for this provision shown by the Corn

This lack of an active role on the part of most farm interests in moving a bill that could well have had a profound impact on them is not easy to explain. As noted earlier, to some degree it reflected a lack of organization, leadership, and coordination within and between the disparate commodity groups. It may also have reflected the assumption that the bill would eventually go through and that their real stake lay with the Uruguay Round negotiation on agriculture.

By the time the Senate bill reached the floor, the administration had already announced that its negotiating position on agriculture in the Round was the elimination of all subsidies—the long-standing nominal position of most of the groups, but still a very awkward basis on which to rally their membership. Washington representatives of the principal farm organizations realized that should negotiations in the Uruguay Round result in an agreement to dramatically cut back worldwide subsidies, the implementing legislation could in fact be used to rewrite fundamental portions of domestic U.S. farm policy and programs. In essence, the authority provided by the fast-track process allowed for the writing of an entire farm bill that, for the first time ever could be moved without the opportunity for filibuster or amendment. This made their stake in the outcome of the bill potentially much greater than that of other private sector interests, a factor the Washington representatives probably understood but hesitated to discuss in detail with their membership.

Labor. Just as labor perceived industry as an active, single-minded, and unified behemoth on the plant closing provision, industry perceived labor the same way. Both were wrong in their assessments. Commented one Labor Committee staffer about the divergence of views in the labor community, "Labor is only unified the day before the vote!"

As noted, with the exception of the United Steelworkers union, organized labor was initially a reluctant participant in the addition of the plant closing provision to the Senate bill. Right from the start, as evidenced by the AFL-CIO's February 1987 meeting in Bal Harbour, Florida, organized labor considered the omnibus bill a part of its "trade," rather than its "labor-management" issues agenda.[22] Its single most important objective for the bill was the Gephardt amendment or some-

---

Growers is difficult to explain in terms of their direct economic stake in the provision, where the production of ethanol at the time accounted for only 350 million bushels of their annual 7 billion bushel output.

[22] It was at this meeting, for example, that AFL-CIO President Lane Kirkland suggested that the Senate-introduced bill was "a box with no contents."

thing close to it. As one labor leader put it, "Frankly, our attitude is that any bill that the president doesn't veto is not worth passing."[23]

The unions had worked to galvanize their rank-and-file and their politicians to the cause of the trade bill. In February and March 1987, for example, the UAW ran a series of television and radio commercials in Washington D.C. and a few other cities, calling for "an effective U.S. trade policy," and demanding "a trade bill with teeth in it." The unions were working for their interests on the bill long before H.R. 3 was introduced. Their principal focus prior to the conference was the Gephardt amendment and, to a lesser but not insignificant degree, worker rights provisions and various funding and training programs for displaced workers. They were less enthusiastic about the congressionally generated TAA provision making training a prerequisite for funds or about the positive adjustment scheme and obligations built into the Senate's Section 201 language. However, on those they were prepared to defer to their supporters on the Ways and Means and Finance Committees who were largely responsible for both.

Yet, in the end the unions found themselves actively advocating the sacrifice of whatever gains they had made on the trade bill in exchange for a political confrontation over plant closing that they fully expected to lose.[24] As with the business groups, this was not a carefully studied decision for most unions. It was more the result of the interplay of a whole series of factors, including inter- and intra-union politics, the rigidity of their positions, and years of confrontation with the Reagan administration and Republicans on the Senate Labor Committee. Together these made negative positions easier to rally around than positive ones.

Both within individual unions and within the AFL-CIO with respect to its affiliate unions and locals, those advocating the "toughest" positions had generally been the victors in internal elections and decision making. Therefore, when it came to plant closing, the group went along with the union and—they presumed—the locals with the most strongly held views on that provision. Moreover, having spent several years focusing on the Gephardt amendment as the be-all and end-all of their trade agenda, when that provision was finally dropped, the unions were

---

[23] Morton Bahr, quoted in Associated Press, "Hill Democrats Pledge AFL-CIO Tough Trade Bill," *Washington Post*, February 17, 1987.

[24] This was certainly the case with respect to the Steelworkers. When asked by a congressman whether he cared that a veto of the omnibus bill with plant closing in it could not be overridden, the union president was reported to have responded, "So be it; the bill isn't worth it without the plants provision."

hard-pressed to explain to their members the provision that had re-placed it—even though several had been directly involved in the drafting process. Part of the reason, suggested one union lobbyist, was that they simply could not explain how, with the end of Gephardt's presidential bid, the Senate "Super 301" language immediately became the ceiling—rather than the floor—of their aspirations for the outcome of the confer-ence. By that point, the plant closing provision was getting more press coverage than any other single issue in the bill and had also taken on major symbolic importance. As the same AFL-CIO representative later commented to Keith Rockwell, a *Journal of Commerce* reporter, "If plants is taken away, we have a very serious problem explaining to our members what is in the bill."

As a general matter, the glass-is-half-full approach was not one orga-nized labor seemed interested in or capable of taking if Republicans were involved in the compromise process. Finally, given the years of bad blood between the unions and the administration, it became appar-ent toward the end that several of the union leaders had convinced themselves that they were better off with the political issue than with any law—regardless of its contents. After all, maybe the next election would bring with it a Democratic president who favored the Gephardt bill. . . .

Organized labor and its congressional boosters had expended a great deal of political capital on two provisions to the virtual exclusion of all others. One became law; one did not. But by the end, most of the congressional actors had decided they wanted a law and were prepared to sacrifice a variety of programs to get it.

Other interests. Various other interests attempted to play a role in the formulation of the omnibus trade bill, with generally limited success. One group of interests was that of foreign government and business entities. Although 1988 was the year when the profile of and backlash against "foreign lobbying" evolved as a significant political issue,[25] for-eign interests experienced a mixed record of success on the trade bill. While most of their efforts were confined to their traditional approach of trying to persuade the executive branch to persuade the Congress, several of the coalitions (combining foreign companies with like-minded importers and retailers) that had been created in response to import-restrictive textile and automobile legislation, attempted to play a more

---

[25] In particular, a great deal was written during the period about the lobbying that took place with respect to the Toshiba/Kongsberg sanctions in the bill. Partly as a re-sult, in October 1988 Congress passed an ethics bill that contained new restrictions on lobbying by former U.S. government officials on behalf of foreign interests.

direct role. Some were involved, for example, in the "pro-trade" group that, as noted earlier, had very little to show for its efforts with respect to Section 201 and other provisions it found objectionable. In fact, the only part of the trade bill where they seemed to make any visible headway was that involving provisions imposing sanctions against Toshiba and Kongsberg, where the most influential opponents were the American companies that considered Toshiba a vital supplier of inputs for their goods. Even then, an extremely strong form of the provision eventually went into law, the lobbying efforts of industry, foreign interests, and the administration notwithstanding.

With respect to foreign governments, the story was pretty much the same—although the EC Commission and a variety of embassies did ratchet up their contacts with the Hill during this period. The head of the EC delegation in Washington, for example, sent Chairman Rostenkowski a detailed letter in March 1987 complaining about multiple provisions in the Ways and Means bill and hinting at mirror legislation or retaliation. A visit by Japanese Prime Minister Nakasone that April also included some discussion of the legislation, but it was generally confined to meetings with executive branch officials and took a back seat to the issue of the administration's semiconductor retaliation. Various written comments on the bill were also received in the 1987–1988 period from the ambassadors of the Association of Southeast Asian Nations (ASEAN) and the embassy of Japan. The Australian embassy lobbied quite heavily against the lamb quota provision. Press statements were issued fairly regularly against the bill in the spring of 1988 by EC, German, French, and Japanese officials.

In July 1987, USTR General Counsel Alan Holmer met with various Washington-based diplomats about the bill and was reported to have suggested, in response to a question, that threats of retaliation "would not be unhelpful."[26] Whether or not they took him at his word, foreign governments had very limited, if any, impact on the outcome of the omnibus bill. At no point was this more evident than at the end of the process, where in spite of their remaining objections to the bill, the United States' trading partners looked on as the administration and

---

[26] Stuart Auerbach, "Other Countries Lobbying Hill," *Washington Post*, July 5, 1987. Obviously, the extent to which foreign positions mirrored those of the administration makes it difficult to differentiate sources of influence. But there was no comparison between foreign influence over the bill and that of either the administration or the U.S. private sector. This was certainly true in comparison to direct Canadian government efforts with respect to implementing legislation for the U.S.-Canada FTA in May 1988. In this case, the Canadian ambassador personally worked several issues in the bill during the course of committee "mock markups," to the point where some members took positions favoring Canada over those of the administration.

the Congress lost themselves in a rabid battle over a solitary *nontrade* issue.

Press and pundits. "Editorial writers who are going to comment on the trade bill should be required to read it first," suggested William Archey of the U.S. Chamber in an interview with the *New York Times*.[27] "If supermarket tabloids were business publications, one can imagine a headline that says 'Trade Bill Eats Baby.' " Of the 386 editorials appearing in the *Washington Post, New York Times,* and *The Wall Street Journal* on international trade and related issues in the two years between October 1986 and September 1988, a quarter involved omnibus trade legislation. Of these, the *Post* issued forty-two editorial opinions about the bill compared with twenty-nine by the *Times* and twenty-three by *The Wall Street Journal,* with an average of 25 percent favorable and 69 percent unfavorable editorial "ratings." There were marked differences, however, in the treatment among papers, and some shifts in editorial opinion were evident with the passage of time. In contrast to the *Post*'s 38 percent positive/55 percent negative and the *Time*'s 24 percent positive/65 percent negative ratings, 100 percent of all *The Wall Street Journal* editorials on the bill were negative. With regard to shifts in editorial opinion over time, the 16 percent positive/74 percent negative assessments of the bill prior to conference had, by the end of the conference, become a 37/60 percent split.[28]

Favored topics in articles and editorials during the course of the bill's initial evolution were executive/legislative branch fights, "protectionist" amendments, and "special interest" provisions (including the tariff suspension bills). Throughout the House-Senate conference, press tracking of developments, primarily through editorial commentary, mainly addressed key substantive provisions. Principal targets of negative editorials were the Gephardt language, sugar duty drawback, the Bryant amendment, and—until summer 1988—plant closing, along with various provisions related to ethanol, Section 201, windfall profits, and AD/CVD law changes.

Particularly active was the *Washington Post,* whose editorial writer, John W. Anderson, probably paid far more attention to issues in the

[27] Susan F. Rasky, "Stock Fall May Affect Trade Bill," *New York Times,* October 30, 1987.

[28] Susan C. Schwab, "Trade and the Media," paper presented at the George Washington University, November 1988. With respect to the *Post,* this shift could be explained in part by the fact that in 95 percent of the cases, the final disposition of the topics it addressed were either consistent with the *Post* editorial position or had at least moved in the paper's direction. Comparable outcome-or-movement percentages for the *Times* and *The Wall Street Journal* were 72 percent and 30 percent, respectively.

House-Senate conference than any member of Congress not directly involved. Conferring with *Post* trade reporter Stuart Auerbach and columnist Hobart Rowen, and calling and being called on by congressional staff, administration officials, and the occasional lobbyist on a specific provision, Anderson developed his own sense of what should and should not stay in the bill. This information he steadily imparted to the public and to the conferees. Launching his series the day after Senate passage of H.R. 3 with an editorial entitled "Time to Trade Up,"[29] he wrote more than a dozen editorials between February 17 and August 5, 1988, tracking progress on the bill. He began with three editorials as the conferees reconvened in February ("Poison Ivy in the Trade Bill," referring to "an abundant growth of poison ivy among the few remaining flowers," "More Poison Ivy," and "Still More Poison Ivy,")[30] that addressed the Gephardt amendment, natural resource subsidies, private right of action, the "scofflaw," and worker rights provisions in the House bill; and lamb quotas, the ESP amendment, mandatory import fees to fund TAA, and the sugar duty drawback provision in the Senate. By the end of the conference in April, he called "The Trade Bill Transformed," criticized the president in May for "An Unwise Veto"—for letting opposition to the plant closing measure take precedence over the bill's negotiating authority—and, in June, following the Senate's failure to override the veto, called on the Congress to "Try Again on Trade."[31]

The Economy

The 1986–1988 period offered some statistical improvement in the U.S. economy with respect to the recession, unemployment, and high dollar earlier in the decade. But it continued to be characterized by latent anxiety among policymakers about both the statistics and the economic policies responsible for them, and came to be totally dominated by the volatility exhibited by the stock market crash in October 1987. While the trade deficit continued to climb through 1987, related developments in the economy that tend to have a more important impact on the politics of trade told a more encouraging story.

Shortly after the 100th Congress convened, the members learned that the U.S. trade deficit for 1986 had reached a record $155 billion, up more than $20 billion from the year before. The deficit continued to climb throughout most of 1987, contrary to the predictions of econo-

---

[29] Editorial, *Washington Post,* July 23, 1987.
[30] Editorials, *Washington Post,* February 17, 21, and 22, 1987.
[31] Ibid., April 4, May 25, and June 10, 1988. By contrast, the May 25, 1988, editorial in the *New York Times* was entitled, "This Trade Bill Deserves to Die."

mists in 1985 that the "*J*-curve" impact of the decline in the relative value of the dollar would have long since been felt. The monthly trade deficit figures fluctuated dramatically throughout 1987. There was, for example, a slight decline in the deficit for the first quarter of 1987 relative to the last quarter of 1986, coinciding with committee action on the bill in the House. On the other hand, the deficits for June and July, the period of Senate floor action on the bill, were found to represent the first and third highest trade deficits, respectively, up to that point in U.S. history. The "honor" of being the largest monthly trade deficit in U.S. history went to the month of October 1987, but was not announced until two months later. By the end of 1987, the U.S. trade deficit had reached an unheard of $170 billion. It began to fall fairly steadily in 1988, and closed the year well short of the records that had been set in 1986 and 1987. By the time the March deficit was announced in May 1988, just as the trade bill was moving through its veto and post-veto stages, for example, it had reached the lowest monthly figure since December 1984.

Yet, in spite of the 1987 trade statistics, at virtually every stage of consideration of the trade bill from January through August 1987, the legislation became less, rather than more protectionist. In fact, long before the stock market crash in October, there was a general sense that in spite of the trade figures, the extreme politics of trade that had characterized the 1985–1986 period were over. This phenomenon can be accounted for by a number of factors, most important among them the steady pace of improvement of other economic statistics and indicators during the same period. The rate of U.S. GNP growth averaged a relatively good 2.5–3.5 percent throughout the 1987–1988 period, in line with that of the previous two years. Even more important was the significant drop in unemployment during the same period. In April 1987, the unemployment rate reached 6.6 percent, the lowest level in seven years; by May it was at 6.3 percent, and shortly after the bill reached the Senate floor in July, a 6.1 percent rate was announced. By 1988, the rate of unemployment had fallen into the 5–6 percent range.

As noted earlier, what did change with the stock market's plunge in October was the nervous attention paid to the announcement of monthly trade figures and, at least for the balance of the year, the trepidation with which politicians approached any modifications of U.S. trade law that might be blamed the next time the market collapsed.

7

CONFERENCE ON A TRADE BILL

All government—indeed, every human benefit and enjoyment, every virtue and every prudent act—is founded on compromise and barter.
—Edmund Burke[1]

PHASE I: GETTING DOWN TO BUSINESS

On the morning of February 17, 1988, Subconference #1 reconvened following nearly a four-month hiatus. From that day until the conference was over, dozens of highly detailed offer-response-counteroffer documents would be exchanged between the two sides. Formal sessions would be rare, as these typed and scrawled papers became the focus of exhaustive (closed) Finance and Ways and Means conferee caucuses, meetings among and between their respective staffers, phone calls across the Capitol and along Pennsylvania Avenue to solidify support for positions, and staff-drafted compromises for the consideration of the members.

It was like starting over, complete with opening statements and two days of staff reviewing the spreadsheets. Rostenkowski announced his plan to divide Subconference #1 topics into "Phase I" and "Phase II," with Phase I matters scheduled to be completed by early March. The first phase would encompass general trade policy, agency, and consultations issues; Section 337 intellectual property rights and Section 232 national security import relief provisions; miscellaneous trade law provisions (including lamb quotas); and controversial tariff and customs law provisions remaining from the October meeting (including the customs fraud scofflaw and sugar duty drawback); and Romanian MFN. Beginning March 7, the conference would turn to Phase II issues, addressing trade-negotiating authority, Section 301, Super 301 and the Gephardt

---

[1] Edmund Burke, "Second Speech on Conciliation with America. The Thirteen Resolutions."

amendment, Section 201 and TAA, antidumping and countervailing duty measures, telecommunications and intellectual property rights provisions, and the proposed repeal of the windfall profits tax.

The approach had been developed by committee staffers Yerxa and Lang as the most practical order in which to have the conferees take up the issues and still leave room for trade-offs across major provisions. By starting with issues considered "doable"—smaller, but not necessarily without controversy—they speculated there was a good chance of making early headway and gathering the momentum needed to tackle the larger issues. Combined with the committees' don't-look-back or a-deal-is-a-deal approach to conferencing—where once closure on an item is achieved it cannot be reopened—the order appeared to offer the best prospect of success.

Rostenkowski had decided the House would make the first offer, so he met with Yerxa and Robert Leonard, the committee's chief counsel, to ponder conference politics and discuss strategy. The House Phase I offer, the chairman concluded, had to be "a big deal." It had to be seen as a "dramatic" step forward for the bill and away from protectionism that would help rally the business community and assist USTR Yeutter in gaining more cooperation from the rest of the administration. He knew the toughest issues were still ahead, but at least his Phase I offer could "get the ball rolling." Rostenkowski and his staff proceeded to accomplish all of the above with a House offer that catapulted the conference process forward in ways not even they had dreamed.

On the afternoon of February 23, the House offer on Phase I was delivered to the Senate, accompanied by a Rostenkowski press statement and background briefing by the Ways and Means staff. In addition to settlements for various noncontroversial items, the House offer proposed to drop almost every controversial provision in the Phase I portions of both House and Senate bills. These included Senate provisions on lamb quotas and private right of action for customs fraud, House customs scofflaw penalties, and identical House-Senate provisions on sugar duty drawback and Romanian MFN. Finance Committee members were stunned, USTR's credibility with other agencies soared, and the press expressed elation. "Fast Start on the Trade Bill," read the *Washington Post* editorial on February 25:

> With one masterful stroke, Rep. Dan Rostenkowski has propelled the House-Senate negotiations on the trade bill to an unexpectedly fast and promising start. He has proposed to the Senate to drop all of the most inflammatory and protectionist sections of the part of the legislation now under discussion.

. . . The Senate conferees are to meet this morning to decide how to respond—whether to join him or to try to defend these attempts to protect specific industries and practices. . . .

Bentsen and the Finance conferees got the message, but were in something of a bind. The House offer was of a type normally considered at the *close* of a conference, not the start, when extraneous material and leftover controversies are occasionally tossed overboard in the rush of waning hours. Instead, they were faced with the options of slowing the process down by arguing each and every item, going along with Ways and Means, or going them one further and picking up the momentum. Whatever they did, they knew the eyes of the press, the administration, and other congressional conferees were upon them and they had a limited time in which to act. They chose to go the House one further. After several hours of closed door deliberations on the morning of February 25, the Finance conferees responded: They accepted virtually all of the House recommendations, including a number they knew the Ways and Means conferees expected them to reject. That offer, too, was made public, leading the *Post* to remark:

> It's astounding. Congressional conferees on the trade bill have now pitched out a long list of flagrantly protectionist provisions that the two houses voted into it last year. Many of the worst and most inflammatory favors to special interests are gone. Disburdened of them, the bill suddenly begins to look less disreputable and a little more like a serious attempt to strengthen trade policy.[2]

The fact that Subconference #1's success with Phase I had generated the only positive media received during the trade bill process to date did not go unnoticed by the congressional leadership, administration, and business community. More to the point, it convinced the bill's most important participants and observers—including the conferees, themselves—that Ways and Means and Finance were serious about writing a law. For the first time it was recognized that the bill could undergo sufficient change to actually render it signable, and that the skeptics and those holding back now did so at the risk of being left behind.

This turning point in the trade bill conference offers insights into the attitudes, motivations, and modes of operation of its principal committee protagonists. Rostenkowski had distributed his proposed Phase I offer to Ways and Means conferees the night before a scheduled caucus in the Capitol. He had, however, called each of his core group members

---

[2] Editorial, "A Good Week's Work," *Washington Post,* February 28, 1988.

in advance to say he had a "bold" offer for the Senate and to ask for their support as early as possible during the caucus. Between these calls and Yerxa's subsequent briefings, Rostenkowski was able to walk into room H-208 of the Capitol the next morning fairly certain he had the votes he needed.

Congressmen Downey, Matsui, Gibbons, and Frenzel launched the caucus by expressing concern about the scofflaw and customs fraud provisions in the bill and support for the chairman's initiative to drop them. This left Russo, Guarini, and Jenkins, who supported the provisions, outnumbered before they even had an chance to make their case. Chairman Peter W. Rodino (D-N.J.), representing the Judiciary Committee on these sections of the bill, then added his support for the draft offer. Rostenkowski, on the very first issue before the caucus, now had a working majority of his conferees who would stay with him for the remainder of the meeting and the rest of the bill.

There followed an abbreviated discussion of other provisions in the proposal, culminating in a brief debate over Romanian MFN. When Crane pointed out that by dropping both House and Senate provisions they were going beyond the scope of conference, Rostenkowski responded that scope would not be an issue. The bill was so big, he reasoned, and was bound to have so many scope problems, that at the end of the conference the Rules Committee would inevitably have to waive the rules for the bill to be taken up on the floor. The Phase I offer was ratified by the Ways and Means conferees almost intact. The scope of conference issue had been aired and set aside early in the process, and the offer was on its way to the Senate.

Bentsen had opened his caucus meeting on the House offer by listing its main points, pointing out that most of what the House had "given up" were Senate provisions, and by noting that the *Washington Post* had really "hung the House offer around the Senate's neck." But as the Finance conferees proceeded through the Ways and Means document, it became clear that they, too, were caught up in the potential engendered by the House offer. On two transfer of authority issues (involving Section 337 and GSP), they sided with the administration and suggested the House recede. On Romanian MFN, they jumped at the offer to drop an amendment that had been imposed on them on the floor. But when the possibility of working out compromise language with USTR on customs fraud was raised, Danforth asked that the issue be deferred pending decisions on lamb and sugar.

Danforth's stated preference was to drop all three provisions because, he contended, if a compromise could be reached on one, it could be reached on three, and then so much for dramatic gestures. So, in quick sequence, the group took up the lamb quota and sugar duty drawback provisions. They were on a roll. Baucus made a brief attempt to justify the lamb quotas, the Finance staff suggested substituting a fast Section 201 case or monitoring provision, and the chairman announced the Senate would recede on lamb with an unspecified amendment to be suggested by staff. On sugar, Moynihan complained that he had been mislead by the provision's private sector authors into assuming it would only be applied prospectively and Bentsen expressed concern about the revenue loss implications. Matsunaga tried to defend it, arguing scope of conference and suggesting a revenue cap. Packwood echoed Danforth's suggestion that all three provisions—customs fraud, lamb, and sugar—be discarded. Bentsen then polled the members on sugar and the provision was summarily dropped by voice vote; the lamb and customs fraud issues were set aside, pending the review of staff-drafted compromises.

The next set of issues pertained to the ITC. Here the Senate accepted the House's proposals, but added entirely new language, proposed by Bentsen, to improve the chances that a former Ways and Means staffer be selected as its next chairman in lieu of an "independent" appointed by the administration to prevent the chairmanship from rotating out of Republican hands.[3] The committee then readily agreed to drop all of the foreign policy trade sanctions that had been added on the Senate floor, with one member reminding his colleagues that they'd been the work of "senators who then voted against the bill anyway."

Returning later that afternoon, the senators addressed the remaining issues: customs fraud, lamb quotas, and a House provision to "reclassify" the import duty on grapefruit juice—effectively raising it from 20 to 35 cents per gallon. Although by this time Senator Heinz's staff and the USTR attorneys had developed a compromise on customs fraud, the members realized that this was a case where the business community was far more concerned about the provision than the administration. Moreover, they once again faced the prospect of adopting "compromise" language on three recognizably unsavory provisions. And so they agreed to drop the grapefruit and customs fraud items entirely. The lamb quota language was left a shadow of its former self, with ITC monitoring of imports and a potential Section 201 case under new expedited procedures for perishable commodities.

---

[3] No two ITC commissioners from the same party can succeed each other in the chairman's position. The committees had become annoyed by several of the Reagan appointees who, the members believed, were using legal or regulatory criteria—extraneous to trade law—to find "no injury" in a disproportionate number of cases. When this provision eventually took effect, the administration left the chairmanship vacant and had its "independent" serve as acting chair until eligible to formally assume the position.

When the Senate response to the House offer was ready, Bentsen went to face the press, announcing he had "met and raised" Ways and Means and calling on other conferees and the administration to take note. When Lang delivered the Senate response to his House counterpart, it was that committee's turn to be taken by surprise. Although Rostenkowski and Gibbons were pleased with the Senate response, a number of House conferees had apparently expected—or at least had hoped—that the Senate would reject the offer on several items. Lang's response to Yerxa: "You pushed a boulder down the hill, it picked up a lot of speed, and then you expect us to stop it halfway?!" Not only had the senators managed to go beyond the House position, they had, in a number of instances, even gone beyond that of the administration, siding with groups in the business community that had earlier sided with them.

The House counteroffer on remaining Phase I issues arrived on Thursday, March 3, including a new proposal on lamb (further weakening of the Senate language), a proposal on ethanol, and a flat rejection of the Senate provision to create an administrative procedure for tariff suspension measures. The Finance conferees met the same day, developed counterproposals on all three and, anticipating the imminent departure of the House for the weekend and a one-week Senate recess, gave Bentsen an open mandate to resolve with Rostenkowski all remaining Phase I issues. Unfortunately, the Ways and Means chairman had not arranged for a comparable mandate and, by 6:15 P.M., found that all his members had gone home or left town. The closeout of Phase I would simply have to wait. It was time to move on to Phase II.

Trade committee members and staff emerged from the Phase I experience, if not elated, then pretty pleased with themselves and optimistic for the bill's future. While some were concerned that the process would now lose momentum, the week ended up contributing a different kind of progress to their endeavors. It was a week of speeches, meetings, and preparations. It was also the week of the Super Tuesday primaries.

The sequence chosen by the chairmen for addressing Phase II issues was a recipe for success from the perspective of the administration and anyone desirous of a signable bill: Each caucus would make the initial offer on the provisions considered most "onerous" in the other's bill. Ways and Means had already transmitted its offer on negotiating authority in the fall; this time it would formulate an offer on the Senate's Section 201 and Trade Adjustment Assistance provisions. The Finance staff used the period to draft proposed Senate responses to the new House offer and to prepare options on the Gephardt amendment, Super 301, and the House antidumping/countervailing duty law changes. The Senate had also insisted on making the first offer on Section 301.

The week was used by various individuals to review the bidding on the bill and to send messages along Pennsylvania Avenue. Wright called a meeting of his subconference chairman for a status assessment. Like a similar meeting in the Senate a week earlier, the session was designed to encourage member "bonding" and to make sure everyone was aware of the progress made in Subconference #1. Rostenkowski spoke at the annual ECAT dinner, reiterating his desire for a bill that the president could sign.[4] And the president closed out the week by devoting both a speech to business executives and his weekly radio address to the trade bill. He characterized Super Tuesday as a victory over protectionism and reiterated his threat to veto any bill that was "antitrade, anticonsumer, antijob and antigrowth." And he made a special point of praising the work of Subconference #1: "We just hope that the rest of the other 16 subconferences will follow the example of flagship subconference number one, and that the flagship subconference will continue this constructive course."

PHASE II: THE HEART OF THE MATTER

The exchanges between conferees on Phase II issues involved a far more plodding process than in Phase I. The issues were more complex and were central to changes in U.S. trade policy and the negotiation of text to effect them. They were also the issues about which the members felt most strongly.

On March 10, the House offer on Section 201 and TAA arrived in the Senate. It was not particularly forthcoming on the Senate's core concepts. While the House was willing to accept a goal of "positive adjustment," Pease and others were still determined that Section 201 remain a vehicle for assisting any industry hit by imports—whether or not it was capable of adjusting. To this end, they proposed that the Senate's "orderly transfer of resources" concept be supplemented by remedies for dislocated workers and impacted communities. They agreed with the Senate's proposed expansion of remedy options, but wanted action to remain largely discretionary by adding a list of considerations falling just short of "national economic interest." And they insisted that adjustment plans and related industry/worker commit-

---

[4] He also used the occasion to suggest that leadership plans for completing the conference and voting on the report by month's end would slip ("if you believe that then you believe pigs can fly.") And he went on to muse: "I get a lot more done with a Republican in the White House. Not because they want me to, though. Presidents want to write history, and I write it for them."

ments be optional. Finally, the House stood by its proposed transfer of presidential authority to the USTR. On TAA, the House tweaked the Senate by refusing to expand eligibility to secondary and oil and gas workers; stuck to its own linkage between TAA benefits and training; and rejected the Senate's mandatory import fee.

When the senators met the following week to develop their counter-offer, they were pleased to learn that "positive adjustment" would be in the final bill. But they faced strong internal differences over the issue of discretion. The debate pitted Chafee and Packwood, who favored more presidential flexibility, against Bentsen and Danforth who did not. While the latter two were less concerned about the nature of the remedy, they were adamant about preventing the president from avoiding action entirely. And so, based on some constructive criticism received from the BRT and ECAT, they set about developing a compromise proposal.

The counteroffer eventually adopted by the Finance conferees made the industry adjustment plan an optional submission, but modified the law in other ways to increase the likelihood that industry would feel compelled to supply one. With respect to presidential discretion, they retained the requirement that the president help facilitate industry ef-forts to achieve positive adjustment, but gave him a wider range of trade and nontrade options from which to chose. This way, they speculated, when they ultimately had to agree to House demands for presidential waivers involving the national economic interest, a president would still find it difficult to meet a "red face test" were he to decide to do nothing at all. They rejected the proposed transfer of 201 authority to the USTR. Finally, they decided to try once again to get the House to focus its definition of "positive adjustment" on competitiveness or the orderly transfer of resources, rather than on relief for dislocation.

The caucus discussion on TAA turned out to be even more heated than the one on Section 201. Bill Brock's absence from the process was a real loss, for they did not trust anyone else in the administration to care enough about TAA to at least *try* for an international agreement on the funding mechanism were it discretionary. And without a funding source, the members were uncomfortable with the revenue implications of their proposals to expand TAA eligibility. While they recognized that the import fee would be an extremely small one, they also realized the improbability of trading partners agreeing to such a move on the part of the United States.

Danforth suggested it was probably worth dropping the mandatory fee if it meant the House and the administration would accept the re-mainder of the Senate's TAA proposal. Moreover, he asserted, it was a "red flag" for those determined to condemn the bill as protectionist.

Packwood agreed, and confirmed that without the fee, the administration would likely buy the rest of the TAA language. It was clear that a majority of senators in the room were ready to back away from the fee, but when the chairman asked for a show of hands, he turned out to have two proxies in his. So the Finance response to the House offer reiterated the expansion of TAA eligibility and retained the mandatory fee. It did, however, add compensation authority.

For purposes of this group of caucus meetings, the last issue on which the senators owed a response to the House related to negotiating authority. Having agreed in the fall to extend fast-track authority for nontariff measure agreements, they had left open the issue of proclamation authority for tariff cuts. This issue, they knew, was likely to be Sam Gibbons' and the administration's sine qua non of the entire bill. They expected to give up eventually on the Senate position requiring fast-track treatment of tariff cuts, but figured it was far too early in the process to do so. And when that time came, they were determined to get something in return. By contrast, on the question of approving the Harmonized System under fast track, they opted to go beyond both House and Senate bills and permit the president to proclaim the new tariff schedule outright, effective January 1, 1989.

The Finance conferees then turned to the preparation of their initial offers to the House on Section 301 and related issues, and antidumping/countervailing duty law changes. Section 301 enjoyed the strongest consensus among the members and their objective for this offer was to move the conference forward without giving up on the core concepts that linked the various components and permutations of Section 301 contained in their bill. In particular, they wanted resolution of the issues of self-initiation and presidential discretion to be held back for the endgame. From their perspective, mandatory self-initiation of Section 301 cases, valuation of foreign barriers, and Super 301 were all variations on the themes of setting priorities and acting on them. With respect to mandatory action under Section 301, the members revisited the notion of "mandatory but not compulsory." While they still did not want to create a legal right to retaliation, they felt it necessary to put enough pressure on the executive to force whatever action was most likely to achieve the desired result, that is, elimination of the adverse foreign practice. For the time being, however, an exact formulation eluded them. Finally, on the matter of transfers of authority to USTR, they made a tactical decision to delay moving any closer to the House.

Having therefore decided not to concede much of anything to the House on Section 301 up to that point, the Senate conferees then turned to the laundry lists in both bills of actionable practices. This was the section on which they would base their own dramatic proposal. In 1984 the Senate had initiated the move toward adding ever more and ever more specific lists of actionable causes to Section 301. Now, they concluded, what they had really done was to undermine their ability to highlight true priorities. And so, they proposed to delete several of the more questionable causes from both bills and to drop entirely all remaining new—as well as all *existing*—causes from the statute, substituting instead detailed report language. They recognized the proposal was one beyond even the administration's wildest dreams, but decided to go ahead anyway. Commented one senator ruefully, "They'll run with anything that's loose and then come back for more."

The next group of issues, the more targeted or sectoral approaches to Section 301-type activities, were easy for the Senate conferees to resolve: On Gephardt versus Super 301, the members opted for a touch of drama as they formally voice voted a unanimous "House recedes." On the stand-alone process for intellectual property rights, the Senate also decided on its own version of the language. And on telecommunications trade, the members agreed to an ad referendum deal on what would later become known as Section 1377. Developed by staff representing Danforth, Matsui, Ways and Means, and USTR, the provision combined the concepts of reciprocity, comparative advantage, and measurable results, and cross-referenced whatever would eventually be agreed with respect to mandatory action under Section 301. It was a provision that Ways and Means had been anxious to resolve at the staff level, so as to avoid a formal meeting of conferees that included House Energy and Commerce. By working out a deal and having it put forward as a Senate offer, Ways and Means could both avoid such a meeting and let the Senate propose dropping language likely to involve the other committee in the statute's implementation. For Finance, the arrangement was a timesaving device and something important to "give" to its House counterpart—namely, the preservation of jurisdiction.

With respect to changes in the antidumping/countervailing duty laws, the senators opted for a Phase I-type approach. They began with the ESP amendment. It had become the single most controversial AD/CVD provision in the Senate bill, and Moynihan read his colleagues the editorials in the *New York Times* and *Washington Post* to prove it. Bentsen asked if they might retain the provision as a bargaining chip and drop it later, to which Packwood responded, "The problem is, they'll take it." The rest concurred, and they agreed to "concede" the amendment to the House. Other such decisions followed, with Finance opting to move the bill fairly steadily in the direction of the administration on AD/CVD matters. A standard of GATT-consistency became its principal criterion for decision and since the committee let USTR and Commerce staff make most of the calls, the Senate offer on AD/CVD issues that was sent to the House on March 15, contained a great many more "House recedes" than "Senate recedes" notations.

When Ways and Means took up the various Senate offers and counteroffers on March 17, they were not particularly well received. Rufus Yerxa began by running through the Senate's proposals for Section 301, which generated a more heated discussion than any other set of proposals from the Senate to date. Guarini was perturbed that the Senate had not yet acquiesced in the full transfer of authority. Pease and several others were furious with the Senate proposal to move all causes of action to report language. And Gephardt wanted to explore differences between his amendment and Super 301, rather than having the debate framed by the Senate as an either-or proposition. Downey reminded his colleagues that they had set the precedent of dropping provisions in both bills, and he urged they at least consider the Senate proposal. Matsui agreed. Meanwhile, he suggested, why not go ahead and accept the telecommunications provisions pending approval by House Energy and Commerce.

When asked by the committee to comment on the Senate proposal, Alan Holmer suggested the administration would not be adverse to setting aside Super 301 until it had a better sense of the outcome of the related Section 301 provisions. On other issues, Holmer's willingness to increasingly assess provisions as something he thought the executive could "live with," was taken as a signal that USTR was becoming progressively more engaged. While this pleased the conferees, they were still plagued by two problems that the USTR officials were unable to address. The first was the extent to which USTR would actually be in a position to pass judgment. The second was the indeterminate number of times such live-with provisions could be worked out without their cumulative effect tipping the scales against the bill as a whole.

On March 22, the House conferees concluded and transmitted to the Senate their response to the offers on Section 301, intellectual property rights, and telecommunications. It was joined the following day by their responses on AD/CVD law modifications, Section 201, and the windfall profits tax. The responses also came with a message: Chairman Rostenkowski was reconvening Subconference #1 beginning the afternoon of Tuesday, March 29, on all remaining Phase II issues; he anticipated the meetings would last the balance of the week and into the evenings until the conference was completed. The House had begun to draw the parameters for the endgame. There would be no further written House offers, and any Senate responses from that point on would be presented at the formal meeting. For both sides it also meant starting to isolate those fundamental issues they wanted to defer until the closing hours.

The latest written House proposals reflected a negotiating stance that anticipated the hard bargaining ahead. On Section 301, the House response employed lots of "Senate recedes," including those on the key issues of initiation and discretion. On the Gephardt language and Super 301, the House counteroffer read "House defers response to Senate offer until basic Section 301 issues are resolved." The Senate proposal to transfer to report language all specific causes of action under Section 301 met with an even less enthusiastic response. Here Ways and Means proposed to leave all but one of the causes in the current law intact, and to add to the statute only those new causes appearing in both bills, namely targeting, worker rights, and anticompetitive practices, all of which were to appear in the definition of "unreasonable" and receive more discretionary treatment.

In its offer on Section 201, the House had pretty much held its ground on major outstanding issues. Finally, with respect to AD/CVD law changes, the House moved toward the Senate positions on non-market economy dumping, accepted Senate offers to recede on its own provisions, and threw in several "Senate recedes with amendments" accompanied by alternative formulations of draft language. Anything they really cared about, the House conferees had obviously concluded, did not yet belong on the negotiating table.

The Senate staffers met to go through all remaining issues the day before the next Finance caucus. They attempted to divide the issues into House counteroffers that were acceptable or could be worked out at staff level and those still reflecting clear policy differences or negotiating leverage. When the senators reconvened, they went along with many of the recommendations, but moved a number of Section 201 and 301 issues from the "compromise or concede" column into that of "defer." For them, the bottom-line issues remained the ones involving presidential discretion, both with respect to the criteria for forcing action and the nature of the action itself, whether the subject was retaliation against foreign barriers or the granting of relief from imports. Moreover, having concluded that the House had held back on its AD/CVD offer, the senators also decided to hold back on the TAA import fee, mandatory self-initiation under Section 301, the remaining transfers of authority, and a handful of items they now assumed Ways and Means opposed more for jurisdictional than substantive reasons. "Let me take [them] into conference," Bentsen asked of his colleagues, and they readily agreed.

Subconference #1 reconvened the afternoon of March 29. Its last formal meeting in mid-February had taken place on the House side and, as was the custom, it was the Senate's turn to host the event. The meeting started 40 minutes late due to votes in both chambers and the conference room in the Hart Building was packed with staff, lobbyists, reporters, and klieg lights. Rostenkowski, Bentsen, and Yeutter all offered introductory remarks and stressed the need for cooperation and compromise. Even then, commented Rostenkowski, it might still take a "miracle" to work out all remaining differences. There followed a rundown of those differences and staff recommendations to resolve a few. The House conferees offered to accept the recommendations on the spot; the Senate conferees wanted to caucus. And so the public meeting was recessed less than an hour after it had started and the committees retired to separate rooms to resume the offer-response process.

Back at the Finance Committee "Exec room," the Senate conferees quickly accepted the staff proposals and settled down to wait for their next set of instructions, treated to a history of the International Labor Organization (ILO) by Senator Moynihan. They had not yet emerged from the Treaty of Versailles when the call came from the House. The Senate was to prepare final offers on telecommunications and intellectual property rights; the House would be making a new offer on TAA and AD/CVD issues.

In the twenty-four hours that followed, the conferees would meet four more times to exchange offers and counteroffers and then disappear into their respective caucuses to consider and formulate responses. During that period, all remaining intellectual property rights and telecommunications issues were resolved and the deals were closed. TAA negotiations were, however, at a standstill, primarily over the link between program expansions and the import fee. This prompted the chairmen to put Senator Roth, Rep. Pease, and the administration together in a room to see what, if anything, they could work out.

It was with respect to the antidumping and countervailing duty law sections of the bill, however, that the most significant progress was made. This was attributable to Rostenkowski's commitment to move the bill in a more signable direction and to the control he and his core group were able to exert over House positions. As the tense and often-bitter dialogue among House conferees progressed, the chairman and his allies forced through more moderate language on anticircumvention. Over carry-out pizza that evening, they agreed to drop cross-statute cumulation language that would have allowed the combining of antidumping and countervailing duty injury assessments. By the afternoon of March 30, they had managed to resolve the bulk of outstanding

AD/CVD issues, including those involving the treatment of multiple offenders and downstream product monitoring. Even with Gephardt's proxy in hand, Russo, Guarini, and Jenkins had been consistently outnumbered.

Late that afternoon, Rostenkowski asked the Senate to make a final offer on all outstanding issues. The senators returned two hours later to present their conclusions to the House. By now the only decisions left to be made were the big ones. The offer-response process had succeeded in progressively narrowing the issues to those where positions were so strongly felt that compromise was either out of the question or would be left up to the two chairman at closeout. It was, therefore, in this context that Finance had come up with its offer: The members refused to budge on Super 301 or their pivotal Section 201 and 301 issues. They conceded on all remaining Ways and Means jurisdictional concerns, as well as on Section 301-related provisions involving mandatory self-initiation of cases and detailed annual valuation of foreign barriers.

The conference session on the Senate offer lasted less than half an hour. Yeutter roundly criticized its Section 201 offer as an "entitlement" to protection, and House members appeared generally disgusted with the whole package.[5] Throughout the day's proceedings, the congressmen had grown increasingly adamant that it was long past time for the *Senate* to make big concessions to the administration on Section 201 and 301 provisions; after all, they reasoned, the *House* had already done so on AD/CVD matters. Commented Rostenkowski, it was probably also long past time to break for the night.

Thursday, March 31, 1988, was the last day before the Easter recess. It was also Congress' latest self-imposed deadline for finalizing the conference on H.R. 3. That guaranteed another long day of short tempers. Rostenkowski made sure everyone knew he had a plane to catch at 7:00 P.M. that evening. It was a standard negotiating tactic, but because everyone was anxious to finish up, it was one of the few not to raise hackles. The Ways and Means conferees got down to business early and made two fundamental decisions. One they shared with the Senate later that morning; the other, they did not. On Section 201, the House agreed to go along with a modified version of the Finance Committee's standard of discretion. The proposal read:

> The USTR shall take all appropriate and feasible action within his power which he determines will facilitate efforts by the domestic industry to make

---

[5] "Furious" was, in fact, the term used by House staffers later to describe member response once their caucus had reconvened.

a positive adjustment and will provide greater economic and social benefits than costs.

Ways and Means then accepted all of the "Senate recedes" from the previous night's offer, made a handful of other suggestions on Section 201, and stood its ground on all major negotiating authority and Section 301 issues. On the Gephardt versus Super 301 issue, the House counteroffer to the Senate simply read "Open." In fact, the second major decision the conferees had made was to drop the Gephardt amendment. At the beginning of the caucus that morning, Gephardt and Pease had arrived with a hastily drafted substitute provision. After a brief but heated discussion, it was voted down in a 6–6 tie; Rostenkowski didn't even need to use the two proxies he had obtained, just in case. Still, rather than concede the point to the Senate outright, they decided to give the administration a chance to seek any modifications of Super 301 it could convince the Senate to accept.[6]

The conference reconvened briefly for presentation of the House counteroffer, and the Finance conferees slipped into a small room down the hall from the Ways and Means hearing room to consider it. They were pleased with the House offer on Section 201, agreeing to the standard of discretion and rejecting the transfer of authority that had come with it. They also decided they were ready to accept the latest House proposal defining "positive adjustment," including its specific reference to adjustment by workers. They discussed the possibility of compromising on conditions for GATT accession of state trading regimes, but decided they did not trust the administration not to approve Soviet accession some day without consulting Congress first. And they decided to leave up to Bentsen the two remaining AD/CVD issues, one pertaining to resource subsidies and the other a minor exception to steel import restraints. That left only Section 301 and Super 301.

Moynihan began the caucus dialogue on Super 301 by suggesting they drop the "finger-pointing" approach in the Senate bill, likening it to the "economic primitiveness" of the Gephardt model. Danforth objected, noting that the country-based focus of Super 301 was fundamental to its design and objective. Besides, he asserted, the NTE was already supposed to achieve a more predictable, systematic basis for addressing egregious practices. Bentsen agreed, listing a number of specific Japanese barriers and reminding his colleagues how little the ad hoc approach to such practices had achieved in the past. Moreover,

---

[6] The subtlety of the House offer notwithstanding, their "quiet" decision on the Gephardt amendment was promptly leaked to the press and Senate conferees.

argued Danforth, "pointing at countries" was still healthier than the practice of "simply haranguing them."

When Yeutter and Holmer arrived, they all agreed to assume for purposes of discussion that the issue of mandatory versus discretionary action under Section 301 (and, therefore, Super 301) had been resolved. Then, said Holmer, from the administration's perspective the only two changes needed in Super 301 were to drop "the name calling" through a shift in focus from "bad actors" to one of "bad actions," and to eliminate the provision permitting follow-up committee initiation of Section 301 cases. This was not what the members wanted to hear, particularly those desirous of a Super 301 with sufficient appeal to the unions that they might rethink their positions on other parts of the bill—like plant closing. The discussion quickly deteriorated into a heated exchange:

Danforth: How can you aggregate the value of the barriers and measure your results if you don't do it by country? . . .

Yeutter: We can aggregate now if we want to.

Danforth: Yes, but you don't. In this case you are going to have to bundle the practices and estimate the total.

Yeutter: We're concerned about a potential negative reaction by the markets.

Bentsen: I'm tired of hearing this, and I'm tired of being blamed for Wall Street's problems.

Moynihan (interjecting): You're talking about my people!

Danforth (to USTR): In my opinion, you have come forward with nothing. We want a concerted effort to open markets and your three [including discretion] objections leave us nothing.

Roth: I agree about the name-calling problem. Maybe we could draft something. . . .

Bentsen: I want to make an offer, but want to hold to our present position.

Baucus (to USTR): *You* should tone down *your* rhetoric. You're helping create the problem yourselves by using phrases like "name calling" and "outlaw."

Moynihan (with exaggerated sigh): I guess we're not going to settle this one by voting. . . .

When the USTR officials left a little while later, nothing of substance had been accomplished. So the senators dispersed—a series of votes had been called on the Senate floor, and several members had to rejoin other subconferences where final deals were being hammered out. Those who made it to the 3:00 P.M. presentation of the latest Senate response to the House, however, were greeted by a very angry Chairman Gibbons, who went on at some length about the paucity of the Senate offer and the absence of tariff proclamation authority for trade agreements. It was definitely time for the two committee chairmen to go off and work out a final package.

Shortly after 4:00 P.M., Bentsen, Rostenkowski, and their key trade staffers disappeared into room H-208 of the Capitol. Yeutter and his people soon joined them, but were asked to sit in an adjoining room. For the next three hours, the two chairmen set about finalizing the deal they would take to their members for approval. They had very different styles, but had worked together successfully in the past. Bentsen was firmly engaged in the substance of the trade debate and contents of the bill, and was well placed to defend the Senate positions. He knew what his members could and could not live with, and approached the meeting as might a conservative poker player. Rostenkowski, too, had a good sense of what would or would not be acceptable to the majority of members he would need for approval of the conference report. Unlike Bentsen, however, he had never claimed—nor was he perceived to be— unduly hung up on the substance of the bill. And in his apparently nonchalant approach at the opening of the meeting, he made that clear. But Rostenkowski wanted a law, and as the staff would be reminded later, his particular strength lay in understanding basic human dynamics.

Bentsen began the meeting by articulating the Senate position on each of the outstanding topics. These included Section 301 issues related to discretion, actionable practices, and transfer of authority; Super 301 and Gephardt; transfer of authority under Section 201, auctioned quotas, and the definition of "positive adjustment"; proclamation authority for tariff agreements and the treatment of state trading regimes in GATT; the two outstanding AC/CVD issues; and, he assumed, TAA, since the last he'd heard, the mini-conference was hopelessly dead-locked. The last item on Bentsen's list was repeal of the oil windfall profits tax. "Don't worry," said Rostenkowski, "oil is yours." There was a brief stunned silence—no one, not even Rostenkowski's staff, had expected that one.[7]

---

[7] Rostenkowski had been advised by staff to hold back on the windfall profits concession until he had exacted various commitments from his counterpart. But Rostenkowski

Considering the issues that remained, they moved on rather rapidly from there. On Section 201, Rufus Yerxa described a potential compromise that he and Jeff Lang had discussed some two months earlier. The remedy standard was agreed, the transfer of authority language was dropped, and auctioned quotas became one of the various presidential remedy options. On TAA, the chairmen decided the mandatory fee would go into effect in two years unless the president determined it was not in the national economic interest and the Congress failed to override that decision. TAA as an entitlement was capped, and oil and gas workers were made eligible. The eligibility of secondary workers was made contingent on the fee going into effect.

On the two remaining AD/CVD issues, a report was substituted for one and the other was dropped entirely. On trade agreement authority, the president would receive proclamation authority for tariff cuts up to 50 percent and could seek fast-track approval for any cuts above that level. Proclamation authority would also apply to the elimination of any tariffs already less than 5 percent ad valorem. The state trading regime provision was to be confined to GATT accession by "major" foreign countries. The Gephardt amendment was dropped and Super 301 was adopted. In the process, they also discarded the provision providing for committee-initiated cases and added a handful of modifications that had finally been worked out late that afternoon by Danforth, Yeutter, and their respective staffs.[8]

The final—and by far the most difficult—set of issues the two chairmen had to resolve related to Section 301. The Senate was prepared to go along with the House transfer of authority to the USTR. On actionable practices, it was willing to add new "unreasonable" causes appearing in both bills and to leave causes in current law intact, if the House would accept the Senate language on worker rights. The real problem was, had always been, and remained the issue of mandatory versus discretionary action. And now whatever formulation they

---

went with his instincts and, as one staffer commented later, "Rostenkowski knew Bentsen was a gentleman; and a gentleman always pays a debt."

[8] Shortly before the chairmen were to meet, Danforth had returned to the Longworth Building to see if he and Yeutter could somehow resolve the "finger-pointing" issue. Retaining the same definitions and measures in the original bill, the staff came up with a formulation whereby "trade liberalization priorities," including both "priority practices" and "priority foreign countries," would be the subject of the program's investigations. Changes applicable to regular Section 301 provisions were left to the chairmen. The decision to drop the committee-initiated 301 process had wisely not been raised again by the executive, but had been suggested and agreed by the members in the interest of avoiding a barrage of requests for formal committee intervention.

adopted would not only apply to regular Section 301 cases, but also to the host of new 301-based provisions applying to intellectual property, telecommunications, and Super 301.

Ultimately, for "unreasonable" and "discriminatory" cases they agreed to retain the discretionary House language that reflected existing law. In view of the new actionable causes, however, they also added report language to enhance the USTR's ability to avoid initiating cases that made little sense:

> In "unreasonable" cases there is a presumption that the USTR would take action on such cases where it has a reasonable indication that such action will be effective in changing the foreign country's practice or barriers.

With respect to trade agreement violations and "unjustifiable" cases, however, they finally had to define the waivers in "mandatory but waivable." To this end, three House exceptions to mandatory action were adopted: a contrary GATT ruling, elimination of the practice, or provision of compensation. The House exception for "national economic interest" was dropped and two new waivers were added. The first was the threat of harm to the U.S. national security. The second waiver, drafted by Lang for Bentsen, read as follows:

> . . . in extraordinary cases, where action would have an adverse impact on the U.S. economy substantially out of proportion to the benefits of the action, taking into account the impact of not acting on the credibility of Section 301.

When the last deal had been cut, the USTR and his staff were invited back into the room. Yeutter expressed reservations about several of the provisions, but was particularly negative about the Section 301 "extraordinary cases" waiver. Bentsen was adamant. In fact, Lang's original draft had read "greatly out of proportion"; Bentsen had scratched out "greatly" and had penciled in "substantially." So, when Yeutter objected to the use of "substantially," Bentsen quietly responded, "I wrote that word, Mr. Ambassador." Subconference #1 was over.

It was 8:30 P.M. by the time Rostenkowski sat down with his Ways and Means conferees to debrief them on the agreement, and a number proved extremely unhappy with the result. At one extreme, Gephardt labeled the final product "insufficient"; at the other, Frenzel lambasted it as "protectionist." Russo and Duncan were unhappy about the outcome of the AD/CVD provisions—the former had wanted more, and the latter had essentially wanted less. Of the fourteen House members, ten ultimately signed the conference agreement for Subconference #1 (Rostenkowski, Gibbons, Downey, Pease, Russo, Guarini, Matsui, Duncan, Archer, and Vander Jagt). Two Democrats (Gephardt and Jenkins) and two Republicans (Frenzel and Crane), did not sign. At 8:55 P.M., Ways and Means called its approval of the package over to the Senate conferees.

Back at the Finance Committee, Bentsen went through each of the items considered by the two chairmen and the manner in which they were settled. A handful of questions were raised, mainly seeking clarification. Then the members voice voted their approval without dissent and broke into a round of applause. A few would have preferred to see more in the deal; several would have liked to see less. All nine Senate conferees agreed to sign the report.

As they were getting ready to leave, Chafee asked if anyone knew what had gone on that day with the rest of the bill. No one did. Packwood speculated that if Subconference #1 were the only conference product, the administration would have surely accepted it. If, however, there were other parts of the bill it disliked, it would certainly be able to identify things in the trade portion it could object to. Although no one mentioned it, all were aware that the plant closing provision had been adopted by the labor issues subconference two days earlier. "Face it," said a Ways and Means staffer later, "if that provision isn't eliminated, the only thing the rest of us are doing is dressing the corpse."

THE OTHER HALF

As Subconference #1 was moving ahead, the other sixteen subconferences and their respective mini-conferences were also making progress. The pace varied from group to group, as did the complexity and controversy surrounding their issues and the willingness of subconference leaders to work with each other and the administration.

Two procedural questions stood out for all participants, however, throughout the conference. Both related to the conference structure and the motivations and control of those theoretically in charge. The first issue was that of closure and what might happen to deadlocked portions of the conference once the main trade part of the bill was complete. The second issue was what, if anything, could or would be done if most of the bill was acceptable to the White House, but the final product of one or more subconferences contained the provision or provisions that would provoke a veto of the entire bill.

The mechanism for dealing with either issue was not entirely clear. Under more normal circumstances, both chambers would have been in a position to vote for deletion of amendments that remained in disagreement when the leadership was ready to proceed with the rest of the bill. The issue was complicated, however, by the approach chosen in the Senate to add S. 1420 to the H.R. 3 vehicle, namely, as a single amendment rather than a series of amendments by title or section. This meant that if there were disagreement on one provision, the entire bill would have to be considered "in disagreement" for purposes of floor votes. The answer was even murkier with respect to options available to deal with veto-provoking provisions. The Senate appointment of conferees had been to the entire conference, rather than to individual subconferences or sections. Had the leadership been inclined to put it to a test, it could have convened the entire group and put individual subconference settlements to a Senate "super-conferee" vote. It turned out that the leadership was not so inclined. Therefore, with no formal mechanism for horse-trading across subconferences, the only option left was one in which a united House-Senate leadership invoked the power of their positions to jawbone the conferees into stripping the bill of such provisions.

All of this was further complicated by the role and attitude of the administration, and as a practical matter, by its difficulty in keeping track of exactly what was going on with respect to individual portions of the bill. "A moving target," complained a USTR official at one of the many interagency meetings held to consider developments in the bill. For the executive, it was hard to draw a line and stick to it when the agencies did not know the precise state of play at any given time. Therefore, had they been inclined to do so, it may well have been impossible for them to alert the leadership during the course of the conference to those provisions moving in a direction likely to prompt a veto of the entire bill.

Whatever the reason, at no point during the conference was the executive branch willing and/or able to offer such a definitive list to congressional leaders, and without such a list, the leadership had little motivation to even consider intervening in subconference deliberations. As a result, everyone was aware that a bill of these proportions guaranteed there would be more than enough for the administration to cite as objectionable if a veto strategy were chosen. It was therefore not surprising that many subconferences closed out with a multitude of provisions the executive found annoying. What was surprising, was the extent to which most of the biggest problems identified by the executive were, in fact, resolved, either to its satisfaction or to a degree where it could "live with" the result.

By the beginning of April, virtually all subconferences had finished their work, with the exception of the mini-conference on the Bryant amendment. The provision in Subconference #1 that turned out to be most objectionable to the administration was that involving TAA. Others, such as transfer of presidential discretion and "mandatory" retaliation under Section 301, rankled but would not have shown up on a veto "short list." With respect to other parts of the bill, the short list of veto items had effectively been narrowed down to the Bryant amendment (were it to be retained), advance notification of plant closing, and Toshiba sanctions. Depending on who was answering the question, the short list also included the agricultural triggered marketing loans, a tripartite competitiveness council, and controls on the export of Alaskan oil.

Opposition to the Bryant amendment on foreign investment disclosure came from various executive branch agencies, the Federal Reserve, and several segments of the private sector. Its principal support came from organized labor, concerned that the growing inflow of foreign capital into production facilities in the United States would bring with it absentee and uncaring management and/or nonunion facilities. These were not the reasons the provision remained in the bill as long as it did, however. That reason lay with the strong and activist support Bryant enjoyed from Speaker Wright and, in conference, from Chairman Dingell. Other House conferees in the mini-conference were not necessarily as strongly committed. Suggested a Republican at one point, most of his colleagues were ready to "take any Senate offer that passes the laugh test."

Once a deal was brokered between Exon and the Treasury Department on the Exon-Florio national security investment language, however, it became clear that the 4–3 Senate margin to drop the Bryant language would hold. Dingell attempted to work out a face-saving compromise for Bryant, but Bryant remained intransigent.

With respect to the plant closing language, it, too, had taken on a life all its own. As Auerbach of the *Washington Post* was later to write, "To business and labor, the plant closing provision took on a symbolic importance far beyond its potential impact, creating a test of labor's ability to get its agenda through a Democratic Congress and big business' ability to stop it."[9] In terms of substantive impact, it was primarily the provision's language on layoffs that would make a difference. As a practical matter, however, that fact was irrelevant because decisions on the provision were by now being made on emotional or political

---

[9] Stuart Auerbach, "On Trade Bill, Game of Chicken Went Too Far: Impasse on Plant Closing Threatens Years of Work," *Washington Post,* April 19, 1988.

grounds, and attempts to seek a compromise had been rejected by both sets of private sector antagonists.

The trade sanctions against Toshiba and Kongsberg were also emotionally driven. In this case the principal proponents were conservative Republicans. Not trusting the administration or the Western allies in COCOM to see that justice was done, they insisted on sanctions that were to be retroactively applied for the 1983–1984 infractions and mandated prospectively for any future violator of COCOM principles.

Senator Jake Garn (R-Utah) was the lead actor for Senate conferees in that subconference. It was a group of conferees from the Senate Banking and House Foreign Affairs Committees known for their extreme differences over export control policy. They had deadlocked over such issues in the past, resulting, on more than one occasion, in presidential authorities for national security export controls to lapse. The four House committees involved in the subconference had narrowly agreed in February to put forward a weaker version of the Senate Toshiba/Kongsberg language. But before the Senate received it, the offer appeared in the Japanese press, infuriating Garn, who vowed to stick with a hard-line approach. Exacerbating the problem was word out of Tokyo on March 22, that the Toshiba executives would receive suspended sentences and $15,000 fines and the vociferous debate that had emerged over foreign lobbying and the former U.S. government officials hired by Toshiba to make its case. Serious questions were also raised about the extent to which U.S. corporate customers of Toshiba semiconductors and parts were objecting to the provision on their own or in response to pressure from their supplier.

As noted earlier, the agricultural marketing loan provision had found its way into the bill due to years of frustration with the United States' inability to persuade the EC to reduce its export subsidies. Its proponents had sought to increase pressure on the executive to act and to increase its leverage in negotiations with the EC. In fact, given the relatively mild form of the provision in the conference report, it was the Department of Agriculture, not the USTR, that perceived a problem.

The limitations on Alaskan oil exports were in the bill for similarly "historical" reasons which, in this case, had little to do with international trade. The regional battle between producers and users of oil over the issue of exports and export bans had been a particularly emotional one since the OPEC oil embargo in the early 1970s, and time had done nothing to dampen each side's strongly held views. The issues were compounded by various shipping regulations and the interests of ports and oil refineries on the continental United States.

Objections raised to the Competitiveness Policy Council, to be made up of representatives of government, industry, and labor, rested more on divergent economic philosophies. Opponents considered it to be a forum for "industrial policy" and at $5 million, a waste of federal funds. But retention of this provision had been almost inevitable: It was in both bills and the subject of its own subconference, comprising one Senate and five House committees. The congressional coauthors were among the conferees. Expecting this group to drop the only provision before it was simply not in the cards.

There had obviously been a great deal of haggling and debate among the conferees, between the conferees and the administration, and within the administration before the most controversial issues had been narrowed down to these key few. Examples of provisions that had had the potential of ending up on the short list of veto items but were ultimately worked out included the Exon-Florio amendment on investment screening for national security purposes, House-passed amendments to the Buy America Act (that Senate conferees and USTR staff had turned into an enforcement mechanism for the GATT Government Procurement Code), and the shipping provisions (that now made action against foreign practices subject to presidential approval). The various controversial finance and debt proposals, including the third world debt facility and reciprocal treatment for primary dealers, were also modified somewhat under strong Treasury Department pressure.

The reasons for conferees accepting these and other changes in the bill that moved it in the direction of the administration varied considerably. As often as not, however, they could be attributed to individual conferees or groups of conferees who simply agreed with the philosophical and policy perspective put forth by the administration and supporting private sector interests. There also was an amorphous concern about what the "super conference" might do to any amendments in disagreement. No one was quite sure how the process would work, but most preferred to modify their language than to find out. Moreover, few subconferences and subconference chairs wanted to be the ones responsible for insisting on the provision that would sink the entire bill.

The decision within the administration to narrow its list of objections to one that could potentially be tackled by the congressional leadership was also difficult to reach. The most important factor was the split between the various agencies, pitting those wanting to work to bring about sufficient change to recommend a presidential signature against those who had already concluded that no amount of work could make the bill salvageable. This divergence of views primarily involved USTR and Commerce on the side of negotiations; OMB, CEA, and the NSC firmly on the other; State generally siding with bill opponents; and

Treasury either uncommitted or leaning toward the trade agencies on issues other than its own. Agriculture and Labor generally favored negotiations, but were lesser players in the debate.

The implications of this split, which was not resolved until after the conference was completed in April, had a confusing impact on signals being sent by the executive to the Congress throughout the conference. It affected decisions on the disclosure of impossibly long versus realistically short lists of objectionable provisions and the ability of officials to offer compromise language (rather than just objections) to conferees. It also resulted in internal debates as to whether to make any specific comments whatsoever that might lead the conferees to believe they could produce a signable bill. Most recognized that without executive input, the need for a veto would become a self-fulfilling prophecy. All of this presented a particular dilemma for Senate Republicans who knew that if the bill were ultimately vetoed, *they* would be expected to provide the margin to sustain that veto. For these conferees, the natural instinct was to try fixing the bill. But if a veto was inevitable, why use the political capital and risk one's integrity with colleagues—just to have to explain in the end you had to vote "no"?

In the absence of clear direction, there evolved a two-tier structure of executive involvement in the conference. Agencies favoring a law harkened back to early presidential declarations of cooperation and embarked on what is commonly known as "freelancing." They held nonmeetings and engaged in phone conversations that never took place, quietly offering suggestions to Hill counterparts they hoped to sustain later on a interagency basis. They sought the support of private sector coalitions to deliver their positions to the Hill. And Baker and Yeutter used their meetings with Senate Republicans to paint a bleak official picture that still offered enough specifics to suggest a possible reconciliation.

On a more official basis, there were administration letters; lots and lots of letters. Some pertained to a single issue; others had multiple lists appended. A great many were signed by what appeared to be the entire Reagan cabinet. Almost all addressed provisions considered objectionable to the executive. Most annoyed the recipients who differed with the positions and were used as ammunition by those who were like-minded. Most contained veto threats of various forms and significance, generally along the lines of "if the final product retains [insert provision] . . . I/we will not be able to recommend that the president sign the bill," or "inclusion of [insert provision] . . . will cause us to recommend Presidential disapproval." The letters (although few of the multi-page attachments) were no doubt read by the cabinet officers who signed them; some were even read by the members to whom they were addressed. Virtually all were designed to get positions—usually drafted and read by staff—on the record.

Throughout the evolution of the bill there had been regular interagency staff-level meetings on its progress and contents. At the subcabinet level meeting of April 1, USTR and Commerce were upbeat in their assessments of the latest accomplishments of the conference, while OMB and CEA, still on a veto track, grudgingly acknowledged there might yet be potential for the settlement of outstanding issues. This was in contrast with a meeting on March 25, where OMB had presented a list of "Major Issues Lost or Being Lost by the Administration," and Yeutter had countered by suggesting it was time to "think of the glass as 80 percent full, not 50 percent empty."

As the dust settled from the last frantic days of the conference and reports of results emerged, a consensus began to develop within the administration around a more manageable list of "bad" provisions. In addition to the six items on the "short list" cited earlier, several agencies continued to object strenuously to the TAA entitlement; various Section 301 provisions (particularly transfer of authority, mandatory retaliation, and worker rights); the "301 clones" (involving Super 301, property rights, procurement, and shipping); the ITC chairmanship language; the debt facility; primary dealer sanctions; and two agricultural issues (that, it turned out later, had actually been resolved).

Those in the administration who were most politically astute, however, were rapidly coming to the conclusion that were their two main concerns—plant closing and the Bryant amendment—eliminated from the bill, there was a very real possibility that a veto could not be sustained over the rest. And so, for the first time, they began to speculate openly among themselves what, if any, potential there might be for working out something with congressional leaders.

On the morning of April 11, Yeutter, James Baker, and several of their key subordinates met in a strategy session. That morning, Baker had appeared on NBC's *Today Show*, carefully moderating his comments about the bill. He avoided a firm veto threat and went out of his way to acknowledge there were "a lot" of provisions that the administration supported. He placed particular emphasis on the plant closing language as a problem, but denied that "Toshiba" rose to the level of "a single issue veto." At the meeting, he and Yeutter agreed that it was probably time to get together with congressional leaders. They had already determined that the plant closing and Bryant provisions had to go. On most other provisions, they expected to have to settle for "whatever we can get," recognizing that no matter what they did, State, Defense, OMB, CEA, and the NSC would probably still recommend a veto.[10] The question they faced was, therefore, if USTR, Treasury, Commerce, Agriculture, and White House Chief of Staff Howard Baker were to recommend that the president sign the bill, would he sign it?

That afternoon, Yeutter and James Baker met with Howard Baker, Ken Duberstein, and Dan Crippen at the White House. Howard Baker agreed that he now needed to get more directly involved. They decided to have a press release issued the next day to signal the president's willingness to engage in a dialogue with Congress over the bill, and to proceed from there to meetings on the Hill. Having both Bakers finally and officially involved was a signal the Congress had been waiting for to show the administration was serious about a signable bill. To date, Howard Baker had only really gotten involved through his staff. James Baker had been active with respect to his own agency's provisions, but had remained detached from the rest of the bill. This was in spite of multiple private requests by members to both asking them to get more engaged. Both were concerned about interfering in the jurisdiction of their cabinet colleagues. More important, however, was their desire to avoid getting "sucked into" the process to the point where they would no longer be assured of a Republican margin to sustain a veto.

On April 12, the White House issued the following release:

> The President has said before that he would like to be able to sign a trade bill that will open markets and improve America's international competitiveness. The 17 subconferences have made notable progress in moving toward such a bill, but further improvements must be made.
>
> The Administration is prepared to continue working with the Congressional leadership and the full Conference on an acceptable bill. As the full Conference moves to complete its work, the President has asked Secretary Baker, Senator Baker and Ambassador Yeutter to make themselves available to resolve the remaining problems.
>
> But, let there be no misunderstanding — the President will not hesitate to veto a trade bill that will hurt America's prosperity.[11]

In the end, however, everything would telescope into a single issue— that of plant closing—as the lines for the last battle were drawn.

---

[10] With respect to the Toshiba language, they decided to leave it up to State and the NSC to work out whatever they could. Under no circumstances would the politics permit even implying a veto over the provision. While they were concerned about a direct intervention on the issue by Japanese Prime Minister Takeshita with President Reagan, when such a message did arrive (citing Toshiba and Super 301), it seems to have made little difference in the outcome.

[11] Office of the Press Secretary, "Statement by Marlin Fitzwater, Assistant to the President for Press Relations," The White House, April 12, 1988.

DECISION TO DERAIL

On April 1, press reports and commentaries about the closeout of the trade bill conference began to appear. Reports in the *Washington Post, New York Times,* and *The Wall Street Journal* were principally descriptive, and—reflecting the dearth of official information reporters had before them—often quite vague. The fact that Congress had gone home for the Easter recess, leaving administration officials to put their "spin" on the bill, was also evident. Virtually all reports noted that while many of the more controversial provisions had either been removed or weakened, each cited various contentious provisions remaining. Few reports identified those elements of the bill that were positive.

Following a statement by Presidential Spokesman Marlin Fitzwater on April 1, a number of the papers then followed up by stressing a "veto threat" theme. Differences began to develop, however, in the direction being taken by their respective editorial writers. At one extreme was *The Wall Street Journal* which, in an April 6 editorial entitled "Creature Feature,"[12] managed to employ every negative trade "buzzword" in common usage at the time, including the words "protectionist" and "protectionism" (once each), "Japan bashing" (twice), "Gephardt" or "Son of Gephardt" (three times), with a reference to "Smoot-Hawley" thrown in for good measure. Its principal acknowledgement that the bill had changed at all was contained in the phrase "the Great Congressional Omnibus Trade Bill Conference of 1988 . . . has huffed and puffed and transformed what would have been truly awful into something that is . . . merely bad." This was in sharp contrast to the approach taken by the *Washington Post* in its "Trade Bill Transformed" editorial appearing on April 4. It noted improvements in the bill from the "three-way negotiation among House, Senate and administration," cited the strengths of the bill, and carefully characterized remaining issues in terms of administration objections. Leaving its options open, the editorial concluded, "over the past two months the trade bill has been transformed. It is now beginning to look like legislation that could genuinely serve the national interest."[13]

The press may have come close to finishing its work on the bill; unfortunately for the Hill staffers, they had not. On April 5, Rufus

---

[12] Editorial, "Creature Feature," *The Wall Street Journal,* April 6, 1988.

[13] The *New York Times* editorial, "Still a Bad Trade Bill," was, on balance, negative. Dated April 2, it commended Bentsen and Rostenkowski for their efforts to improve the bill, but suggested that the "main reason for a veto" of the bill in its "current form" was "posturing colleagues [who] still want to 'get tough' with foreigners, especially Japan," and that "the bill [was] smeared with protectionist fingerprints."

Yerxa and Jeff Lang called a meeting of all subconference staffs in the Ways and Means hearing room. As the conference chairman's representative, Yerxa chaired the lengthy discussion that followed on what needed to be accomplished before the bill was ready for the next stage of the deliberative process.

The leadership had asked that the conference results be finalized and filed by April 15. By then, formal drafts of the statutory language had to be completed and submitted to the legislative counsel's office to be melded together and given new section numbers and a unified table of contents. Statement of Managers (conference report) language had to be written and the Congressional Budget Office (CBO) needed to provide the requisite budget assessment for the entire bill. Once everything was written, agreed, and put together, signature sheets for conferees would be distributed.[14] At that point, the House Rules Committee would have to arrange for waiving points of order and the other "technicalities" of proceeding to floor action. It was also agreed that each subconference would write detailed summaries of accomplishments, to let everyone know what, in fact, had ended up in the bill. Finally, each subconference had to ensure that *Congressional Quarterly* reporters were fully briefed on conference report specifics since it was considered the most likely source for others seeking information on the bill.

The staff was aware that regardless of the bill's fate, all of these tasks would have to be completed. They discussed whether executive branch staff should be allowed to review and provide technical comments on the draft text and report language, but decided each subconference could make its own decision. Ways and Means and Finance staffers fully intended to share their drafts with their USTR and Commerce Department counterparts. House Energy and Commerce had never done so before and had no intention of starting now. When the group began to speculate about the treatment of unresolved issues, they were reminded by Lang that Rostenkowski and Bentsen had agreed not to distribute signature sheets until everything in the bill was resolved, one way or another. As to plant closing or any other provision that could turn out to be a veto item, *these* decisions, they agreed, were clearly "above their pay grade."[15]

---

[14] Four copies of each signature sheet were needed. The convoluted House assignment of conferees meant that over 130 pages of signature sheets would be required; one of the conferees was expected to sign his name eighty times.

[15] Before adjourning, Yerxa suggested they agree on the "short title" for the bill. Someone jokingly raised, and the group promptly discarded, the "Fortress America Act." They opted for the Senate's less cumbersome "Omnibus Trade and Competitiveness Act."

Several small principals meetings were held in advance of the planned meeting between James Baker, Yeutter, and the Finance Committee leadership. On April 11, for example, Yeutter and Danforth met to go through the administration's "short list." They discussed the key decision makers who had to be involved if minor changes were to be made to the Toshiba, marketing loan, and TAA provisions. It was understood that plant closing and the Bryant amendment needed to be out of the bill entirely to avoid a veto. But Danforth cautioned that when they met with Bentsen, the administration needed to sound far more "upbeat" about the bill's prospects, for if they took a "nickel and diming" approach with Bentsen, they were sure to meet with a negative reaction.

When Danforth met alone with Bentsen later that afternoon, he was proven right. While the chairman agreed that the Bryant provision needed to stay out of the bill, he had concluded that the plant closing language had some merit. As to the other issues, Bentsen rhetorically asked, would the executive ever run out of changes it wanted to make? Danforth suggested Bentsen should view the exercise more positively, for with the exception of TAA, all the trade provisions for which they had worked so hard were now considered acceptable. Moreover, he asserted, the remaining problems were extraneous to what they had set out to accomplish. They had known for almost a year that the choice could come down to a trade law that omitted plant closing or a bill with plant closing that never became law.

When the meeting between James Baker, Yeutter, Bentsen, Packwood, and Danforth took place following the White House press release of April 12, the two administration officials struck a positive tone. Before they could begin detailing their short list, however, Bentsen proceeded to read aloud the contents of a list—four pages long—detailing the "concessions" already made by the conferees to the administration. The trade bill could simply not be reopened, he asserted, and any discussion with the leadership would have to be confined to Bryant and plant closing. He had, he said, a meeting scheduled the next morning with Byrd, Wright, and Rostenkowski; could he tell them that if Bryant and plant closing were out that the president would sign the bill? But Baker and Yeutter could not commit. The meeting closed with Bentsen promising to try to sell that formulation to the leaders, but warning that more specific assurances would be needed before any final decisions could be made.

On the morning of April 13, Byrd, Wright, Rostenkowski, and Bentsen got together to decide what to do about the bill. Rostenkowski, Bentsen, and Byrd all agreed that their strong preference was for a law, and acknowledged that the chances of overriding a veto with the plant closing provision in the bill were extremely slim. The same was true for the Bryant amendment, but as far as they were concerned, the provision remained in disagreement and, therefore, was already out of the bill. Wright was not happy about the prospect of losing out completely on Bryant, but finally accepted the inevitable. They all agreed to see if the unions would let them drop plant closing from the trade bill and move it on another vehicle.

At 3:00 that afternoon, they met again in Byrd's office with various union representatives. Byrd had invited the presidents of each union, but only Richard Trumka of the United Mine Workers was able to attend. Lane Kirkland of the AFL-CIO was in hospital, and Owen Bieber of the UAW and Lynn Williams of the Steelworkers were unable or chose not to be there. This meant that the congressional leadership found themselves negotiating primarily with the unions' Washington-based legislative representatives who, no matter how competent or well-meaning, were bound to take a far more cautious and hard-line position than might their bosses.

The congressional leaders tried to point out the reasons why labor should be pleased with the trade bill with or without the plant closing provision. Wright read a list of "good things for the working man," and joined his Democratic colleagues in noting that what they were after was a bill signed or otherwise enacted into law. While there were apparently no real objections when they noted that the deadlock on Bryant meant it would have to go, on plant closing they got a very different response. The AFL-CIO representative, for example, suggested that if plant closing were taken out of the bill, the unions would "oppose the bill, but not fight it."[16] But what began as a fairly subdued effort by the leadership to get the unions to endorse splitting the bills in two, ended two-and-a-half hours later in a vociferous argument, with the labor representatives and Senator Kennedy (who had arrived sometime during the meeting) reportedly "stomping" out a back door.

For the four congressional leaders who remained in the room, it had been an exercise in frustration. They had wanted labor to agree to support the bill without plant closing, not to offer acquiescence, and certainly not opposition and an argument. The leaders already felt they were taking something of a risk in pushing for the deletion of plant closing before receiving final confirmation from the White House that the result would be a bill signed into law. But above all, they were angry

---

[16] By this he could either have meant that the unions would not actively work against the bill, or that the trade bill vote would not appear later in the AFL-CIO "key votes" list used to tally member "COPE" (Committee on Political Education) ratings.

with the inflexibility shown by the unions and their Senate colleagues, particularly since they thought they had received assurances that the plant closing language would be dropped were it ultimately to jeopardize the rest of the bill. They left the room with the understanding that they would probably have to force the issue with the union presidents, but agreed not to make a final decision until after meeting the following day with James and Howard Baker. They left the bill, commented a staffer later, "poised somewhere between a signature and certain death."

The meeting between Byrd, Wright, and the two White House representatives was scheduled for 1:30 P.M. on April 14. The issue, however, was pretty much decided before it ever took place. The unions used the eighteen hours between meetings to generate opposition to dropping the plant closing provision among their Democratic allies in the House. Calls were made by several union presidents to various House members to have them put pressure on Wright. The result was what one House observer called "a palace revolt," with House Education and Labor conferees and Democratic members from Michigan (led by Dingell), Ohio, and Wisconsin threatening to walk away from the conference report on the bill.

What was to have been the definitive executive-legislative summit on the omnibus trade bill lasted 20 minutes. It was described by both sides as "amiable." Byrd and Wright explained that they were "thinking of making changes," but they "weren't sure yet." The two Bakers stated that inclusion of either Bryant or plant closing would result in a veto; that without them, other provisions would guarantee a divided cabinet, but that they "expected the president would take [their] recommendation to sign."

When the two administration officials left, it was understood that the next move was up to the Congress. Both had expected to reach an agreement there and then, but speculated that the leaders were not yet ready and had been too embarrassed to cancel the meeting. As they walked out, however, they were optimistic that a deal was imminent. They were mistaken, for the Democratic leadership had pretty much given up on any resolution of plant closing shortly before the meeting. Byrd, in a lengthy telephone conversation with Wright later that afternoon had urged his colleague to call the unions' bluff, but Wright was simply not willing to take the risk. Byrd's decision not to activate the Senate "super conference" for a vote on the provision was presumably made to avoid a public battle among his Democratic chairmen.

Late that afternoon, Byrd called Howard Baker to let him know what to expect. Both Bakers then made calls to alert and begin lining up key

Republicans. "What will you do?" asked James Baker of Danforth. "I'll vote to override," Danforth responded, "but don't worry, it won't be much of a fight. The votes just aren't there." Byrd and Wright issued a joint press release announcing their "decision" to retain the plant closing measure in the bill and vowing to go forward for enactment. Bentsen and Byrd cited a sharp and unexpected increase in the trade deficit announced that day and pointed to the 101 point drop in the Dow that had accompanied it as among the reasons for pushing ahead. Rostenkowski issued a curt release, noting the three years that had gone into the bill and making a point he would later reiterate on the floor: "The country deserves better than to have this bill die in a crossfire of competing interest groups."

Journalists who had been tracking the events of the previous days fairly closely attributed the decision to the Democratic leaders' reluctance to take on organized labor. The White House issued a release with its version of what had transpired the following day. After reiterating support for specific items in the bill and citing plant closing and "other non-trade provisions" opposed by the administration, the statement closed with:

> . . . Our negotiators yesterday were encouraged to believe that the plant closing provision would be eliminated. Later, however, we were told that after certain consultations took place they could not remove that provision. The labor unions apparently would sacrifice the entire trade bill for this provision.
> . . . If the bill reaches the President in its present form, the President will veto it.[17]

The developments leading up to what happened with the plant closing provision were tailor-made for the "what if" games often associated with events in policymaking that went one way but could just as easily have gone another. While the weeks following the decision were steeped in bitterness and recriminations, it was evident that virtually everyone involved in the issue—business, labor, and members on both sides of the aisle—regretted the position in which they now found themselves. An analysis by Stuart Auerbach of the *Post* on April 19 probably offered the best summation of what had, in fact, taken place:

> A game of chicken carried too far by the Reagan administration, the Democratic congressional leadership, business and labor may have doomed for this year a trade bill that has elements all sides like. . . .

[17] Office of the Press Secretary, "Statement by Marlin Fitzwater," The White House, April 15, 1988.

There was general agreement that the situation resulted from miscalculations by both the administration and Congress, who spent last week testing each other's limits instead of seeking accommodation.

"THE TRADE BILL IS DEAD; LONG LIVE THE TRADE BILL"[18]

The axioms that "nothing is over until it's over" and "hope springs eternal" represent fundamental truths in the operation of the U.S. Congress. While the congressional apparatus ground through its preparations for passage of what it now knew to be a doomed bill, Byrd, Bentsen, and their respective staffs still explored any and all means to turn enough votes to override the president's veto. Meanwhile, a flurry of quiet conversations were already taking place about the possibility of a second bill—a new "breakout" strategy. Rostenkowski raised the idea with Wright as soon as he realized the way things would break on plant closing, and early on the morning of April 15, it was discussed between USTR, White House, Danforth, and Rostenkowski staff.

The two months that followed were a time of high politics and intense maneuvering, as the administration and the Democratic and Republican leaders in the Congress prepared for the votes on the conference report and the votes to sustain or override the veto they all knew would follow. Some of the tactics employed were common to both parties and both chambers, others tailored to unique circumstances in each. Both sets of antagonists—the Democratic leadership and the administration—galvanized their private sector supporters in business and labor circles to make calls, lobby, write letters, and send telegrams to lock in allies and to persuade the undecided to their way of thinking.

Labor was informed by the Democratic leadership that either it delivered the votes to override the veto, or it could forget the rest of its legislative agenda for the year. Meanwhile, the administration was off promising major business groups that if the veto on the omnibus bill were sustained, there would be a second bill; a promise emphatically denied by the Democratic leadership. It was not, however, the trade portions of the bill, albeit important, that appeared to generate the most intense debate about the prospect of a second bill, it was repeal of the oil windfall profits tax. The American Petroleum Institute (API) was one of the only major business groups not working to oppose H.R. 3, and it influenced a great many votes in both chambers.[19]

---

[18] National Association of Manufacturers Newsletter, *Trade and Industry* VI, no. 4 (June 29, 1988).

[19] The position taken by the petroleum lobby in favor of the bill resulted in an interest-

Party leaders on both sides of the Capitol worked to shore up party discipline, and where necessary to offer sufficient political cover or exert enough political heat to bring their members into line. Party caucuses dwelt on the upcoming presidential election and the need to show solidarity. At a meeting of Senate Republicans on April 25, for example, there was a great deal of discussion about the importance of being "team players" and not weakening the president's position by voting against him. Commented one senator wryly, "and when the team is told to jump over a cliff, we jump over a cliff; once a week we're given another cliff to jump over." Letters were sent by the administration to Republican leaders to distribute to wavering members, including one from the president stating, "I want a trade bill. I will work vigorously to secure one. And I will urge the Leadership to schedule prompt action on a bill immediately after the Congress sustains in forthcoming veto of H.R. 3."

In the Senate, the closeness of previous votes on the bill, the volatility of party discipline on the issues, and the critical role a handful of Republican votes would play in determining the existence of a veto-proof margin for the bill, meant that the battle would be fought one senator at a time. The most obvious targets for pressure from both sides were the original "yes, but . . . " senators, along with the two Alaskans who made it known they would vote whichever way was most likely to stop the oil export ban from ever becoming law. In the end, these Republicans, Senator Proxmire (who opposed the bill's FCPA provisions), and at least two southern Democrats became the focus of all the courting, lobbying, promises, and threats so characteristic of this kind of political guerilla warfare.

The Republicans were called on individually by cabinet members and their Senate leaders; they were taken to the White House to see the president; they were called on by Byrd and Bentsen; and they were offered quiet assurances that, should they vote for the bill, labor would take a low profile in their upcoming Senate races. Oil state senators were told by Democrats there would be no second bill; and they were told by the Republican leadership that either another vehicle would be found for windfall profits or the administration would consider adding it to the Canadian FTA bill. The Democratic leadership even offered the Alaskans—and got through the House—a concurrent resolution making a "technical correction" that deleted the oil export ban in the not-yet-enrolled trade bill. It was blocked in the Senate.

---

ing case of politics making strange bedfellows, to the point where the API and the unions were sharing headcounts and dividing targets for lobbying purposes.

On April 21, after four hours of debate, the House voted overwhelmingly in favor of H.R. 3. The 312–107 vote constituted a 3-to-1 margin of victory, and 23 more votes than the 289 that would be needed to override a veto. All of the Democrats (other than Gephardt and Robert J. Mrazek [D-N.Y.]) and 68 Republicans voted in favor.[20] Although the size of the margin came as a surprise to both sides, the fact that there would be enough votes to override a veto in the House had been expected. By contrast, right up until the vote on the Senate floor, it was unclear whether there would be sufficient votes to portend a veto override. When the vote finally occurred on April 27—coming, the *Congressional Quarterly* noted "after four days of leisurely debate and intense, behind-the-scenes politicking"[21]—the bill's proponents were not surprised to find themselves three votes short of the number needed and fading fast. The vote was 63–36 in favor of H.R. 3, with all Democrats but Proxmire and eleven Republicans voting for.[22]

Under the circumstances, the debate was remarkably subdued. Bentsen, in his closing remarks on the bill immediately prior to the vote, addressed the question of a second bill. Without denying the possibility entirely, he made sure his colleagues understood why the odds were against it:

> My concern is that this trade bill is not a Phoenix that is going to rise suddenly from the ashes, pure in form.
> . . . For those who think we will automatically have a new bill, that is not the way it is. All those amendments that were offered before can be offered again. . . . The House can have a closed rule, but that is not the case here under our rules. The fight would have to be taken up again. The weeks and weeks we spent on the floor of the Senate and the months and months we

---

[20] The *Congressional Quarterly* attributed the unexpectedly wide margin to oil, textile, and labor interests favoring the bill, and to lack of party discipline in the Republican ranks. Earlier the House had voted 340–61 for a rule waiving all points of order against the conference report. It had also voted 167–253 against a Michel motion to recommit the report with instructions to report it back without the plant closing language. This move was later credited as enabling those in both parties who objected to the language to cast a symbolic vote against it, and then turn around and vote in favor of the omnibus bill. Elizabeth Wehr, "Congress May Yet Send Reagan A Veto-Proof Trade Measure," *Congressional Quarterly*, April 23, 1988, 1059.

[21] Wehr, "Trade Bill Passes Senate, Heads for Certain Veto," *Congressional Quarterly*, April 30, 1988, 1131.

[22] At least one (and possibly more) of the Republicans who voted for the bill were prepared, if necessary, to vote on the other side. This included one who delayed casting his "yea" vote until the leadership signaled that it had the 34 votes it needed. Of Republicans on the Finance Committee, 6 of 9 had voted for the bill.

spent in conference negotiating out the differences, those are the choices. That is what we face again.[23]

But with the vote concluded, Danforth returned to the floor. The Democratic leadership might have wanted to see through the override ride votes before declaring the bill dead, but Danforth had other ideas:

> Mr. President. . . . Is it possible for there to be a second bill? . . .
>
> It is partly up to the administration. What will the veto message look like? If the veto message focuses on plant closing, and maybe the Alaskan oil issue—a very short list—I think that would be a very encouraging sign from the administration. If, on the other hand, the administration has a very long list of all the complaints anybody can think of . . . that clearly would be a sign to the Congress that the administration is not serious about trade legislation this year.
>
> Similarly, the question . . . is partly up to the leadership of the Congress. Are our friends on the other side of the aisle willing to press forward with a bill that does not have the plant-closing provision in it? Do they want a trade bill passed this year or do they not? All of us are politicians, and I understand the value some may see in having this bill as a political issue rather than as the law of the land. But that is a question that will have to be asked on the other side of the aisle.[24]

Back at the other end of Pennsylvania Avenue, the debate was just beginning about the nature of the president's veto message. State and CEA fought for the "long list" version of the message backed, ironically, by Senate Republicans concerned about voting to sustain a veto solely on the basis of an increasingly popular plant closing provision. Baker, Baker, and Yeutter, while accepting the need for some cover on the override vote, still pushed for the "short list" version of the message so as to improve the chances of a second bill.

By the time H.R. 3 arrived at the White House on Friday, May 13, the timing and content of the veto message were still in doubt. Although breakout strategy proponents realized that every day that passed moved them and a crowded Senate calendar that much closer to the politically charged election season, it was a battle they were willing to fight. When the veto message was finally issued on the morning of May 24, it was characterized by a conciliatory tone, stressed the positive trade provisions of the bill, and concluded with "I urge prompt action on a second bill immediately after the Congress sustains my veto." Moreover, with

---

[23] Congress, *Congressional Record* (22 April 1988), S4545.
[24] Ibid., S4927.

respect to the plant closing language, it "encourage[d] the Congress in any subsequent trade bill to include a program that provides incentives for such notice."[25] While four provisions in addition to plant closing and the Alaskan oil issue were cited as rationale for the veto, they did not include provisions, such as the Toshiba sanctions or triggered marketing loans that were in fact still considered serious veto items by several agencies.[26]

The vote to override followed shortly thereafter in the House, with 308 voting to override and 113 voting against. When the Senate took up the issue on June 3, there were 61 "yeas" to 37 "nays," sustaining the president's veto by a comfortable margin.[27]

But the Democratic leaders in both chambers had, by that time, also decided that they wanted a law—two laws, if they could arrange it. The leaders felt they had gotten whatever political mileage they could out of the president's veto of H.R. 3, with polling data showing that a vast majority of Americans now favored the plant closing provision. Now they were concerned that the trade issue itself could be turned against them by Republicans claiming the Democrats had sacrificed the bill to "special interests." Moreover, they were hearing regularly from members of their own party who still wanted to see their provisions enacted into law. The leadership decided to try a two-bill strategy, beginning with a stand-alone plant closing measure. Once that got through the Senate and was enacted into law, the president would then receive the rest of the omnibus bill, *provided* that it could be moved quickly through the Senate and that no amendments would be added that would necessitate another conference. It was a risky strategy but was, as a practical matter, the only option they had left once the decision was made to try for both bills.

To improve the chances that the strategy would succeed, its Democratic architects in the Senate knew they had to convince organized

---

[25] Congress, House, "Omnibus Trade and Competitiveness Act of 1988—Veto Message from the President of the United States (H. Doc. No. 100–200)," *Congressional Record* (May 24, 1988), vol. 134, no. 74, H3531.

[26] The four other issues cited in the message were "industrial policy planning" through the competitiveness council, "a new centralized international institution to arrange the forgiveness of billions of dollars of debt," "expanded ethanol imports that could harm U.S. grain producers," and an "amendment to the Trading with the Enemy Act that prevents the President from moving swiftly to block blatant enemy propaganda material from entering the United States."

[27] With two members who probably would have voted for the override absent that day, only thirty-three votes were needed to sustain the veto. One of the votes to sustain had, however, been cast by Byrd to give himself the option of moving to reconsider the vote at a later date had a senator changed his/her mind.

labor. Bentsen took the lead, as his and Riegle's staff reviewed previous vote counts on plant closing and on the remainder of the bill to show that while they could not be enacted together, each enjoyed sufficient support to be enacted separately. Above all, they wanted to ensure that once the omnibus bill was taken up again in the Senate that it would be treated by the majority of members more like a conference report than original text—namely, immune from amendments. Bentsen and his colleagues were convinced the strategy could work, and while James Baker expressed some skepticism, he and his White House colleagues agreed to give it a try.

The day after the Senate voted to sustain the veto, the president made calls to several key senators, pledging to work with them on a second trade bill. By early the following week, Packwood and Danforth were on the Senate floor with clipboards collecting cosponsors. Wright held a press conference on June 15 to announce his intention to proceed, following the enthusiastic endorsement of the plan at a caucus of his members.[28] The trade bill now appeared on the "must list" for both chambers' pre-adjournment business.

S. 2527, a bill identical to the plant closing provision from the omnibus trade bill, was taken up in the Senate on June 22. A vote to block the motion to proceed to consideration of the bill failed on a vote of 30 yeas and 61 nays. The Senate debated the bill for seven days, adopting several minor clarifying amendments and rejecting all challenges to the provision's fundamentals. Several cloture petitions to limit debate were introduced, with the second vote on cloture passing by a decisive 88–5. The bill was approved by the Senate on a vote of 72–23 shortly thereafter. By then it was July 6. That day, Byrd introduced, on behalf of Senators Bentsen, Danforth, himself, Packwood, and sixty-six others, S. 2613, the Omnibus Trade and Competitiveness Act of 1988, a bill identical to the original, but for the deletion of plant closing and the Alaskan oil export provision. The House had in the meantime introduced H.R. 4848, the same measure, and on July 13 passed both H.R. 4848 (by a vote of 376–45) and S. 2527 on plant closing (by a vote of 286–136).

On August 2, the White House issued a statement by the president, announcing that he would allow the plant closing bill to become law without his signature. That day, the Senate took up consideration of H.R. 4848, lifting it directly from the calendar and bypassing committee

---

[28] No such formal announcement was made in the Senate. The ethics probe that later brought about Wright's resignation was also getting underway at that time, which may have contributed to the high profile he gave this event.

action. The leadership on both sides of the aisle was anxious to move
the bill as quickly as possible and to prevent it from getting bogged
down in amendments and yet another conference. They arrived at a
unanimous consent agreement providing for a maximum of twenty specific amendments and, most important, an agreement that the vote on
final passage would occur no later than 6:00 the following evening. Of
the possible amendments, one dealt with imports of Soviet furskins, five
with ethanol, three were efforts to weaken the bill's provisions on Section 301, five involved striking unspecified "pork provisions," and the
remainder addressed foreign policy-related trade issues or were not specifically identified. When the bill was taken up the following day, only
five of the amendments were, in fact, offered, of which four were rejected and one was withdrawn. When the Senate voted final passage of
H.R. 4848, it was by a margin of 85–11 and without amendment.

On the evening of August 3, almost one year from the date of the first
conference meeting on H.R. 3, the White House issued the following
statement by the president:

> I am pleased the Senate has . . . joined the House by quickly approving—by
> an overwhelming bipartisan vote—a responsible trade bill that includes re-
> peal of the windfall profits tax and many of the elements proposed as part
> of my 1987 competitiveness initiative. While this bill is not perfect—no
> bill 1,128 pages in length ever is—on balance it will strengthen America's
> international competitiveness. The bill therefore merits my approval when it
> reaches my desk.[29]

On August 23, 1988, the Omnibus Trade and Competitiveness Act
of 1988 was signed into law.

---

[29] Office of the Press Secretary, "Statement by the President," The White House,
August 3, 1988.

8

THE END OF AN ERA IN U.S. TRADE POLICY?

Politics is not an exact science.
—Otto von Bismarck[1]

The purpose of this study was to tell a story; a story offering special insights into a trade law and U.S. trade policymaking. Consistent with its underlying "law as a prism" premise, however, it is appropriate to close with a look at the Omnibus Trade and Competitiveness Act in terms of its place in and implications for contemporary U.S. trade policy. Applicable questions include: To what extent did the 1988 act exhibit the qualities that set the second era in U.S. trade policy apart from the first? Was there evidence of new trade policy themes or a reversion to the themes of the past? Was the act an aberration or a portent of things to come?

Just as the historical analysis of the 1988 act required the juxtaposition of its procedural and substantive components, so too does any discussion of trade policy trends. Regardless of one's frame of reference, the Omnibus Trade Act was an unusual piece of legislation. This would be true solely by virtue of its status as a major piece of discretionary legislation that was first vetoed and then enacted almost intact by presidential signature during a single congressional term. When we differentiate between process and substance, however, we find that most of the evidence suggesting a return to pre-1934 themes in U.S. trade policy can be found in the bill's process-related attributes. For example, any number of statistical assessments of the bill would lead one to conclude that something had changed radically since the three-page act of 1934.

---

[1] Otto von Bismarck, Speech to the Prussian Upper Chamber [*Herrenhaus*], December 18, 1863.

The Omnibus Trade Act was over 467 statutory pages in length, of which well over half pertained to trade. This compared to 31 pages making up the 1962 trade act, and 98 and 173 pages, respectively, for the 1974 and 1979 acts. The 1930 act had encompassed some 200 pages, in sharp contrast to a 5-page act in 1816.[2]

Other statistics offer similar comparisons between the first era in U.S. trade policy and the 1988 act. While the 129 amendments added during thirteen days on the Senate floor in 1987 do not begin to approach the 1,112 added during Senate consideration of the Smoot-Hawley Tariff Act, it is still a high figure relative to the 29 amendments added to the Trade Act of 1974 or the 44 amendments added to the Trade and Tariff Act of 1984.[3] Another statistic, cited during consideration of H.R. 3, was that the bill contained "30 new Federal and State agencies, offices, advisory panels, and commissions. . . . [and] between 100 and 165 new reports, studies, reviews." This, too, far exceeded comparable numbers in previous trade laws.[4]

All of these page, amendment, and content statistics certainly provide evidence of the overwhelming amount of material in the 1988 act. They also reflect a trend discussed later involving the proliferation of issues and actors in U.S. trade policy. And they show the exhaustive detail in legislative drafting that has come with enhanced congressional scrutiny and the reassertion of prerogative. These statistics do not, however, say much more about the substance of the law. Nor do they necessarily correspond to the number of provisions that might be considered protectionist, as was the case with virtually all amendments to the Smoot-Hawley Act. Indeed, as the history of the 1988 act shows, several of the Senate floor amendments added more flexibility for the executive branch to keep the U.S. market open than had existed in the underlying bill. Moreover, many of the reports, panels, and reviews were actually added as compromise alternatives to what would otherwise have been action-forcing mandates.

---

[2] Destler, *American Trade Politics*, 2d ed., 95; and Schattschneider, 22. There are several ways to count pages of legislation. For example, the 1988 act also took up over 150 pages in the *Congressional Record* and 1,100 pages of double-spaced legislative text as H.R. 4848.

[3] "Congress Clears Trade Bill on Final Day," *Congressional Quarterly Almanac* 30 (1974): 553–562; Destler, *Making Foreign Economic Policy*, 187; and Congress, Senate, Consideration of Miscellaneous Tariff, Trade, and Customs Matters, H.R. 3398, 98th Cong., 2d sess., *Congressional Record* (September 17–20, 1984), vol. 130, nos. 116–119, D1155, D1163, D1176, and D1187. Senate action on the 1974 and 1984 acts took four days.

[4] Congress, Senate, Statement of Senator Pete Domenici on H.R. 3, *Congressional Record* (April 27, 1988), S4849.

As to the question of whether these statistics reflect a pervasive new trend or an anomalous occurrence, they appear to represent a very real trend. However, this trend is one applicable not just to trade, but to a great many other legislative activities as well, implying a more fundamental shift in the structure of executive-legislative interaction. The same can be said with respect to statistics pertaining to the number of committees and members of Congress involved in the trade bill conference. Here, the advent of government-by-omnibus has occurred in concert with a progressive diffusion of power once concentrated in standing committees of jurisdiction.[5]

Taken together, the process characteristics identified and examined in the context of the 1988 act indicate that important changes have occurred since 1934 in the way Congress writes trade law. While the statistical evidence of these changes could either be interpreted as a throwback to the pre-1930 era or a major acceleration of trends evident since the early 1970s, it tells us little about future U.S. trade policy until considered alongside the substantive law it produced. What *can* be asserted on the basis of the process characteristics alone, however, is that the proliferation of actors and provisions has created a legislative environment far more vulnerable to narrow interests inclined to favor trade protectionism than at any time since Smoot-Hawley.

Substantively, the Omnibus Trade Act of 1988 could be seen to differ from the Reciprocal Trade Agreements Act of 1934 by any number of qualitative and quantitative measures. While the comparison is less extreme when the 1988 act is compared to those of 1984, 1979, 1974, and even to the act of 1962, the number and nature of congressional add-ons in the 1988 act clearly represented a significant acceleration of a trend over all previous post-1934 trade laws.

The 1988 act also marked a slight shift in the balance of control over U.S. trade policy away from the executive and toward the Congress, and a diffusion of control by a market-oriented policy elite to a more complex group of interests. These shifts were evident in both process and substance, including the fact that this was the first major trade law since 1930 to be drafted in the Congress, rather than in the executive. Substantive evidence includes trade decisions made directly by Congress in the bill (such as on Japanese construction and Toshiba sanctions);

---

[5] Stanley Bach of the CRS concluded in 1988 that while the standing committees "remain very influential in shaping the final form of legislation," the nature of conference committees had changed with the growing use of omnibus legislation. He related this to the weakening of the power of seniority in the mid-1970s and the dramatic expansion of committee size. Bach, "Conference Committees: Reflecting Change in Congress," 27–28.

the specificity of changes governing administration of U.S. trade law (involving, for example, causes of action and retaliation under Section 301 and its various clones); and other examples where Congress enhanced its own role in the implementation of U.S. trade policy (including the "reverse" fast track and fast-track extension processes).

Based on these substantive considerations, therefore, it could be argued that were the velocity of change in the 1988 act to continue in future trade laws, there could well be a critical mass beyond which trade-liberalizing agreement authority may not be worth the price. Contributing to this possibility is the fact that major market-opening agreements have become progressively more complex and hard to reach, with a resulting gravitation of policymakers toward minimalist multinational or bilateral and plurilateral agreement solutions.

When it comes to the fundamentals, however, it is evident that the 1988 act was fully consistent with the other trade laws of the second era. Here one need look no further than the conformity of its composition with the "$(X - Y) + Z$" formula of every major U.S. trade law enacted since 1934. It contained relatively expansive trade liberalizing authorities, limits on the use of those authorities, and various congressional quids pro quo. In the absence of an executive branch request for the agreement authority in 1986, Congress was unable to enact its own trade bill. Similarly, had the executive insisted in 1988 that the authority be unfettered by add-ons, it would not have prevailed.

All trade legislation enacted since the 1988 act pursuant to its terms has also been consistent with the formula.[6] This was particularly evident with respect to the commitments and side agreements the Clinton administration found necessary to achieve enactment of the NAFTA in 1993—that were inevitably labeled "pork" by the media. The pitched battles between Congress and the executive over enactment of this law and over the 1991 extension of the fast track, however, still raise questions about the future of the fast-track process and trade-protective cost of trade-liberalizing agreements.[7]

---

[6] Trade measures considered by Congress under the terms of the 1988 act include a 1991 resolution of disapproval of the two-year extension of fast-track authority, and implementing legislation for the NAFTA and the Uruguay Round GATT accords. A brief extension of the 1988 fast track was approved by Congress in 1993 as a stand-alone measure, but it, too, was entirely in keeping with the $(X - Y) + Z$ equation, emerging with its own set of executive branch promises about the NAFTA and Uruguay Round.

[7] In May 1991, the House rejected the resolution disapproving the otherwise automatic two-year extension of fast track by a vote of 231–192; the Senate by a vote of 59–36. The controversy leading up to the vote, as organized labor and environmental groups tried to prevent the use of the fast track to enact the Bush administration's anticipated NAFTA, turned out to be a preview of the 1993 fight over the NAFTA itself.

Ultimately, in judging the add-ons contained in the 1988 act, it is useful to differentiate between action taken or required to be taken in statute and action authorized to be taken by the executive. In some cases, it is also useful to consider the progression of the legislation through the process and the underlying motivation of its authors. It is worth noting, for example, that most of the Section 301-related provisions were motivated by members seeking to open—rather than close—markets, and that the provisions consisted largely of mandates for the executive to exercise more actively *existing* authorities.[8] To the extent the original bills contained increased micromanagement of the AD/CVD laws or restrictive product-specific initiatives, most were either diluted or stripped entirely. And whether intentional or not, the shift in emphasis from import relief to adjustment in Section 201 probably made it an even more difficult means to obtain trade protection.

Considered in this way, a number of the 1988 act's key provisions can be seen to have actually reinforced the principal themes of the post-1934 era. Still, when the issue of balance among the component parts of the formula is raised, a case could be made that the magnitude of "Z" items relative to that of the "X − Y" authorities in the 1988 act exceeded any such ratio in previous trade laws. Here the Section 301 data noted above could be interpreted quite differently—namely, that the number and magnitude of action-forcing statutory triggers and "red-face tests" in the 1988 act could prompt sufficient trade-restrictive action to outweigh any trade-liberalizing impact from implemented agreements. In this case, any final assessment of the act's trade-restrictive "costs" relative to its trade-liberalizing "benefits" must inevitably await experience with the NAFTA and Uruguay Round agreements and the 1988 act's action-forcing mandates.

The fact that neither the NAFTA nor the GATT agreements were enacted prior to the expiration of the original 1988 fast-track authority marked the first time in the history of contemporary U.S. trade policy

---

Although the Clinton administration negotiated new side agreements on labor and the environment, the depth of the controversy, delays in executive branch marshaling of support, and the fact the NAFTA vote became a proxy for various other issues, ultimately required the president to become directly and actively involved in lining up votes. In the end, the House voted 234–200 to approve the measure; the Senate vote was 61–38. It is worth noting that authors of the fast-track extension language in 1988 had not expected it to result in much of a fight, if any at all. But then no one in Congress directly involved in the 1988 act seriously considered the prospect of a NAFTA.

[8] Destler's analysis of the 1988 act in terms of its "free trade" versus "protectionist" characteristics concludes that "the final bill was not so much 'protectionist,' as often claimed, as it was aggressive and unilateralist . . . [with respect to] foreign trade barriers." Destler, "Delegating Trade Policy."

that a major multiyear delegation of trade-liberalizing authority was not used to implement trade agreements. Moreover, as noted earlier, the bruising battle in 1991 to extend the fast track and the temporary extension enacted in 1993 carried with them their own price tags.[9] Recalling the way the formula is constructed, whether or not trade-liberalizing agreements are reached, whether they represent major or minimalist accomplishments, and regardless of whether Congress votes them up or down, the quid pro quo "Zs" in a major trade law become and often remain law in perpetuity.

Having considered both process and substance in the 1988 act, it is safe to rule out a reversion of U.S. trade policy to the Smoot-Hawley era. But this should not preclude speculation that the second and current era in U.S. trade policy may be coming to a close. For this purpose it is necessary to consider both the magnitude of trends evident in the act and whether they reflect variations on existing trade policy themes or significant new underlying forces.

An example of a relatively new trend in U.S. trade policy can be found in the 1988 act's heavy emphasis on action premised on a "negative" rather than a "positive" approach to reciprocity in trade. For the executive, the act offered the potential for trade liberalization through the reciprocal exchange of concessions. By contrast, most in Congress were far more interested in Section 301-type activities that threatened denial of access to the U.S. market as leverage against foreign barriers. Therefore, while both branches embraced market openness in a manner generally consistent with the economic theories of Smith and Ricardo, Congress' approach emphasized strategic concepts more often associated with conflict resolution and game theory.[10]

Whether this trend signals a fundamental change in U.S. trade policy again rests with how the law is administered. In a global trade environment characterized by low tariffs and government intervention, and by trading partners reluctant to make concessions, this approach to

[9] In this regard, it is also worth noting several occasions in the late 1980s and early 1990s, when attempts were made to eliminate the fast-track process through a Senate rules change. Although they failed, such efforts by the maritime industry, and threats by the textile lobby, had the effect of persuading the administration to take the former industry off the negotiating table in the Uruguay Round and to moderate its negotiating stance with respect to the latter.

[10] Examples of works on conflict resolution/game theory that can be readily applied to trade policy include Robert Axelrod, *The Evolution of Cooperation* (New York: Basic Books, 1984); and Thomas Schelling, *The Strategy of Conflict* (Cambridge, Mass.: Harvard University Press, 1960).

reciprocity may in fact make strategic sense. It would, however, guarantee a more activist use of trade policy tools, making the process more prone to misjudgment and an inadvertent spiraling into market closure.

Assuming this proverbial slippery slope is averted, an activist "muddling through" scenario for U.S. trade policy is most likely in the near term. As to the future of U.S. trade policy, consider the following observations to be benchmarks for analyzing developments as they occur:

(1) The proliferation of issues in U.S. trade policy evident during and since passage of the 1988 act may pose the greatest threat to its future direction, if the pursuit of global trade enhancement is consistently undermined or overtaken by other nontrade policy goals. This "square pegs" phenomenon, which became far more pronounced in debates over NAFTA and MFN for China, includes the search for trade solutions to address problems not necessarily caused by trade. It also includes the use of trade tools to promote increasingly diverse U.S. policy objectives. Competitiveness, nonproliferation, human rights, and environmental protection are all important and legitimate policy goals. However, relying on trade tools for their promotion risks relegating trade to afterthought policy status and reducing the potential economic value of new export opportunities to be gained from negotiations. It also raises the specter of such policy objectives being used as a stalking horse by those with protectionist intent.

(2) Policymaker economic philosophy and leadership may be the most important determinants of whether the dominant focus and goal of U.S. trade policy remain global market opening and expanded world trade. As long as key players in the executive and legislative branches of government, in the private sector, and in the media believe international trade offers a positive- rather than zero-sum game, existing U.S. trade law and the way in which it is administered can contribute to trade enhancement. However, even this commitment to market principles could be undermined by the impact of the federal budget deficit on U.S. policy options. In a post-Cold War era where domestic concerns take precedence over foreign policy issues, and where the principal medium of international influence is likely to be economic rather than military, concerns about the deficit could well make denial of access to the U.S. market—perceived as a "no-cost" policy tool—the inevitable tool of first resort for policymakers. At the same time, the budget deficit will make it progressively more difficult to move "costly" market-liberalizing tariff cuts through the legislative process.

(3) In terms of trade politics, the experience of the 1988 act would

lead one to conclude that the efforts of some individuals and groups notwithstanding, trade need not be overtaken by partisan and/or populist motivations: the most partisan issue in the 1988 trade bill was plant closing, a nontrade provision; and generally bipartisan treatment of the bill in conference and in the Senate helped to a consolidate a policy middle ground that held against the fringes in both political parties. This phenomenon was even more evident in the strong bipartisan character of the 1993 vote on NAFTA. Trade has always been an easy target for demagoguery and xenophobia, with protectionism simply the economic manifestation of isolationism. In the absence of bipartisanship, there would almost certainly be a statistical majority in Congress favoring import protection—consisting of a partisan block from one party and just enough members from the other with strong import-sensitive constituencies.

(4) Process characteristics of U.S. trade policy should not automatically be equated with a substantive trade-liberalizing or trade-restrictive motivation or outcome. The length of a trade bill, the number of amendments or side deals generated, and stepped up activity levels need not necessarily equate with trade "protectionism." Congressional activism in the 1980s, for example, often represented efforts to reinforce—rather than to undermine—an executive-led market-oriented trade policy. Process-related characteristics, such as the diffusion of control cited earlier may, however, increase the vulnerability of the policy process to the motives of narrower interest groups, including trade protectionism. The legislative fast track is one of the few processes used by Congress that works in a timely manner and can be counted on to deliver a straight "yes" or "no" vote. The fate of the mechanism and, therefore, of future U.S. trade agreements is of particular concern, since pressure to expand its application to nontrade issues or to dilute traditional trade committee control could eventually translate into its actual or de facto elimination.

(5) Finally, it is worth acknowledging again for the record that legislating on trade, as with other policy endeavors, remains a remarkably human business. In the case of the 1988 act, individual philosophies, personalities, and motivations, along with the leadership capabilities and competence of those at the helm, had a great deal to do with the outcome. Furthermore, in contrast to several of the stereotypical images popularly attributed to Congress, the history of the 1988 act would suggest that members of Congress can be extremely hardworking, are not necessarily led blindly by staff, often seek to contribute to what they perceive to be the greater good, and are not always captive of "special interests."

* * *

It would appear then, that the only development certain to bring with it an end to the current era in U.S. trade policy would be the ascent to control of policymakers who had abandoned a market-oriented trade philosophy. Events signaling this sea change could include congressional rejection of a major trade agreement, a refusal by Congress to grant trade agreement authority, the elimination of the fast-track process, or a president rejecting negotiated solutions in favor of a largely unilateralist approach. Any one of these would likely mean that the post-1934 approach to U.S. trade policy had run its course and that the Omnibus Trade and Competitive Act of 1988 was, indeed, the last of its era. Only when Congress and the executive next come together to forge a major new trade law, however, will we know for sure.

BIBLIOGRAPHY

BOOKS AND ARTICLES

Aberbach, Joel D., Robert D. Putnam, and Bert A. Rockman. *Bureaucrats & Politicians in Western Democracies*. Cambridge, Mass.: Harvard University Press, 1981.

Adams, William, and Fay Schreibman, eds. *Television Network News: Issues in Content Research*. Washington, D.C.: George Washington University, 1978.

Ahearn, Raymond J., and Alfred Reifman. "Trade Policymaking in Congress." In *NBER Conference Report: Recent Issues and Initiatives in U.S. Trade Policy*, ed. Robert E. Baldwin. Cambridge, Mass.: National Bureau of Economic Research, 1984.

————. "U.S. Trade Policy: Congress Sends a Message." In *NBER Conference Report: Current U.S. Trade Policy: Analysis, Agenda and Administration*, eds. Robert E. Baldwin and J. David Richardson. Cambridge, Mass.: National Bureau of Economic Research, 1986.

————. "Trade Legislation in 1987: Congress Takes Charge." In *NBER Conference Report: Issues in the Uruguay Round*, eds. Robert E. Baldwin and J. David Richardson. Cambridge, Mass.: National Bureau of Economic Research, 1988.

Aho, C. Michael, and Jonathan David Aronson. *Trade Talks: America Better Listen!* New York: Council on Foreign Relations, 1985.

Alderfer, E. B., and H. E. Michl. *Economics of American Industry*. 2d ed. New York: McGraw-Hill, 1950.

Allison, Graham T. *The Essence of Decision: Explaining the Cuban Missile Crisis*. Boston: Little, Brown, 1971.

Axelrod, Robert. *The Evolution of Cooperation*. New York: Basic Books, 1984.

Babbie, Earl R. *Survey Research Methods*. Belmont, Calif.: Wadsworth Publishing, 1973.

Baldwin, Robert E., and Anne O. Krueger, eds. *The Structure and Evolution of Recent U.S. Trade Policy*. Chicago: University of Chicago Press, 1984.

Barber, William J. *A History of Economic Thought*. Middlesex, England: Penguin Books, 1967; reprint 1985.

Barone, Michael, and Grant Ujifusa. *The Almanac of American Politics 1988*. Washington, D.C.: National Journal, 1987.

Barry, John M. *The Ambition and the Power: The Fall of Jim Wright: A True Story of Washington.* New York: Viking Penguin, 1989.

Bartlett, Ruhl J., ed. *The Record of American Diplomacy: Documents and Readings in the History of American Foreign Relations.* New York: Alfred A. Knopf, 1948.

Bauer, Raymond A., Ithiel de Sola Pool, and Anthony Lewis Dexter. *American Business and Public Policy,* 2d ed. Chicago: Aldine-Atherton, 1972.

Beck, Roy Howard. "Coalition Hammers Out Protective Trade Bill," *Jackson (Michigan) Citizen Patriot,* August 9, 1987.

Bello, Judith H., and Alan F. Holmer. *Guide to the U.S.-Canada Free-Trade Agreement: Text, Commentary, Source Materials.* New Jersey: Prentice-Hall Law & Business, 1990.

Bergsten, C. Fred. *Toward a New International Economic Order: Selected Papers of C. Fred Bergsten, 1972–74.* Lexington, Mass.: Lexington Books, 1975.

Birnbaum, Jeffrey H., and Alan S. Murray. *Showdown at Gucci Gulch.* New York: Vintage Books, 1987.

Bisnow, Mark. *In the Shadow of the Dome: Chronicles of a Capitol Hill Aide.* New York: William Morrow, 1990.

Blaker, Michael K. "Probe, Push and Panic: The Japanese Tactical Style in International Negotiations." In *The Foreign Policy of Modern Japan,* ed. Robert A. Scalapino. Berkeley: University of California Press, 1977.

Cassidy, Robert C. "Negotiating About Negotiations: The Geneva Multilateral Trade Talks." In *The Tethered Presidency,* ed. Thomas M. Franck. New York: New York University Press, 1981.

Cater, Douglass. *The Fourth Branch of Government.* New York: Random House, 1959; reprint, New York: Vintage Books, 1977.

Choate Pat. *Agents of Influence.* New York: Alfred A. Knopf, 1990.

Cohen, Richard E. "The Hill People." *National Journal: The Hill People,* May 16, 1987, 1170–1172.

———. *Washington at Work: Back Rooms and Clean Air.* New York: Macmillan Publishing, 1992.

Congressional Quarterly. *Trade: U.S. Policy Since 1945.* Washington, D.C.: Congressional Quarterly, Inc., 1984.

Culbertson, William S. *International Economic Policies.* New York: D. Appleton, 1925.

———. *Reciprocity: A National Policy for Foreign Trade.* New York: Whittlesey House (McGraw-Hill), 1937.

Curtis, Thomas, and John Robert Vastine. *The Kennedy Round and the Future of American Trade.* New York: Praeger, 1971.

Dahl, Robert A. *Congress and Foreign Policy.* New York: Harcourt Brace, 1950.

———. *Pluralist Democracy in the United States: Conflict and Consent.* Chicago: Rand McNally & Company, 1967.

Dahl, Robert A., and Charles E. Lindblom. *Politics, Economics, and Welfare.* New York: Harper & Row (Harper Torchbooks), 1953.

Dam, Kenneth W. *The GATT: Law and International Economic Organization.* Chicago: University of Chicago Press, 1970.

Davidson, Roger H., and Walter J. Oleszek. *Congress and Its Members*, 2d ed. Washington, D.C.: Congressional Quarterly Press, 1981, 1985.

Deakin, James. *The Lobbyists*. Washington, D.C.: Public Affairs Press, 1966.

Destler, I. M. *Making Foreign Economic Policy*. Washington, D.C.: The Brookings Institution, 1980.

———. *American Trade Politics: System Under Stress*. Washington, D.C.: Institute for International Economics and New York: The Twentieth Century Fund, 1986.

———. "Protecting Congress or Protecting Trade?" *Foreign Policy* 62 (Spring 1986): 96–107.

———. *American Trade Politics*, 2d ed. Washington, D.C.: Institute for International Economics and New York: The Twentieth Century Fund, 1992.

———. "Deregulating Trade Policy." In *Congress, the Executive, and the Making of American Foreign Policy*, ed. Paul E. Peterson. Norman: University of Oklahoma Press, 1994.

Destler, I. M., and Thomas R. Graham. "United States Congress and the Tokyo Round: Lessons of a Success Story." *The World Economy* 3, no. 1. The Netherlands: Trade Policy Research Centre, 1980.

Destler, I. M., Haruhiro Fukui, and Hideo Sato. *The Textile Wrangle*. Ithaca: Cornell University Press, 1979.

Destler, I. M., and John S. Odell. *Anti-Protection: Changing Forces in United States Trade Politics*. Washington, D.C.: Institute for International Economics, 1987.

Dexter, Lewis Anthony. *How Organizations are Represented in Washington*. Indianapolis: Bobbs-Merrill, 1969.

———. *Elite and Specialized Interviewing*. Evanston, Illinois: Northwestern University Press, 1970.

Dobson, John M. *Two Centuries of Tariffs: The Background and Emergence of the United States International Trade Commission*. Washington, D.C.: GPO, 1976.

Dodd, Lawrence C., and Bruce I. Oppenheimer, eds. *Congress Reconsidered*. Washington, D.C.: Congressional Quarterly Press, 1981.

Evans, John W. *U.S. Trade Policy: New Legislation for the New Round*. New York: Council on Foreign Relations/Harper & Row, 1967.

———. *The Kennedy Round in American Trade Policy*. Cambridge, Mass.: Harvard University Press, 1971.

Faulkner, Harold Underwood. *American Economic History*, 6th ed. New York: American Economic History, 1949.

Fenno, Richard J., Jr. *The Power of the Purse: Appropriations Politics in Congress*. Boston: Little, Brown and Co., 1966.

Fisher, Louis. *The Politics of Shared Power: Congress and the Executive*, 2d ed. Washington, D.C.: Congressional Quarterly Press, 1987.

Freeman, J. Leiper. *The Political Process: Executive Bureau-Legislative Committee Relations*. New York: Random House, 1955. 1965.

Frey, Bruno S. *International Political Economics*. Oxford and New York: Basil Blackwell Inc., 1984, 1986.

———. "The Political Economy of Protection." In *Current Issues in International Trade*, ed. David Greenaway. New York: St. Martins Press, 1985.

Gilpin, Robert. *The Political Economy of International Relations*. Princeton, N.J.: Princeton University Press, 1987.

Glennon, Michael J., Thomas M. Frank, and Robert C. Cassidy, Jr., eds. *United States Foreign Relations Law: Documents and Sources*. Vol. IV. New York: Oceana Publications, 1984.

Glover, John G. and William B. Cornell, eds. *The Development of American Industries*. New York: Prentice-Hall, 1936.

Griffith, Ernest S. *The Impasse of Democracy*. New York: Harrison-Hilton Books, 1939.

Hamilton, Alexander. *Selected Writings and Speeches of Alexander Hamilton*, ed. Morton J. Frisch. Washington, D.C.: American Enterprise Institute, 1985.

Harris, Louis. *Inside America*. New York: Vintage Books, 1987.

Heckscher, Eli F. *Mercantilism*. Translated by Mendel Shapiro. London: George Allen & Unwin, 1934.

Heilbroner, Robert L. *The Worldly Philosophers*. New York: Simon and Schuster, 1980.

Hess, Stephen. *The Ultimate Insiders*. Washington, D.C.: The Brookings Institution, 1986.

Holmer, Alan F., and Judith Hippler Bello. "The 1988 Trade Bill: Is it Protectionist?" In *International Trade Reporter*. Washington, D.C.: Bureau of National Affairs, October 5, 1988.

Hudec, Robert. *The GATT Legal System and World Trade Diplomacy*. New York: Praeger, 1975.

Hufbauer, Gary Clyde, and Jeffrey J. Schott. *Trading for Growth: The Next Round of Trade Negotiations*. Washington, D.C.: Institute for International Economics, 1985.

Hufbauer, Gary Clyde, Diane T. Berliner, Kimberly Ann Elliott. *Trade Protection in the United States: 31 Case Studies*. Washington, D.C.: Institute for International Economics, 1986.

Hull, Cordell. *The Memoirs of Cordell Hull*. New York: Macmillan Company, 1948.

Jackson, John. *World Trade and the Law of the GATT*. New York: Bobbs Merrill, 1969.

Kelley, William B., Jr. "Antecedents of Present Commercial Policy, 1922–1934." In *Law of International Trade*, ed. Stanley D. Metzger, 253–330. Washington, D.C.: Lerner Law Book Co., 1965, 1966.

Key, V. O., Jr. *Politics, Parties, & Pressure Groups*, 5th ed. New York: Thomas Y. Crowell Company, 1964.

Keynes, John Maynard. *The General Theory of Employment Interest and Money*. New York: Harcourt Brace, 1936.

Koh, Harold Hongju. "Congressional Controls on Presidential Trade Policy-making After I.N.S. v. Chadha." *Journal of International Law and Politics* 18, no. 4 (Summer 1986). New York: New York University.

Kress, Andrew J., ed. *The Economics of Diplomacy*. Washington D.C.: Georgetown University School of Foreign Service, 1949.

Kuttner, Robert. *The Life of the Party: Democratic Prospects in 1988 and Beyond*. New York: Penguin Books, 1987.

Lande, Stephen L., and Craig VanGrasstek. *The Trade and Tariff Act of 1984.* Lexington, Mass.: Lexington Books, 1986.

Lindert, Peter H. *International Economics,* 8th ed. Homewood, Ill.: Richard D. Irwin, 1986.

Lipset, Seymour Martin, and William Schneider. *The Confidence Gap: Business, Labor, and Government in the Public Mind,* 2d ed. Baltimore: Johns Hopkins University Press, 1987.

McGowan, Ada G. *The Congressional Conference Committee.* New York: Columbia University, 1927.

Malbin, Michael J. *Unelected Representatives.* New York: Basic Books, 1980.

Malmgren, Harald B. *International Economic Peacekeeping in Phase II.* New York: Quadrangle Books, 1972.

Mann, Thomas E., and Norman J. Ornstein. *The New Congress.* Washington, D.C.: American Enterprise Institute, 1981.

Matthews, Christopher. *Hardball.* New York: Harper & Row, 1989.

Metzger, Stanley D., ed. *Law of International Trade.* Washington, D.C.: Lerner Law Book Co., 1965, 1966.

Miller, James A. *Running In Place.* New York: Simon & Schuster, 1986.

Mills, C. Wright. *The Power Elite.* New York: Oxford University Press, 1956.

Nachmias, David, and Chava Nachmias. *Research Methods in the Social Sciences,* 3d ed. New York: St. Martin's Press, 1987.

O'Herron, Thomas F., ed. *Terms of Trade: The Language of International Trade Policy, Law, and Diplomacy.* Washington, D.C.: International Advisory Services Group Ltd., 1990.

Oleszek, Walter J. *Congressional Procedures and the Policy Process,* 2d ed. Washington, D.C.: Congressional Quarterly Press, 1984.

Ornstein, Norman J., ed. *Congress in Change.* New York: Praeger, 1975.

Ornstein, Norman J., Thomas E. Mann, Michael J. Malbin, Allen Schick, and John F. Bibby. *Vital Statistics on Congress, 1984–85 Edition.* Washington, D.C.: American Enterprise Institute, 1984.

Ornstein, Norman J., Thomas E. Mann, and Michael J. Malbin. *Vital Statistics on Congress, 1987–1988.* Washington, D.C.: Congressional Quarterly Inc., 1987.

Pastor, Robert A. *Congress and the Politics of U.S. Foreign Economic Policy, 1929–1976.* Berkeley: University of California Press, 1980.

Preeg, Ernest. *Traders and Diplomats.* Washington, D.C.: The Brookings Institution, 1970.

Prestowitz, Clyde V., Jr., *Trading Places.* New York: Basic Books, 1988.

Redman, Eric. *The Dance of Legislation.* New York: Simon & Schuster, 1973.

Reid, T. R. *Congressional Odyssey: The Saga of a Senate Bill.* San Francisco: W. H. Freeman and Company, 1980.

Ricardo, David. *The Principles of Political Economy and Taxation,* 3d ed. (1821); reprint, London: J.M. Dent & Sons Ltd., Everyman's Library, 1911.

Rogers, Lindsay. *The Pollsters: Public Opinion, Politics, and Democratic Leadership.* New York: Alfred A. Knopf, 1949.

Rossiter, Clinton. *Parties and Politics in America.* New York: The New American Library (A Signet Book), 1960.

Rourke, Francis E., ed. *Bureaucratic Power in National Politics,* 2d and 3d eds. Boston: Little, Brown and Company, 1972, 1978.

Schattschneider, E. E. *Politics, Pressures and the Tariff.* New York: Prentice-Hall, 1935.

Schelling, Thomas. *The Strategy of Conflict.* Cambridge, Mass.: Harvard University Press, 1960.

Schick, Allen, ed. *Making Economic Policy in Congress.* Washington, D.C.: American Enterprise Institute, 1983.

Schriftgiesser, Karl. *The Lobbyists.* Boston: Little, Brown, 1951.

Schwab, Susan C. "Japan and the U.S. Congress." *Journal of International Affairs* 37, no. 1 (Summer 1983). New York: Columbia University School of International and Public Affairs.

———. "Politics, Economics and U.S. Trade Policy." *Stanford Journal of International Law* XXIII, no. 1 (Spring 1987). Stanford, California: Stanford University School of Law.

———. "The Last U.S. Trade Bill?" *The International Economy,* 1, no. 1 (October/November 1987).

———. "The Omnibus Trade and Competitiveness Act of 1988: The End of an Era in U.S. Trade Policy?" Ph.D. diss., George Washington University, 1993.

Schwab, Susan C., and Ira Wolff. "Korea: A Congressional Commentary." In *Korea-U.S. Relations,* eds. Robert A. Scalapino and Hongkoo Lee, 147–156. Berkeley: Institute of East Asian Studies/University of California, 1988.

Selznick, Philip. *TVA and the Grass Roots.* Berkeley: University of California Press, 1949.

Silk, Leonard. *Economics in the Real World.* New York: Simon & Schuster, 1984.

Soule, George. *Ideas of the Great Economists.* New York: The New American Library, 1952.

Spero, Joan Edelman. *The Politics of International Economic Relations,* 2d ed. New York: St. Martin's Press, 1981.

Stanley, Howard W., and Richard Niemi. *Vital Statistics on American Politics.* Washington, D.C.: Congressional Quarterly Press, 1988.

Steiner, Gilbert. *The Congressional Conference Committee, Seventieth to Eightieth Congresses.* Urbana: University of Illinois Press, 1951.

Stockman, David A. *The Triumph of Politics.* New York: Avon Books, 1986.

Stokes, Bruce. "Bentsen and Hedges." *National Journal: The Hill People,* May 16, 1987, 1212–1214.

———. "Rosty Reigns Here." *National Journal: The Hill People,* May 16, 1987, 1298–1301.

———. *The Inevitability of Managed Trade: The Future Strategic Trade Policy Debate.* New York: Japan Society, 1990.

Taussig, F. W. *The Tariff History of the United States,* 8th ed. New York: G. P. Putnam's, 1931.

Thwing, Eugene, ed. *Political Cyclopedia.* New York: Funk & Wagnalls, The Literary Digest, 1932.

Tolchin, Martin, and Susan Tolchin. *Buying Into America*. New York: Times Books, 1988.

Tumlir, Jan. *Protectionism: Trade Policy in Democratic Societies*. Washington, D.C.: American Enterprise Institute, 1985.

Twiggs, Joan E. *The Tokyo Round of Multilateral Trade Negotiations: A Case Study in Building Domestic Support for Diplomacy*. Washington, D.C.: Georgetown University, Institute for the Study of Diplomacy, and Lanham, Maryland: University Press of America, 1987.

Viner, Jacob. *Studies in the Theory of International Trade*. New York: Harper & Brothers, 1937.

Vogler, David J. *The Third House: Conference Committees in the United States Congress*. Evanston: Northwestern University Press, 1971.

Weatherford, J. McIver. *Tribes on the Hill*. New York: Rawson, Wade Publishers, 1981.

Webb, Eugene J., Donald T. Campbell, Richard D. Schwartz, and Lee Sechrest. *Unobtrusive Measures: Nonreactive Research in the Social Sciences*. Chicago: Rand McNally, 1966.

Williams, Benjamin H. *Economic Foreign Policy of the United States*. New York: Howard Fertig, 1929.

Winham, Gilbert R. "Robert Strauss, the MTN and the Control of Faction." *Journal of World Trade* 14 (September-October 1980).

———. *International Trade and Tokyo Round Negotiations*. Princeton: Princeton University Press, 1986.

Young, John Parke. *The International Economy*. New York: The Ronald Press, 1942.

PUBLIC DOCUMENTS (CHRONOLOGICAL ORDER)

U.S. Congress. House. Committee on Ways and Means. *Overview and Compilation of U.S. Trade Statutes*. Prepared for the use of the Committee on Ways and Means by its staff. 101st Cong., 1st sess., 1989. Committee Print 101-14.

United States-Canada Free-Trade Implementation Act of 1988. Public Law 100-449, 100th Congress. 102 Stat. 1851, 19 USC 2112.

Omnibus Trade and Competitiveness Act of 1988. Public Law 100-418, 100th Congress. 102 Stat. 1107, 19 USC 2901.

U.S. Congress. Senate. Committee on Finance. *Changes Made by H.R. 4848 (P.L. 100-418) in Pre-existing Laws Under Finance Committee Jurisdiction*. Prepared by the Staff for use of the Committee on Finance. 100th Cong., 2d sess., 1988. Senate Print 100-147.

———. House. *Omnibus Trade and Competitiveness Act of 1988*. 100th Cong., 2d sess., H.R. 4848.

———. House. *Omnibus Trade and Competitiveness Act of 1988: Conference Report to accompany H.R. 3*. 100th Cong., 2d sess., 1988. Report 100-576.

———. *Summary of the Conference Agreement on H.R. 3: The Omnibus Trade and Competitiveness Act of 1988*. 100th Cong., 2d sess., April 19, 1988. Conference Committee Print.

———. *H.R. 3, Omnibus Trade and Competitiveness Legislation: Comparison of House and Senate Provisions.* 100th Cong., 1st sess., October 6, 1987. Committee Print.

———. Senate. *Omnibus Trade and Competitiveness Act of 1987.* 100th Cong., 1st sess., Amendment in the nature of a substitute to H.R. 3.

———. House. *Trade and International Economic Policy Reform Act of 1987.* 100th Cong., 1st sess., H.R. 3.

———. Senate. *Omnibus Trade and Competitiveness Act of 1987.* 100th Cong., 1st sess., S. 1420.

———. Senate. Committee on Finance. *Omnibus Trade Act of 1987: Report of the Committee on Finance on S. 490.* 100th Cong., 1st sess., 1987. Report 100-71.

———. House. Committee on Ways and Means. *Trade and International Economic Policy Reform Act of 1987: Report of the Committee on Ways and Means to accompany H.R. 3.* 100th Cong., 1st sess., 1987. Report 100-40, Part 1.

———. House. Committee on Ways and Means. *Summary of Titles I, II, and VIII of H.R. 3 "Trade and Economic Policy Reform Act of 1987."* Prepared by the staff for use of the Committee on Ways and Means. 100th Cong., 1st sess., March 26, 1987. Ways and Means Committee Print 100-7.

———. Senate. *Omnibus Trade Act of 1987.* 100th Cong., 1st sess., S. 490.

———. House. *The Trade, Employment, and Productivity Act of 1987.* Message from the President of the United States Transmitting A Draft of Proposed Legislation. 100th Cong., 1st sess., 1987. House Document 100-33.

———. Senate. Committee on Finance. *Mastering the World Economy: Hearings before the Committee on Finance.* 100th Cong., 1st sess.; January 13, 15, 20, 22 and February 3, 5, 19, 1987. Senate Hearing 100-6, Parts 1-4.

———. House. Committee on Ways and Means. *Overview and Compilation of U.S. Trade Statutes.* Prepared for the use of the Committee on Ways and Means by its staff. 100th Cong., 1st sess., 1987. Committee Print 100-1.

———. Senate. *Standing Rules of the Senate and Congressional Budget and Impoundment Control Act of 1974, as Amended.* 100th Cong., 1st sess., 1987. Senate Document 100-4.

———. House. *Trade and International Economic Policy Reform Act of 1986.* 99th Cong., 2d sess., H.R. 4800.

———. House. Committee on Ways and Means. *Comprehensive Trade Policy Reform Act of 1986: Report to accompany H.R. 4750.* 99th Cong., 2d sess., 1986. Report 99-581, Part 1.

———. Joint. Committee on Foreign Affairs and Committee on Foreign Relations. *Legislation on Foreign Relations Through 1985.* Volume II. Joint Committee Print. Washington, D.C.: GPO, 1986.

———. House. Committee on Ways and Means. *Telecommunications Trade Act of 1986: Report to accompany H.R. 3131.* 99th Cong., 2d sess., 1986. Report 99-471, Part 2.

———. Senate. *Trade Enhancement Act.* 99th Cong., 1st sess., S. 1860.

Office of the United States Trade Representative. *Annual Report on National Trade Estimates: 1985 ("as requested by Section 303 of the Trade and Tariff Act of 1984 [P.L. 98-573, 98 Stat. 2950, October 30, 1984]").* Washington, D.C.: Executive Office of the President, 1985.

U.S. Congress. Senate. *The United States Senate 1787–1801: A Dissertation on the First Fourteen Years of the Upper Legislative Body.* Prepared by Roy Swanstrom. 99th Cong., 1st sess., 1985. Document 99-19. Washington, D.C.: GPO, 1985.

———. House. *Telecommunications Trade Act.* 99th Cong., 1st sess., H.R. 3131.

———. Senate. Committee on Finance. *Promoting Expansion of International Trade in Telecommunications Equipment and Services: Report to accompany S. 942.* 99th Cong., 1st sess., 1985. Report 99-204.

———. Senate. *Telecommunications Trade Act.* 99th Cong., 1st sess., S. 942.

Trade and Tariff Act of 1984. Public Law 98-573, 98th Congress. 98 Stat. 2948, 19 USC 1654.

U.S. Congress. House. *Trade and Tariff Act of 1984: Conference Report to accompany H.R. 3398.* 98th Cong., 2d sess., 1984. Report 98-1156.

———. House. Committee on Ways and Means. Subcommittee on Trade. *Overview of Current Provisions of U.S. Trade Law.* Prepared for the use of the Committee on Ways and Means by its staff. 98th Cong., 2d sess., 1984. Committee Print 98-40.

———. Senate. *Telecommunications Trade Act.* 98th Cong., 2d sess., S. 2618.

———. Senate. Committee on Governmental Affairs. *Trade Reorganization Act of 1983: Hearings before the Committee on Governmental Affairs on S. 121.* 98th Cong., 1st sess.; March 17, April 26, May 11 and 12, June 24 and 29, September 14 and 15, 1983. Senate Hearing 98-474.

Office of the United States Trade Representative. *A Preface to Trade.* Washington, D.C.: Executive Office of the President, 1982.

Office of the President. Executive Order. "Reorganization Plan No. 3 of 1979." Executive Order 12188. (January 4, 1980). 44 *Federal Register* 69273.

Trade Agreements Act of 1979. Public Law 96-39, 96th Congress. 93 Stat. 144, 19 USC 2501.

U.S. Congress. Senate. Committee on Finance. *Trade Agreements Act of 1979: Report of the Committee on Finance on H.R. 4537.* 96th Cong., 1st sess., 1979. Report 96-249.

———. House. Committee on Ways and Means. *Trade Agreements Act of 1979: Report of the Committee on Ways and Means to accompany H.R. 4537.* 96th Cong., 1st sess., 1979. House Report 96-317.

———. Senate. Committee on Finance. *Private Advisory Committee Reports on the Tokyo Round of Multilateral Trade Negotiations.* 96th Cong., 1st sess., 1979. Committee Print 96-28.

———. Senate. Committee on Finance. *Trade Agreements Act of 1979: Hearings before the Subcommittee on International Trade on S. 1376.* 96th Cong., 1st sess.; July 10 and 11, 1979. Parts 1 and 2.

———. Senate. Committee on Finance. *MTN Studies: Reports Prepared at the Request of the Subcommittee on International Trade.* 5 Vols. 96th Cong., 1st sess., 1979. Committee Prints 96-11 through 15.

Advisory Committee for Trade Negotiations. *Report to the President, the Congress and the Special Representative for Trade Negotiations.* June 1979.

U.S. Congress. Senate. Committee on Finance. *History of the Committee on Finance.* 95th Cong., 1st sess., 1977. Senate Document 95-27.

———. Senate. Committee on Finance. *United States International Trade Policy and the Trade Act of 1974.* Prepared by the Staff for the use of the Committee on Finance. 94th Cong., 2d sess. Committee Print. Washington, D.C.: GPO, 1976.

———. Congressional Research Service. Foreign Affairs Division. *The Role of Advisory Committees in U.S. Foreign Policy.* Prepared for the Senate Committee on Foreign Relations and the House Committee on International Relations. 94th Cong., 1st sess. Joint Committee Print. Washington, D.C.: GPO, 1975.

Trade Act of 1974. Public Law 93-618, 93d Congress. 88 Stat. 1978, 19 USC 2101.

U.S. Congress. Senate. Committee on Finance. *Trade Reform Act of 1974: Report of the Committee on Finance on H.R. 10710.* 93d Cong., 2d sess., 1974. Report 93-1298.

———. House. Committee on Ways and Means. *Trade Reform Act of 1973: Report of the Committee on Ways and Means to accompany H.R. 10710.* 93d Cong., 1st sess., 1973. Report 93-571.

Commission on International Trade and Economic Policy, *United States International Economic Policy in an Interdependent World.* Report to the President submitted by the Commission on International Trade and Investment Policy. July 1971. Washington, D.C.: GPO, 1971.

General Agreement on Tariffs and Trade: Basic Instruments and Selected Documents. Volume IV. Geneva, Switzerland: GATT, 1969.

Trade Expansion Act of 1962. Public Law 87-794, 87th Congress. 76 Stat. 872, 19 USC 1351.

U.S. Congress. House. *Trade Expansion Act of 1962: Conference Report to accompany H.R. 11970.* 87th Cong., 2d sess., 1962. Report No. 2518.

———. Senate. Committee on Finance. *Trade Expansion Act of 1962: Report to accompany H.R. 11970.* 87th Cong., 2d sess., 1962. Report No. 2059. 76 Stat. 872, 19 USC.

———. House. Committee on Ways and Means. *Trade Expansion Act of 1962: Report of the Committee on Ways and Means to accompany H.R. 11970.* 87th Cong., 2d sess., 1962. House Report No. 1818.

———. Senate. Committee on Finance. *Text of Statements submitted by Governmental Departments and Brief Analyses of Testimony and Written Statements by Industry Representatives on H.R. 11970.* 87th Cong., 2d sess., 1962. Confidential Committee Print.

———. Senate. Committee on Finance. *Trade Expansion Act of 1962: Hearings before the Committee on Finance on H.R. 11970.* 87th Cong., 2d sess.; August 7, 8, 9, and 10, 1962. Part 3.

Trade Agreements Extension Act of 1958. Public Law 85-686. 72 Stat. 673.

Agricultural Act of 1956. Section 204. Public Law 84-540, 84th Congress. 70 Stat. 188, 7 USC 1854.

Trade Agreements Extension Act of 1955. Public Law 84-86. 69 Stat. 162.

Trade Agreements Extension Act of 1954. Public Law 83-464. 68 Stat. 360.

Trade Agreements Extension Act of 1953. Public Law 83-215. 67 Stat. 472.

Trade Agreements Extension Act of 1951. Public Law 82-50. 65 Stat. 72.

Trade Agreements Extension Act of 1949. Public Law 81-307. 63 Stat. 697.

U.S. Tariff Commission. *Operation of the Trade Agreements Program June 1934 to April 1948.* Washington, D.C., 1948. Report No. 160. Second Series. Part I, Summary.

Trade Agreements Extension Act of 1948. Public Law 80-792. 62 Stat. 1053.

Trade Agreements Extension Act of 1945. Public Law 79-130. 59 Stat. 410.

Joint Resolution of 1943: To extend the authority of the President under section 350 of the Tariff Act of 1930, as amended. Public Law 78-66. 57 Stat. 125.

Joint Resolution of 1940: To extend the authority of the President under section 350 of the Tariff Act of 1930, as amended. Public Resolution 76-61. 54 Stat. 107.

Joint Resolution of 1937: To extend the authority of the President under section 350 of the Tariff Act of 1930, as amended. Public Resolution 75-10. 50 Stat. 24.

Reciprocal Trade Agreements Act of 1934. Public Law 73-316. 48 Stat. 943, 19 USC 1001, 1201, 1351–1354.

U.S. Congress. Senate. Committee on Finance. *Reciprocal Trade Agreements: Report of the Committee on Finance to accompany H.R. 8687.* 73d Cong., 2d sess., 1934.

———. Senate. Committee on Finance. *Hearings before the Committee on Finance on H.R. 8687: An Act to Amend the Tariff Act of 1930.* 73d Cong., 2d sess.; April 26, 27, 30, and May 1, 1934.

———. House. Committee on Ways and Means. *An Act to Amend the Tariff Act of 1930: Report of the Committee on Ways and Means to accompany H.R. 8687.* 73d Cong., 2d sess., 1934.

Agricultural Adjustment Act of 1933. (Act of May 12, 1933). Section 22, as added by Public Law 74-320. 48 Stat. 31, 7 USC 624.

Buy American Act. (Title III of the Act of March 3, 1933). Public Law 72-428. 47 Stat. 1520, 41 USC 10a–10d.

Tariff Act of 1930. Public Law 71-361. 46 Stat. 590.

GLOSSARY OF TRADE TERMS

accession: The process of becoming a contracting party (CP) to the GATT. Negotiations with established CPs determine the obligations a nonmember country must undertake before it will be entitled to full GATT membership benefits.

ACTN: *See* Advisory Committee for Trade Negotiations.

ACTPN: *See* Advisory Committee for Trade Policy and Negotiations.

AD/CVD: Antidumping/Countervailing Duties. *See* countervailing duties, dumping.

adjustment assistance: Financial and technical assistance available to firms, workers, and communities to help them adjust to increased competition from imports. The program for workers, known as Trade Adjustment Assistance (TAA), is the largest of the three federal programs.

ad referendum ("ad ref") agreement: An agreement reached pending final approval by ultimate decision makers.

ad valorem tariff/rate: An import duty assessed on the basis of a percentage of the import's value. For contrast *see* specific tariff/duty.

Advisory Committee for Trade Negotiations (ACTN): A private sector advisory group established under the Trade Act of 1974 to provide broad policy advice to the president and Congress on trade agreements. Committee role and name were expanded in 1988. *See also* Advisory Committee for Trade Policy and Negotiations.

Note: Descriptions are drawn and adapted from various sources, including Office of the United States Trade Representative, *A Preface to Trade* (Washington D.C.: Executive Office of the President, 1982); Thomas F. O'Herron, ed., *Terms of Trade: The Language of International Trade Policy, Law, and Diplomacy* (Washington, D.C.: International Advisory Services Groups Ltd., 1990); John M. Dobson, *Two Centuries of Tariffs: The Background and Emergence of the United States International Trade Commission* (Washington D.C.: U.S. Government Printing Office, 1976); and U.S. Congress, House, Committee on Ways and Means, *Overview and Compilation of U.S. Trade Statutes,* prepared for the use of the Committee on Ways and Means by its staff, 101st Cong., 1st sess., 1989, Committee Print 101-14.

Advisory Committee for Trade Policy and Negotiations (ACTPN): Name given to the ACTN in the Omnibus Trade Act of 1988 to reflect its new role in U.S. trade policy. *See also* Advisory Committee for Trade Negotiations.

Agricultural Policy Advisory Committee (APAC): A private sector advisory committee established pursuant to the Trade Act of 1974 to advise Congress and the executive on general agricultural implications of trade agreements.

Agricultural Technical Advisory Committee (ATAC): Sectoral committees established pursuant to the Trade Act of 1974 to advise Congress and the executive on specific agricultural sector implications of trade agreements.

American Selling Price (ASP): A method of calculating tariffs applied to a limited number of U.S. imports, such as benzenoid chemicals, under the Fordney-McCumber Tariff Act of 1922. For these products, the import duty was based on the price level of competing American products, rather than on the import's value. The ASP method was eliminated in connection with the GATT Tokyo Round Customs Valuation Code. *See also* valuation.

antidumping (AD): *See* dumping.

Antidumping Code: A multilateral code of conduct negotiated during the GATT Kennedy and Tokyo Rounds involving procedural and substantive standards for national antidumping rules. U.S. acceptance and implementation of the code is contained in the Trade Agreements Act of 1979.

APAC: *See* Agricultural Policy Advisory Committee.

applied tariff rate: The actual tariff rate imposed on an import, as distinct from the bound rate under GATT agreements. For contrast *see* bound rates.

ASP: *See* American Selling Price.

ATAC: *See* Agricultural Technical Advisory Committee.

bilateral agreement: An agreement between two countries.

bind/binding: *See* bound rates.

border tax adjustments: The remission of taxes on exported goods, including sales and value-added taxes. Such adjustments are legal under the GATT.

bound rates: Tariff rates extended on a Most-Favored-Nation (MFN) basis under the GATT. A nation binds its rates in connection with tariff reductions and/or a commitment not to raise rates above existing levels. See also applied tariff rate.

Bretton Woods Conference: A 1944 meeting held in Bretton Woods, New Hampshire, to consider international measures to increase cooperation in trade and finance. Among the results of the conference were the establishment of the International Monetary Fund and the World Bank.

Buy American: Refers to the Buy American Act of 1933 and its successors by amendment, which give preference to American bidders on U.S. government contracts. *See also* Government Procurement Code.

CAP: *See* Common Agricultural Policy.

Caribbean Basin Initiative (CBI): A presidential initiative to support the economic development and well-being of various Caribbean and Central American countries. Trade provisions of the Caribbean Basin Economic Recovery Act of 1983 provide for duty-free treatment of certain U.S. imports from beneficiary countries. Apparel, sugar, and other import-sensitive products are not covered by the program.

CBI: *See* Caribbean Basin Initiative.

C.I.F.: Cost, Insurance, Freight. A valuation system based on the value of imports at the port of entry in the United States. It includes freight, insurance, and charges other than import duties.

COCOM: Coordinating Committee on Multilateral Export Controls. A 16-nation committee that sets guidelines for exports, particularly related to the transfer of sensitive technology in East-West trade. Discontinued 1994.

code of conduct: The term used to describe international instruments governing trade-related disciplines. Included in the GATT Tokyo Round agreements were several codes governing the use of nontariff measures. *See* Government Procurement Code, Standards Code, and so forth.

Column 1 rates: Tariff rates under the U.S. tariff schedule that have been lowered in the context of trade agreements; extended to all countries which enjoy MFN status with the United States. Column 1 is divided into "General" and "Special" categories, with the latter subcolumn listing rates such as those applicable under FTA agreements and the Generalized System of Preferences (GSP).

Column 2 rates: The highest tariff rates in the United States tariff schedule; applied to countries to which the United States does not extend MFN treatment. These rates were generally established in the Tariff Act of 1930.

commitments policy: A term used to describe U.S. policy under provisions of the 1979 Trade Agreements Act involving the application of an injury test in countervailing duty cases to nonsignatories to the GATT Subsidies Code, if such countries have made commitments on the use of export subsidies substantially equivalent to those in the code.

Common Agricultural Policy (CAP): The agricultural policies and programs maintained by the European Community (EC). Among the principal policy tools are the variable levy and restitution payments (subsidies to exports of commodities that cannot be sold within the EC at target prices). *See also* variable levy.

comparative advantage: The central concept in trade theory developed by David Ricardo. A country has "comparative advantage" in the production of goods it can produce relatively more efficiently, and should export those goods while importing goods in which it has the greatest comparative disadvantage.

compensation: The GATT principle under which any country that raises a tariff, withdraws a tariff binding, or otherwise impairs a trade concession must compensate its affected trading partners by making other tariff or trade concessions.

concession: Tariff or other import barrier-reduction commitments granted in connection with trade agreements. Under GATT, modification of previous concessions requires compensation or allows the affected countries to modify or withdraw previous concessions of its own.

constructed value: *See* dumping.

consultations: *See* dispute settlement.

contracting party (CP): A GATT member/signatory, accepting the specified obligations and benefits of GATT agreements.

countervailing duties (CVD): An additional duty imposed by a country on imports enjoying subsidies offered by the government of the country of export. *See* export subsidies.

CP: *See* contracting party.

cumulate: A verb meaning to accumulate or combine into a single number that is commonly used in connection with injury determinations where the impact from imports from several sources is combined to assess overall injury. The term "cumulation" is the noun most often used in this context.

Customs Union: A group of countries that has eliminated tariffs between themselves and set a common external tariff.

CVD: *See* Countervailing Duties.

Dillon Round: Multilateral trade negotiations that took place under the auspices of the GATT between 1960 and 1961, the fourth such round of negotiations since the GATT's creation in 1947.

DISC: *See* Domestic International Sales Corporation.

discrimination: Inequality of treatment by an importing nation through the application of preferential tariff rates or trade restrictions to the products of certain exporting countries, but not others. For contrast *see* most-favored-nation treatment.

dispute settlement: Various procedures under the GATT providing for legal redress in cases of violation, nullification, or impairment of trade benefits protected by GATT agreements.

domestic content requirements: Production origin requirements imposed by governments, generally to maximize the proportion of a manufactured good originating in that country.

Domestic International Sales Corporation (DISC): A type of corporation, provided for under a 1971 law, that is entitled to defer taxes on income from export profits. DISCs were found to be inconsistent with the GATT and the law was eventually amended to provide for arms-length pricing and the establishment of Foreign International Sales Corporations (FISCs).

dumping: The sale of a product or commodity in a foreign market at less than fair value. Under U.S. law, fair value is considered to be the price of the product in the producer's home market or in a third market, but can also be calculated on the basis of its estimated cost of production ("constructed value"). Dumping is considered an unfair trade practice under the GATT, which permits the imposition of antidumping duties equal to the margin of dumping.

duty: *See* tariff.

duty drawback: The return by government, in whole or in part, of import duties (and certain domestic taxes) on goods imported into special zones for transformation into different products before formal entry into the United States or subsequent reexport.

duty suspension: A temporary reduction in tariffs.

escape clause: Provisions of U.S. trade law and international trade rules providing temporary relief to domestic industries injured by virtue of increased imports. The multilateral basis for such U.S. law is found in GATT articles which permit the withdrawal of previously granted trade concessions to respond to a severe adverse impact on producers from increased imports. *See* Section 201.

export subsidies: Government payments or other economic benefits given to domestic producers of goods that are sold in foreign markets. The GATT recognizes that export subsidies may distort commerce and imposes certain disciplines on their use.

F.A.S.: Free-Along-Side. A valuation basis at U.S. port of exportation for exports and at foreign port of exportation for imports.

fast track: The term for authority periodically granted by Congress to the executive, providing for accelerated consideration of legislation to implement trade agreements. "Fast track" refers to special rules of House and Senate procedure that preclude filibuster and amendment of such legislation, thereby guaranteeing an up-or-down vote within a specified time frame. It was first granted in the Trade Act of 1974 for implementation of Tokyo Round non-tariff measure (NTM) agreements.

FCPA: *See* Foreign Corrupt Practices Act.

FISC: Foreign International Sales Corporation. *See* Domestic International Sales Corporation.

Florence Agreement: A UN-sponsored agreement that provides for duty-free entry of certain scientific, educational, and artistic materials under specified conditions.

F.O.B.: Free-On-Board. A term of valuation referring to the seller's delivery of goods to a named destination at his risk (insurance) and cost (transportation).

Foreign Corrupt Practices Act (FCPA): The U.S. law enacted in 1977 designed to prevent corporate bribery of foreign officials. Penalties for violation include fines and/or imprisonment.

Free Trade Area (FTA): An agreement between countries to eliminate barriers to trade among themselves while still maintaining their individual tariff schedules vis-a-vis other trading partners. The GATT permits such differential treatment where substantially all trade between the countries involved is covered by the agreement.

FTA: *See* Free Trade Area.

GATT: *See* General Agreement on Tariffs and Trade.

General Agreement on Tariffs and Trade (GATT): A multilateral instrument created in 1947–1948 that is subscribed by over ninety countries accounting for more than four-fifths of global trade. The GATT is both a set of agreed rules governing trade and an institution headquartered in Geneva that provides the framework through which the agreements are negotiated and enforced. The primary objective of the GATT is to liberalize trade and place it on a secure basis, thereby contributing to world economic growth. U.S. participation is based on an executive agreement that did not require Senate ratification as a treaty. Replaced by the World Trade Organization (WTO) in 1995 by the Uruguay Round agreements.

Generalized System of Preferences (GSP): A GATT-consistent system of nonreciprocal tariff preferences provided by industrialized nations to developing countries. Each country maintaining such a program establishes its own eligibility criteria and product coverage. The U.S. system was first authorized in 1974. *See also* graduation.

Government Procurement Code: A GATT code of conduct negotiated during the Tokyo Round that established procedures to ensure transparency, nondiscrimination, and national treatment in government purchasing. Signatories to the code commit to apply these procedures to the products of other signatory countries with respect to specific government entities agreed on during the negotiations. U.S. participation includes the use of waivers to the Buy American Act.

graduation: The treatment of trade obligations and preferences involving LDCs as they advance in their level of development. Under GATT, such countries are expected to accept obligations commensurate with their level of development. Under the U.S. GSP program, advanced developing countries "graduate" from eligibility for its benefits.

grandfather clause: A provision in an agreement that exempts an existing practice that would otherwise contradict the new agreement's terms. Under GATT, original signatories were allowed to retain certain GATT-inconsistent practices. *See also* waiver.

GSP: *See* Generalized System of Preferences.

Harmonized System: Also known as the "Harmonized Code." A system of tariff nomenclature emerging from a 10-year negotiation of the International Convention on the Harmonized Commodity Description and Coding System. The United States adopted the Harmonized System in the 1988 Omnibus Trade Act. *See also* tariff schedule.

HS/HTS: *See* Harmonized System.

import quota: A quantitative restraint on imports, generally calculated in volume terms and implemented through a system of licenses. By reducing the quantity of the imported product, the price and/or market share commanded by domestic producers is expected to exceed the level that would otherwise have occurred.

import relief: Remedies provided to domestic producers and workers considered to be injured by imports. *See* adjustment assistance, import quota, tariff. *See also* escape clause, Section 201.

import restrictions: Limits placed on imports, such as through the use of tariffs or quotas, import licensing, discriminatory standards, and other forms of nontariff barriers.

import surcharge: A fee placed on imports on top of the normal tariff; generally calculated in percentage terms relative to the value of the import.

Industry Policy Advisory Committee (IPAC): A private sector advisory committee established pursuant to the Trade Act of 1974 to advise Congress and the executive on broad industry implications of trade agreements.

Industry Sector Advisory Committee (ISAC): Sectoral committees established pursuant to the Trade Act of 1974 to advise Congress and the executive on specific industrial sector implications of trade agreements.

infant industry protection: The use of import restrictions as a means to stimulate manufacturing at early states of industrialization. Proponents justify the policy based on the high start-up costs of an emerging industry.

investment performance requirements: Special conditions imposed on foreign direct investment by recipient countries, such as minimum export requirements for production output and domestic content requirements.

intellectual property rights: Legally protected intellectual property such as patents, trademarks, and copyrights.

International Trade Commission (ITC): An independent bipartisan commission and agency that serves an investigative and quasi-judicial function under U.S. trade law. The ITC conducts studies and makes determinations and recommendations involving the competitiveness of U.S. industry in connection with trade negotiations, injury from imports under the U.S. escape clause statute and antidumping/countervailing duty laws, and Section 337 intellectual property rights cases. Established by statute in 1916 as the U.S. Tariff Commission; renamed in the Trade Act of 1974 with expanded responsibilities.

IPAC: *See* Industry Policy Advisory Committee.

ISAC: *See* Industry Sector Advisory Committee.

ITC: *See* International Trade Commission.

Kennedy Round: The sixth round of multilateral trade negotiations under the GATT (1963–1967). Involved forty-eight countries and resulted in major global tariff reductions, including the first linear cuts used in any such round. An antidumping code was also negotiated, along with government commitments to provide food aid to developing countries. *See* Trade Expansion Act of 1962.

LDC: lesser-developed country. LDCs are also referred to as developing countries, third-world countries, and, for those in more advanced stages of development, newly industrialized countries (NICs).

linear tariff cuts: Tariff cuts taken on an across-the-board basis, rather than negotiated individually by item. Generally implemented through use of a negotiated formula, allowing for only a few exceptions for particularly "sensitive" products.

local content: *See* domestic content.

Long-Term Agreement on International Trade in Cotton Textiles (LTA): *See* Multi-Fiber Arrangement.

LTA: Long-Term Agreement on International Trade in Cotton Textiles. *See* Multi-Fiber Arrangement.

manufacturing clause: A provision of U.S. copyright law from 1897 to 1986 that effectively banned imports of works by U.S. authors not manufactured in the U.S. or Canada.

market access: Availability of a national market to exporting countries, reflecting the extent to which that country's market is protected by barriers.

MFA: *See* Multi-Fiber Arrangement.

MFN: *See* most-favored-nation treatment.

most-favored-nation treatment (MFN): Application by a country to another country of the lowest rates of duty it applies to any third country. An agreement with an "unconditional" MFN provision is a commitment to automatically grant to the trading partner any tariff reduction or privilege negotiated with any other country.

MTN: *See* multilateral trade negotiation.

Multi-Fiber Arrangement (MFA): An international arrangement between textile and apparel producing and consuming countries providing for quantitative restraint arrangements between participants that would otherwise be inconsistent with GATT. The MFA has been renewed periodically since its inception in 1974. It succeeded and expanded the scope of the Long-Term Agreement on International Trade in Cotton Textiles (LTA) which went into effect in 1962.

multilateral agreement: An agreement between three or more countries.

multilateral trade negotiation (MTN): The term (often used in acronym form) to refer to any one of the multi-nation "rounds" of trade-liberalizing negotiations under the GATT.

NAFTA: *See* North American Free Trade Area.

National Trade Estimates (NTE) report: An annual report listing major barriers or distortions to U.S. trade, including foreign restrictions on trade in goods and services, violations of intellectual property rights, and barriers to foreign direct investment. Required by the Trade and Tariff Act of 1984.

national treatment: Treatment accorded foreign products or entities by a country that is no less favorable than that granted to its own domestic products or firms.

NIC: newly industrialized country. *See* LDC.

NME: *See* nonmarket economy.

nonmarket economy (NME): A term used to describe countries with centrally planned or managed economic policies, where pricing and cost of factors of production are not determined by market forces. Generally used to describe the economies of Communist or former Communist countries still in transition.

nontariff barrier (NTB)/nontariff measure (NTM): An impediment to imports that are not in the form of tariffs. These may include border measures, such as quantitative restrictions, or other practices that have the same effect of limiting imports.

North American Free Trade Area (NAFTA): A free trade area (FTA) agreement negotiated between the U.S., Mexico, and Canada. Negotiations were completed in 1992, with congressional approval voted in 1993 pursuant to fast-track implementing authority contained in the Omnibus Trade Act of 1988.

NTB: *See* nontariff barrier.

NTE: *See* National Trade Estimate report.

NTM: nontariff measure. *See* nontariff barrier.

OMA: *See* orderly marketing agreements.

Omnibus Trade and Competitiveness Act of 1988: A multi-provision trade and competitiveness law, containing trade agreement implementing authority for the Uruguay Round MTN and the North American Free Trade Area (NAFTA), and a variety of other trade provisions. Often referred to as the Omnibus Trade Act of 1988. *See also* Special 301, Super 301.

orderly marketing agreements (OMAs): Negotiated agreements between producer and consuming nations under which the producing nation commits to limit its exports so as not to "disrupt" the market for producers in the importing country.

performance requirements: *See* investment performance requirements.

peril point: A provision enacted in the 1948 Trade Agreements Extension Act whereby in advance of negotiations to reduce tariffs, the U.S. Tariff Commission was required to investigate whether or not a threat of injury existed to any industry whose tariff might be reduced. The provision had the effect of restricting U.S. negotiator flexibility. It was repealed in 1949 and reinstated in 1951 in a modified form. The procedure was supplanted by provisions in the 1962 Trade Expansion Act.

positive adjustment: Concept similar to "structural adjustment," with greater emphasis on the overall beneficial impact on economies of structural change. Also used to imply government facilitation to either promote change or to ease related dislocations. *See* structural adjustment.

preferential treatment: Special favorable treatment accorded imports from certain countries, such as duty-free treatment granted developing countries under the Generalized System of Preferences (GSP) program.

principal supplier: The country that is its trading partner's most important source of a product. Countries generally negotiate individual tariff reductions in exchange for concessions from these principal beneficiaries, and then apply them to other trading partners on an MFN basis.

proclamation authority: Tariff reduction authority granted by Congress since 1934, in advance of a trade negotiation, that permits presidential implementation of agreements without subsequent legislative approval.

quantitative restriction (QR): Limits placed on the importation of a product, generally on a volume basis. *See* import quota.

quota: *See* import quota.

QR: *See* quantitative restriction.

Reciprocal Trade Agreements Act of 1934: The first major U.S. trade law providing advance authority for the president to enter into bilateral reciprocal tariff agreements, including the application of concessions on an MFN basis. Used to implement various trade-liberalizing agreements, it was extended and modified on several occasions until superseded by the Trade Expansion Act of 1962. *See also* Trade Agreements Extension Acts.

reciprocity: The exchange of trade concessions between two countries. A concept that implies comparability or a general equality in the value of exchanged concessions.

Reorganization Plan No. 3: An executive branch trade reorganization prompted by the Trade Agreements Act of 1979; implemented by Executive Order 12188 of January 4, 1980. It enhanced the responsibilities of USTR as the lead agency in U.S. trade policy, shifted administration of U.S. antidumping and countervailing duty laws from the Department of Treasury to the Department of Commerce, and transferred Foreign Commercial Service export promotion activities from the Department of State to the Department of Commerce.

retaliation: The imposition of an import restriction in response to a foreign practice that adversely affects the exporting country. The GATT permits retaliation in certain circumstances, particularly in response to foreign actions inconsistent with trade concessions granted in negotiated agreements.

round: One in a series of multilateral trade negotiations held periodically since 1947 under GATT auspices, culminating in simultaneous agreements among participating countries to reduce trade barriers. *See* Kennedy Round, Tokyo Round, and so forth.

safeguard: *See* escape clause.

SECO: Section 126 of the Trade Act of 1974 required the president to determine if any major industrialized country had failed to make concessions providing "substantially equivalent competitive opportunities" for the commerce of the United States relative to that granted by the United States in the Tokyo Round MTN. Used to convey the concept of reciprocal nondiscriminatory treatment, the phrase also appeared in draft telecommunications sector trade legislation in the 1980s.

Section 22: A provision of the Agricultural Act of 1933, added as an amendment in 1935, authorizing the president to impose import quotas on certain commodities where imports would interfere with domestic agricultural support programs. Used primarily to restrict imports of dairy products. Grandfathered in original GATT agreements.

Section 201: Refers to Sections 201–204 of the Trade Act of 1974, as amended, which provide escape clause authority, procedures, and criteria for the president to grant temporary relief for industries seriously injured or threatened with injury by virtue of increased imports (based on a finding and recommendation by the ITC). The law originated with executive orders issued beginning 1947, a 1951 law, and the 1962 Trade Expansion Act, which included the concept of trade adjustment assistance. The law has been modified several times since 1974, including 1988 act amendments designed to promote positive adjustment of injured industries. *See also* adjustment assistance, escape clause, structural adjustment.

Section 204: Refers to Section 204 of the Agricultural Act of 1956, as amended in 1962, which provides authority to the president to negotiate and enforce agreements with foreign governments to limit their exports to the U.S. of certain farm products (mainly meat), and textile and apparel products under the Multi-Fiber Arrangement.

Section 232: A provision of the 1962 Trade Expansion Act involving the treatment of imports that may threaten national security. It precludes the reduction of import restrictions on such products and provides for the imposition of protective barriers.

Section 301: Refers to Sections 301–309 of the Trade Act of 1974, as amended, which provide authorities and procedures for enforcement of U.S. rights under trade agreements and responses to unfair foreign practices considered unjustifiable, unreasonable, or discriminatory that burden or restrict U.S. commerce. Based on a provision in the Trade Expansion Act of 1962, the 1974 act provisions have since been amended to specify the types of practices subject to investigations, time limits for action, and criteria for acting or avoiding action (including retaliation). Section 301 is also the basis for action under "Super 301" involving major foreign barriers and "Special 301" pertaining to intellectual property rights.

Section 332: A provision of the Tariff Act of 1930, originating with 1922 legislation, that has become the basis for ITC authority to conduct investigations on trade-related topics.

Section 337: Refers to a section of the Tariff Act of 1930 involving foreign unfair practices in trade and competition; now used primarily to exclude from U.S. commerce products infringing U.S. patents, trademarks, and copyrights. Administered by the ITC in a manner similar to regulatory enforcement of federal unfair competition and anti-trust law.

Section 406: An escape clause statute similar to Section 201 of the 1974 Trade Act that provides for relief from market disruption by imports from Communist countries. It has a lower standard of injury causation than Section 201.

sensitive products: A product whose cost of production is sufficiently high relative to its international competition that a reduction in its protective tariff or nontariff barrier is considered likely to threaten the producer's survival.

Smoot-Hawley Tariff Act: *See* Tariff Act of 1930.

Special 301: The name commonly given to Section 182 of the Trade Act of 1974, as added by amendment in 1988. The provision established new procedures for a systematic U.S. response to foreign violations of U.S. intellectual property rights.

specific tariff/duty: An import tax set at a fixed amount per unit or per unit of measure of an import regardless of its value.

standards: Technical specifications for products that establish certain required characteristics, such as levels of quality, performance, safety, or dimensions. They may involve terminology, symbols, testing and test methods, packaging, marking, or labeling requirements.

Standards Code: Under the Tokyo Round, individual national standards are permitted under a GATT "Agreement on Technical Barriers to Trade" for the legitimate protection of health, safety, and welfare. Technical standards and related testing and certification requirements are not, however, to be designed and used as barriers to trade.

state trading enterprises: Government-run or controlled entities (as distinct from private corporations), that conduct much of the international trade of a country. Generally found in state trading nations/nonmarket economies.

state trading nation: Countries that rely heavily on government entities instead of private corporations to conduct their trade with other countries. The largest of these through the 1980s, the Soviet Union and China, were not members of GATT. Several Eastern European countries, however, joined GATT beginning in the 1970s under special arrangements designed to ensure the steady expansion of their imports from other GATT members (despite the limited impact of tariffs on import decisions in a state trading nation). *See also* nonmarket economy.

STR: Special Trade Representative. *See* United States Trade Representative.

structural adjustment: Fundamental (as distinct from cyclical) changes over time in the productive components of a national or international economy, generally involving shifts in comparative advantage associated with technological developments and the relative cost and movement of resources among productive pursuits. Such adjustment can take place between sectors, between regions, and among nations (as reflected in the composition of imports and exports). *See also* comparative advantage.

subsidy: *See* export subsidies.

Subsidies Code: A multilateral code of conduct negotiated in the Tokyo Round that built on previous GATT rules governing the treatment of subsidies and countervailing duties. The code prohibits the use of export subsidies in manufactured goods, and attempts to discipline the use of domestic subsidies that would have an adverse impact on the trade of other code signatories.

Super 301: The name commonly used to describe a provision of the Omnibus Trade Act of 1988, requiring a multiyear program of self-initiated Section 301 cases against the major barriers of countries found to be maintaining a pattern of such barriers. It included time limits for the resolution of such cases and required some degree of results-based measurement. The provision is technically Section 310 of the Trade Act of 1974, added as an amendment by the 1988 act.

TAA: Trade Adjustment Assistance. *See* adjustment assistance.

targeting: A term used to refer to a variety of government practices designed to enhance the export competitiveness of specific domestic industries.

tariff: A tax imposed on imports at the border. Also the rate at which imported goods are taxed. *See also* ad valorem tariff, bound rates, Column 1 Rates, and Column 2 Rates, specific tariff/duty.

Tariff Act of 1930: Also known as the Smoot-Hawley Tariff Act, named for Sen. Reed Smoot (R-Utah) and Rep. Willis C. Hawley (R-Ore.). The act represented the culmination of a highly protectionist era in U.S. trade policy and contained specific tariff increases that resulted in an average 53 percent tariff on dutiable U.S. imports. Most 1930 tariff rates appear today in Column 2 of the U.S. tariff schedule. A handful of other trade provisions still in effect originated with this act. *See also* Column 2 rates, Section 332, Section 337.

Tariff Commission: *See* International Trade Commission.

tariff quotas: A combination of tariffs and quotas whereby two different tariff rates are applied to an imported product, the lower one on a finite quantity (or quota) of imports first entering the market, and the higher rate on products entering above that quantity.

tariff schedule: A comprehensive list of goods which a country may import and the import duties applicable to each product. In 1989, the Harmonized Tariff Schedule (HTS) replaced the Tariff Schedules of the United States (TSUS). The TSUS was enacted in 1962, and had originated with the Tariff Act of 1930. *See also* Harmonized System.

Tokyo Round: The seventh round of GATT multilateral trade negotiations (1973–1979). It differed from previous rounds in that it addressed disciplines on nontariff as well as tariff barriers to trade and involved developing countries and several nonmarket economy countries. *See also* code of conduct, nontariff measure.

TPC: *See* Trade Policy Committee.

TPM: *See* Trigger Price Mechanism.

TPRG: *See* Trade Policy Review Group.

TPSC: *See* Trade Policy Staff Committee.

Trade Act of 1974: Legislation authorizing U.S. negotiation and implementation of GATT Tokyo Round agreements. In addition to tariff-cutting authority, the act contained the first fast-track legislative mechanism to implement nontariff barrier agreements. It also contains the statutory basis for trade remedy laws involving foreign barriers to U.S. exports and import relief for industries injured by imports, and authority to waive the denial of MFN to communist countries (the Jackson-Vanik freedom of emigration provision). *See also* fast track, Generalized System of Preferences, Section 201, Section 301.

Trade Adjustment Assistance (TAA): *See* adjustment assistance.

Trade Agreements Act of 1934: *See* Reciprocal Trade Agreements Act of 1934.

Trade Agreements Act of 1979: Legislation approving and implementing U.S. commitments made during the GATT Tokyo Round; enacted under fast-track provisions of the Trade Act of 1974. It incorporated into U.S. law provisions related to NTM codes of conduct, contained extensive changes to U.S. antidumping and countervailing duty laws, required the president to reorganize executive agency trade functions, and extended presidential access to fast-track authority for eight years. *See also* antidumping, code of conduct, Government Procurement Code, Reorganization Plan No. 3, Standards Code, Subsidies Code, Tokyo Round.

Trade Agreements Extension Acts: A series of eight laws enacted between 1945 and 1958 that extended and modified provisions of the Reciprocal Trade Agreements Act of 1934 to authorize the implementation of tariff agreements.

Trade Agreements Program: The phrase used to describe U.S. trade policy since enactment of the Reciprocal Trade Agreements Act of 1934, based on the negotiation of trade-liberalizing agreements with foreign countries.

Trade and Tariff Act of 1984: A trade law that renewed the U.S. GSP program, authorized use of fast-track authority to implement a bilateral FTA agreement with Israel, and established a process for implementing other FTA agreements. It also mandated an annual report on trade barriers, established a process for USTR self-initiation of Section 301 cases, and expanded causes of action under Section 301 to include intellectual property rights violations and investment performance requirements. *See also* National Trade Estimate (NTE) Report.

Trade Expansion Act of 1962: Legislative authority for U.S. participation in the GATT Kennedy Round. In addition to tariff-cutting authority, it established Trade Adjustment Assistance programs for workers and firms, and created the position of Special Representative for Trade Negotiations. *See also* Kennedy Round, United States Trade Representative.

Trade Policy Committee (TPC): Created in 1975 as the senior-most interagency committee on U.S. trade policy pursuant to the Trade Expansion Act of 1962. It is chaired by the USTR. Since the early 1980s its intended function has generally been superseded by other cabinet-level councils.

Trade Policy Review Group (TPRG): The subcabinet level interagency trade committee subordinate to the TPC; generally chaired by the Deputy USTR.

Trade Policy Staff Committee (TPSC): The office director level interagency trade committee, chaired by USTR staff, that is subordinate to the TPRG.

Trigger Price Mechanism (TPM): A system for monitoring the price of steel imports used between 1978 and 1982. It attempted to identify prices, based on the landed price of products from Japan, below which formal antidumping cases could be triggered.

TSUS: Tariff Schedule of the United States. *See* tariff schedule.

unfair trade practices: Used to describe practices by firms or governments considered to result in an artificial competitive advantage for the benefitting firms in international trade. Most frequently cited in the context of export subsidies, dumping, and various practices involving trade agreement violations. *See also* Section 301.

unilateral: Action taken by a country on its own initiative, not dependent or conditioned on action by another country or group of countries.

United States Trade Representative (USTR): The cabinet-level official who is the principal adviser to the president on U.S. trade policy and negotiations. Also refers to the Office of the U.S. Trade Representative, in the Executive Office of the President, that the official heads. The position was originally created by the Trade Expansion Act of 1962 as the president's Special Representative for Trade Negotiations (STR).

Uruguay Round: The eighth round of multilateral trade negotiations under GATT auspices which commenced in 1986 with a GATT Ministerial meeting in Punta del Este, Uruguay, and ended in 1993.

USITC: *See* International Trade Commission.

USTR: *See* United States Trade Representative.

valuation: The appraisal of worth of imported goods by customs officials for the purpose of assessing import duties. The Customs Valuation Code of the GATT Tokyo Round established transaction value as the primary method of valuation, i.e., based on the price actually paid or payable for the imported good, as distinct from that price combined with other costs and charges associated with its importation.

variable levy: A tariff that is adjusted to reflect changes in world market prices, designed to ensure that the import price after payment of duty will equal a predetermined "gate" price. The best known example is the variable levy system, applied to commodity imports under the EC Common Agricultural Policy, that sets tariffs at the difference between the lowest available market price and the target price for domestic producers.

VER: *See* voluntary export restraint.

voluntary export restraint (VER): A unilateral limit placed on exports of a product by the exporting country. *See also* voluntary restraint agreement (VRA).

Voluntary Restraint Agreement/Arrangement (VRA): Arrangements by which producers voluntarily limit exports of certain products in order to avoid economic dislocation in the importing country and/or the imposition of mandatory import restrictions by that country. Unlike formal orderly marketing agreements (OMAs), VRAs do not require offsetting compensation under GATT by the importing country.

VRA: *See* voluntary restraint agreement/arrangement.

waiver: A formal exemption of a right or claim. Under GATT, a waiver is a formal agreement by the contracting parties to relinquish or forgo legal rights, or to suspend the application of specific GATT provisions.

Williams Commission: A prestigious panel appointed by President Nixon in 1970 to explore U.S. trade policy interests. The Commission's recommendations ultimately led to U.S. involvement in the GATT Tokyo Round and enactment of the Trade Act of 1974.

World Trade Organization (WTO): *See* GATT.

GLOSSARY OF CONGRESSIONAL TERMS

act: Legislation that has been approved by both houses of Congress and signed into law by the president or enacted through a veto override.

amendment: A proposal to change part or all of a bill or resolution. Examples of different types of amendments include amendments in the nature of a substitute, amendments in the first or second degrees, and perfecting amendments.

amendment in disagreement: Provision/amendment considered in a House-Senate conference where House and Senate versions of the language differ. Conferees may adopt the provision from either one of the bills or compromise language between the two. *See also* scope (of conference).

amendment in the second degree: An amendment to an original ("first degree") amendment.

amendment "tree": There are rules limiting the number and types of amendments that may be considered to a specific provision at any given time. Once those limits have been reached the amendment "tree" is said to be filled and no further amendments are allowed.

bill: A legislative proposal before Congress, designated H.R. in the House of Representatives and S. in the Senate. They are numbered in the order in which they are introduced during each two-year congressional term. Specific numbers can be reserved by the leadership.

budget reconciliation: A step mandated by the 1974 Budget Act used to bring existing law into conformity with decisions contained in congressional budget resolutions. The process generally involves an omnibus fiscal measure that is used to adjust spending and revenue programs.

Note: Descriptions are drawn and adapted from various sources, including Congress, Senate, Republican Policy Committee, *Glossary of Senate Terms . . . A Guide for New Hires,* 102d Congress, 1st sess., July 1991; Walter J. Oleszek, *Congressional Procedures and the Policy Process* 2d ed. (Washington, D.C.: Congressional Quarterly Press, 1984); Congress, Senate, *Standing Rules of the Senate and Congressional Budget and Impoundment Control Act of 1974, as Amended,* 100th Cong., 1st sess., 1987, Senate Document 100-4; and Robert Dove (former Senate parliamentarian), interviews by author, 1992.

by request: Legislation submitted by a member of Congress at the request of someone else (e.g., the administration).

chairman's mark: *See* mark.

clean bill: A bill to which amendments have not been added. After the process of amending a bill, it may be reintroduced or reported as a single new measure or clean bill.

closed rule: A rule governing action on a measure on the House floor that precludes the addition of amendments. *See also* rules.

cloture: A method of limiting debate in the Senate. A cloture petition must be signed by at least sixteen senators. Once filed, one day must elapse before it can be voted on. Three-fifths of all senators must vote in the affirmative for cloture to be invoked on most items. Once cloture is invoked, a 30-hour limit is placed on further consideration of the bill or amendment, and senators are limited in the amount of time they are allowed to speak. Except by unanimous consent, no new amendments can be proposed after cloture is invoked. Initial cloture votes to shut off debate during a filibuster often fail because many senators vote against any first attempt to attain cloture, regardless of the issue, to protect the rights of the minority.

companion bill: A bill introduced in one chamber that is identical (or very similar) to legislation submitted in the other.

concurrent resolution: A resolution that must be passed by both houses of Congress, but does not go to the president for signature and is not legally binding. Often used to express the sense of the Congress on various issues or for internal congressional matters (such as adjournment resolutions).

conference: An ad hoc committee of representatives ("managers") from the House and Senate appointed to reconcile the differences between House and Senate versions of legislation. Also the process of reconciling legislation in a conference committee. Participants are appointed by leaders in each chamber and are generally drawn from committees of legislative jurisdiction, based on seniority. Various rules and practices govern conference committee activities. *See also* conference report, scope (of conference).

conference report: The final version of a bill emerging from a House-Senate conference that reconciles House- and Senate-passed versions. It is accompanied by a "Statement of Managers" that details the disposition of various provisions and amendments in conference. A majority of the managers for each house must agree on the conference report and both chambers must approve it for the bill to be sent to the president for signature. Conference reports cannot be amended on the floor; they can, however, be amended by concurrent resolution making corrections to the bill prior to enrollment. *See also* conference, enrolled bill.

Congress: In addition to the name of the U.S. legislature, the term also refers to the two-year congressional term during which the body meets. Each Congress is numbered sequentially and is made up of two one-year "sessions."

congressional intent: The meaning or purpose Congress intended with respect to a legislative measure, generally expressed in committee or conference reports accompanying bills, floor statements by members during consideration of those bills, etc.

Congressional Record: The transcript of debate and proceedings in Congress, printed daily when Congress is in session. Transcripts of verbatim debate may be edited by members before printing, but only as to grammar, not as to substance.

Continuing Resolution (CR): When a fiscal year ends without an appropriation for each executive department or agency for the following fiscal year having been approved, a continuing resolution is enacted allowing departments to continue spending at a specific rate (usually based on that of the previous year).

cosponsor: One who joins in sponsoring legislation. "Original" sponsors or cosponsors are the members who joined when a measure was initially introduced. Their names appear on the printed text of the measure.

"Dear Colleague": A general term of salutation used in letters sent by members of Congress to many or all other members in the same legislative body. Such letters are often used to seek sponsors for legislation or support for amendments.

enacting clause: The opening phrase of a bill, which reads "Be it enacted by the Senate and the House of Representatives . . ."

enrolled bill: The final copy of a bill which has been passed in identical form by both chambers. It is certified by an officer of the house of origin and then sent on for signatures of the House Speaker, the Senate president, and the U.S. president. An enrolled bill is printed on parchment.

fast track: A legislative mechanism providing for accelerated treatment by Congress of trade agreements. The process, granted periodically to the executive branch since the Trade Act of 1974, involves special rules of procedure employed by each chamber that preclude filibuster and amendment of agreement implementing legislation, thereby guaranteeing an up-or-down vote within a specified time frame.

filibuster: A time-honored Senate delaying tactic, the filibuster is a talkathon designed to balance minority rights with the principle of rule by the majority. By threatening a filibuster, a senator or group of senators can force the majority to amend or even abandon a particular piece of legislation. A filibuster can last for many days and is a tactic of last resort for a determined minority. There are complicated rules for ending a filibuster. *See also* cloture.

final passage: Final approval of a legislative measure by a chamber of Congress.

germane: Directly relevant to the subject at hand. Germaneness rules apply to certain legislative activities.

"the Hill": Commonly used to refer to the Congress or Capitol Hill.

hold: A senator can place a "hold" on a piece of legislation on the Senate calendar, asking his or her party leadership to delay floor consideration of it. The majority leader will honor holds for a reasonable period of time.

Holds are not in any way official; they are part of the unwritten code of "senatorial courtesy" and can be overridden by the majority leader, who has broad discretion to set the Senate's program.

House recede/Senate recede: Notations used in House-Senate conference documents to indicate a compromise offer or agreement whereby one chamber accepts the other's provision in lieu of its own.

joint resolution: A resolution passed by both houses of Congress in the same form. Legally binding since both houses approve the same document for presidential signature. A veto of a joint resolution can be overridden by a two-thirds vote of Congress. This form of resolution has become the principal substitute for the one house legislative veto, found unconstitutional in the Supreme Court ruling on *I.N.S.* v. *Chadha.*

legislative veto: A procedure by which Congress (or a house of Congress) overturns an action or regulation issued by the executive branch. Various forms of the legislative veto were written into law prior to the Supreme Court ruling on *I.N.S.* v. *Chadha* in 1983. The court's ruling greatly restricted the use of the legislative veto as inconsistent with lawmaking procedures set out in the Constitution. Legislative vetoes can still occur by a joint resolution of Congress.

majority leader: Leader of the majority party in the Senate; second ranking leadership position (after the Speaker) in the majority party in the House. Leaders are elected by their party colleagues.

mark: Used to refer to the document that is the basis for a committee markup. *See* markup.

markup: The process of considering and amending legislation in congressional committees, prior to voting and reporting bills out of committee for consideration by the full chamber.

member(s): Commonly used to refer to members of Congress, of the House or Senate, or of a congressional committee, such as in "the members voted to approve the bill."

minority leader: Leader of the minority party in the House or Senate. "Republican leader" (or "Democratic leader") are increasingly used instead by individuals in the position.

modified rule: A rule for action on the House floor that sets parameters for action, generally including specified amendments and time limits. Also referred to as "modified closed" or "modified open" rules. *See also* rules.

motion to recommit: A motion to send a bill back to the committee that reported it. Generally, a motion to recommit, if adopted, means the end of floor consideration of the bill unless the motion is accompanied by instructions.

motion to recommit with instructions: A motion to send a bill back to the committee that reported it, with specific instructions to report it back to the floor, usually within a specified time period and with modifications, amendments, etc.

motion to table: *See* table.

"Mr. President": Used by senators to seek recognition, begin a statement, or address the presiding officer on the Senate floor.

open rule: A rule for action on the House floor that permits unlimited amendments. *See also* rules.

override: *See* veto override.

pocket veto: A veto of legislation by virtue of the president not signing it after the Congress has adjourned. When Congress is in session, a bill goes into law if the president does not act on it within ten days of its receipt.

point of order: An objection raised by a member that the chamber is acting in a manner not consistent with the rules governing the business of that chamber. In the case of a conference report, if the presiding officer sustains the point of order, the report is rejected and may be sent back to conference. Rules may be suspended (waived) by unanimous consent to avoid points of order. *See also* rules.

proxy: The authority to act on behalf of another person. In Congress, proxies are generally put in writing and are used during committee action. Proxies are not allowed in floor votes.

quorum: The number of members who must be present in the chamber or in committee for the conduct of business. A majority of the membership constitutes a quorum in the House or Senate.

recess: A break in congressional activity that, unlike adjournment, does not end the official legislative day and therefore does not interrupt unfinished business. The Senate often recesses from one calendar day to the next, remaining in the same legislative day for a sustained period of time.

recorded vote: A vote where each member takes a formal position, usually by formal roll call vote in the Senate and electronic recording of votes in the House.

report: "To report" is the act that follows committee approval or disapproval of a bill and the process of sending it on to the full chamber for consideration. When used as a noun, a "report" refers to the document issued by the committee in connection with the legislation and describes the purpose and scope of a bill, together with supporting rationale and intent. The report lists and explains amendments adopted by the committee and usually includes departmental comments on the bill. Minority views by those opposing the measure may also be included.

resolution: A simple resolution, designated as H. Res. or S. Res., deals with matters entirely within the prerogative of one chamber or the other. It does not have the force of law. *See also* concurrent resolution, joint resolution, Sense of the Congress.

revenue origination clause: Article I, Section 7 of the Constitution states "All bills for raising revenue shall originate in the House of Representatives; but the Senate may propose or concur with amendments as on other bills." In practice, both houses act on tax and trade measures, but the Senate generally takes H.R.-numbered revenue measures, strips everything after the enacting clause, and substitutes its own language. The House limits the Senate's access to revenue vehicles by "bundling" revenue measures into the fewest possible bills. If the Senate passes a revenue measure on an S.-numbered bill, it is "blue slipped" by the House, i.e., returned to the Senate accompanied by a resolution reiterating House constitutional prerogatives.

rules: A set of parameters governing the conduct of business in the House or Senate, including permanent rules in each chamber on the order of business and parliamentary procedures. In the House, a rule is also a resolution reported by the Committee on Rules that establishes the terms (length of debate, allowable amendments, etc.) under which a bill is considered on the floor. *See also* closed rule, modified rule, open rule, point of order.

scope (of conference): Rules governing the work of House-Senate conference committees that preclude (1) the insertion of material in a conference report that was not contained in either the House- or Senate-passed bills or (2) the deletion of material contained in both bills. A point of order may be raised against any conference report not in conformity with these rules. *See also* conference, conference report, point of order.

second degree amendment: *See* amendment in the second degree.

Sense of the Congress/Senate: An expression of sentiment, opinion, or intent on the part of the Senate or House contained in a bill, resolution, or amendment. *See also* resolution.

session (of Congress): One year of a congressional term; each such "Congress" consists of two years.

sine die adjournment: The term used for long-term adjournment at the end of a session of Congress. "Sine die" translates from Latin as "without day," i.e., indefinitely.

Speaker (of the House): Leader of the majority party in the House. Elected by party colleagues to the post.

Statement of Managers: *See* conference report.

suspend (rules): A waiver or temporary suspension of a chamber's rules applicable to the treatment of legislation in that chamber.

table (a bill/an amendment): A tabling motion, if carried, postpones consideration of a matter before the chamber and usually has the effect of killing it. Tabling of a motion to reconsider an action taken (e.g., a vote) has the effect of confirming that action. Tabled motions are nondebatable.

unanimous consent (UC): A term generally used in connection with action on the Senate floor to express the implicit approval of all members relative to some procedural motion. Almost anything can be done in the Senate by unanimous consent, but it takes the objection of only one senator present on the floor at the time to prevent a unanimous consent request from being agreed to.

unanimous consent agreement: A vehicle used to facilitate action on the Senate floor. Unanimous consent agreements act as the Senate's "game plan" with regard to time of debate, allowable amendments, time on amendments, etc.

They usually state (1) hours to be spent debating a bill, (2) time to be spent debating amendments or procedural motions, and (3) time to be spent on named amendments. Specific times and dates for final disposition of legislation may be included in such agreements.

veto: The disapproval by a president of a bill (or joint resolution). The president must veto the legislation within ten days of receiving it or it goes into law without his signature.

veto override: Enactment into law over a president's veto. Legislation vetoed by the president may be enacted by a two-thirds majority of each chamber voting to override.

voice vote: A vote on a pending matter with members answering "aye" or "no" in chorus. Specific votes of individual members are not recorded. Most congressional actions are taken by voice vote to expedite business.

waive (rules): *See* suspend (rules).

whip: A member of the party leadership in a chamber, appointed by each party to assist in carrying out the party's legislative agenda. These party leaders often disseminate information to other members, conduct headcounts and build coalitions to support party initiatives, etc. Assistant whips may also be appointed.

yeas and nays: A recorded vote required by the Constitution if requested by one-fifth of the members. If the "yeas and nays" are ordered on a measure, it means that a recorded vote will occur when there are no further amendments or when all the allotted time for the measure has expired.

INDEX